JOE PUBLIC 2030

Five Potent Predictions Reshaping
How Consumers Engage Healthcare

CHRIS BEVOLO

RUTLEDGE
HILL

Published by HarperCollins Leadership, an imprint of HarperCollins Focus LLC.

Any Internet addresses, phone numbers, or company or product information printed in this book are offered as a resource and are not intended in any way to be or to imply an endorsement by HarperCollins Leadership, nor does HarperCollins Leadership vouch for the existence, content, or services of these sites, phone numbers, companies, or products beyond the life of this book.

Any people depicted in stock imagery provided by Getty Images are models, and such images are being used for illustrative purposes only. Certain stock imagery © Getty Images.

Library of Congress Cataloging-in-Publication Data

Library of Congress Control Number: 2021921735

ISBN: 978-1-4002-2707-5 (HC)
ISBN: 978-1-4002-2708-2 (E)

Printed in the United States of America.

Rutledge Hill rev. date: 02/21/2022

CONTENTS

Acknowledgments. vii
About the Author ix

CHAPTER 1
Introduction. 1

CHAPTER 2
Our Process, Caveats, and Whatnot. 17

CHAPTER 3
Twenty Questions 24

CHAPTER 4
Prediction - The Copernican Consumer. 55

CHAPTER 5
Prediction - Constricted Consumerism. 89

CHAPTER 6
Prediction - The Funnel Wars. 117

CHAPTER 7
Prediction - The Rise of Health Sects. 155

CHAPTER 8
Prediction - Disparity Dystopia 196

CHAPTER 9
Conclusion 229

Appendix 233
Endnotes. 255

ACKNOWLEDGMENTS

One of the coolest aspects of writing the Joe Public series of books is how the number of people who shaped the content increased along the way. Back in 2011, I wrote *Joe Public Doesn't Care About Your Hospital* on my own, which was both fun and daunting at the same time. With *Joe Public II: Embracing the New Paradigm*, I co-authored the content with Adam Meyer, without whom there was no way in hell I'd be able to speak with authority on topics such as digital marketing. *Joe Public III: The End of Hospital Advertising* was driven by the input of 12 industry leaders and the amazing accomplishments they shared for the book. For *The Gospel of Growth*, I shared authorship with Vicki Amalfitano and Brandon Edwards. Now *Joe Public 2030*, a book shaped by the contributions of three dozen experts, thinkers, and influencers in the healthcare space. The opportunity to sit at the center of this group, take all the incredible inputs and ideas, and shape them into this book has been and honor and a privilege.

So first, thank you to all the industry experts who were willing to share their expertise and insights for this book: Marco Bevolo, Adam Brase, Yumin Choi, Danny Fell, David Goldhill, Matt Gove, Bryan Hamilton, Nate Kaufman, Wright Lassiter, Jarrett Lewis, Kevan Mabbutt, Sandra Mackey, Paul Matsen, Russ Meyer, Wendell Potter, Kyle Rolfing, Dr. Jaewon Ryu, Suzanne Sawyer, Laura Schoen, Dr. Erica Taylor, Scott Weber, and Kristen Hall Wevers. (Full bios are found in the Appendix.)

Next, thank you to all my peeps in Team 2030, the brains responsible for generating the five predictions at the heart of this book: Christian Barnett, Sasha Boghosian, Desiree Duncan, Brandon Edwards, Bjorn Gunnerud, Shannon McIntyre Hooper, Josh Schoonover, Jeff Speer, Jared Usrey, Kris Wickline, and Stephanie Wierwille, with special shout-outs to team members Lucy Whitfield, for all of her research support, and Kayla Johnson, for incredible project coordination throughout the process.

Thank you to Jayne Alexander for all her help in managing the publishing process, as well as our publishers at Rutledge Hills. Thank you (again) to Brandon Edwards, Executive Chairman at Revive, and Joanne Thornton, Chief Executive Officer at Revive, for encouraging and supporting this project every step of the way. Thanks (again) to Des Duncan for all her guidance on issues of health disparities and inequities. Thank you to Jill Tannenbaum and Josh Kaufman from Weber Shandwick for their review of the text. And thanks (again) to Shannon McIntyre Hooper for keeping me honest.

Thank you to all the people in healthcare who have shaped my thoughts, opinions, and passions over the past 20 years, and maybe most importantly to those who share with me the meaning these books have had for them. It's that reinforcement that gives me the courage to keep going back out there.

And finally, as always, thank you to my family for all of their love and support – to my dad, my wife, Tonya, and my three amazing daughters, Amber, Julia, and Callie.

This book is dedicated to my mom, who passed away in April of 2021. I didn't tell you enough about all the great ways you shaped who I am today. This is for you.

ABOUT THE AUTHOR

Joe Public 2030: Five Potent Predictions Reshaping How Consumers Engage Healthcare was written by Chris Bevolo. A nationally recognized futurist, author, and speaker on healthcare marketing, strategy, and branding, he has spent his career helping organizations better understand and leverage key trends in healthcare competition, branding, and consumerism. This is Chris' seventh book, and his 2011 book, *Joe Public Doesn't Care About Your Hospital* (RockBench Publishing), became a field guide for driving transformation in hospital marketing departments across the country. His other books include *The Gospel of Growth* (Revive, 2020), *Joe Public III: The End of Hospital Marketing* (RockBench Publishing, 2018), *Joe Public II: Embracing the New Paradigm* (Interval, 2014), *A Marketer's Guide to Measuring Results* (HealthLeaders Media, 2010), and *A Marketer's Guide to Brand Strategy* (HealthLeaders Media, 2008). Chris has written dozens of articles and papers and is a frequent keynote speaker and featured presenter at national healthcare conferences on the topics of marketing, branding, innovation, and consumer trends.

Chris founded Interval, a nationally-recognized healthcare marketing firm, in 1995 and has worked with dozens of hospitals and health systems across the U.S. to develop successful marketing and branding initiatives. In 2014, Interval was acquired by Revive, and Chris now serves as Chief Brand Officer at the agency. Chris earned an M.B.A. at the University of St. Thomas in Minneapolis and holds a B.S. in journalism and mass communication from Iowa State University.

Chapter 1

Introduction

You will not agree with the contents of this book. At least not some of it. Or maybe even all of it. The team responsible for developing the predictions you will find here don't agree with all the content in this book. The 20+ industry experts we talked with don't agree with all the content in this book. Even *I don't agree* with all the content in this book. But that's ok. In fact, that's somewhat the point. After all, we're setting out to predict how consumers will engage with healthcare 10 years from now, which is both a vast area of focus and a long time away. We conducted an enormous amount of due diligence – studying reams of articles, research, and data. We conducted in-depth interviews with 21 experts from around the globe and from some of the most respected health brands in the world, such as Mayo Clinic, Geisinger, Intermountain Healthcare, Johns Hopkins Medicine, CVS Health, Optum, and Bain Capital. And we engaged a team of some of the smartest people I know to sort through it all and generate the five predictions found here. Which is why it's critical to point out that these aren't *my* ideas – they represent the ideas of our team of predictors. And I don't convey that as a CYA, but rather to ensure credit is given where credit is due. While I contributed to the development of these ideas, I had the humble privilege of pulling them all together in the form you see here.

And yet, I can hear one of those experts loud and clear in my mind, when I ran one of our predictions by him for validation: "No way – that sounds like it comes from someone who doesn't know anything about healthcare." So, we expect some, shall we say, polite disagreement on what we've set out here. That's not only ok, it's healthy and desired. Our goal in publishing the five predictions you'll find here is not to be right as much as it is to spark conversation. Because the truth is, in all five cases, the trends we're predicting are already under way. In some cases, that may be a good thing; in others, clearly not a good thing. Yet by sparking conversation now, maybe there are those who read these predictions who will set out to either ensure they do happen as articulated, or who will fight like mad to prevent them. Either way, having the conversation now about how consumers and healthcare will change in 10 years will, at a minimum, better prepare all of us in the healthcare industry for what may come. And given some of the predictions, that is a very important goal indeed.

The idea for *Joe Public 2030* comes from the publishing of the first book in the series, *Joe Public Doesn't Care About Your Hospital,* 10 years ago in 2011. Since then, we have published two other books in the series, and when the idea of continuing the series came up, we wondered what else we could talk about? The first book, what I called a "manifesto for change," rattled more than a few cages with our call for transformation in the hospital and health system space. It was also widely praised as a true driver of change in the industry, and I still have people today who reach out and let me know the impact it had on them personally, as well as on their organizations. The two subsequent books kept the theme of change front and center, with *Joe Public II: Embracing the New Paradigm* (2014) calling for hospitals and health systems to hurry up and dive headfirst into digital engagement, and *Joe Public III: The End of Hospital Marketing,* celebrating the progress the industry had made in engaging consumers in more effective ways. And so when the question of the topic of a fourth (and *definitely* final) book in the series came up, we decided to honor the decade since its inception by looking 10 years into the future.

Importantly, our focus changed midway through our process (which I've outlined in the following chapter). Like all the other books in the series, *Joe Public 2030* was intended to focus on my primary area of experience and expertise, and that of the agency I work for, Revive, which is marketing, communications, and branding. But as our team explored the future, we kept landing on concepts and concerns that were far broader, and far higher-level, than the disciplines of marketing and communications. Our research and discussion kept coming back to opportunities and challenges for the healthcare industry as a whole. Most of us who participated in the book-development process have spent a lot of personal and professional time studying the business of healthcare and the way the healthcare system is changing over time, which better prepares us to help those looking to improve how they market and brand to consumers. So it probably shouldn't have been a surprise when we kept returning to themes such as health disparities, political tribalism, or AI and digital twinning.

For those familiar with the previous *Joe Public* books, our target audience for this content is different than in the past. On a broad scale, *Joe Public 2030* will provide value for anyone interested in the future of healthcare in the United States. More specifically, though, this book has value for those organizations that provide health or healthcare services to consumers – hospitals, health systems, physicians and physician practices, newer provider companies in the areas of urgent care and primary care, virtual care providers, retail health companies, vertically-integrated health insurance companies, or others – as well as any companies, firms, agencies, and consultants who support the broader provider sector. Unlike past books in the *Joe Public* series, this content is not aimed at only those responsible for branding, marketing, communications, and the consumer experience at provider organizations (though the content found here will absolutely affect those disciplines moving into the next decade). Anyone in a leadership position at a provider organization, or any other of the organizations listed above, from CEO to CFO and COO to CNO to CIO and on down, should find the content here thought-provoking. We hope those thoughts turn into actionable strategies, too.

The five predictions

This book posits five predictions about the state of healthcare in the U.S. that are powerful, compelling, and somewhat "non-obvious" (more on that in the next chapter). As I explain in the next chapter, we went beyond the fundamental trends we're all familiar with, such as the advancement of value-based care, or the weight of Baby Boomers on the health system in the U.S., or the explosion of virtual care as a result of the Covid-19 pandemic. We actually give a synopsis of 20 such foundational trends in Chapter Three for context. Instead, these more common trends became the building blocks for higher-level predictions. Even where a prediction seems somewhat singular in nature, such as Constricted Consumerism, the rationale for the prediction goes beyond just understanding consumerism itself to include how that trend intersects with others, such as the increase in vertical integration by health insurers, or the continued acceleration of industry consolidation. There is a lot of value in the 30,000-foot view as well as the street map.

It's also important to note the intentionality behind the active, current-tense voice used in the subtitle of our book, "Five Potent Predictions **Reshaping** How Consumers Engage with Healthcare." Not "that will shape" or that "could shape," but "reshaping," as in, "*already* shaping." That's because in each case our predictions have already started to take root. They are founded in where we are now, and where we have been. These are not wild-hair guesses that have no grounding in reality, but instead are visions based on what is *already* occurring in the healthcare space. In each case, we build on what we see around us and take it to a potential future conclusion or dynamic. So while one could dismiss where our predictions end up, it's impossible to dismiss their existence, to one degree or another, in today's reality. People of a certain generation remember the cool artwork that consisted of a dense pattern of dots, and when viewed the right way showed a hidden picture inside the pattern. Our challenge here was to paint that concentration of dots, then to look for the subtly hidden and critically important picture that emerged as a result.

Here's a highlight of each of our five predictions:

> Prediction – The Copernican Consumer
> *Consumers will become the center of their own health universe more than ever before, enabled by sensors, AI, and other technology, as well as services geared toward empowering them, leading to profound implications for*

both consumers and healthcare organizations. Potential results could include a dramatic reduction in the need for primary care clinicians, an entirely new sector devoted to personal health management, true precision medicine combined with health management, and more.

Prediction – Constricted Consumerism
While consumers will become increasingly responsible for their own health and use of healthcare services, they will actually become less and less empowered in the choices they have for care, especially in higher-acuity, higher-cost situations. While many in the industry will continue to sing the praises of choice, the reality is most consumers will have far fewer choices moving forward, often in ways they might never ever consider or see.

Prediction – The Funnel Wars
Today we tend to consider hospitals and health systems as birds of the same feather in terms of business model, with variances based on size, scope of services, for-profit/non-profit, and other factors. Moving forward, we could see the splitting of the health system model, with some systems moving even further to the larger, more comprehensive "health" organizations, others retracting into solely acute-care destinations – the "giant ICU on a hill" – and others somewhere in the middle. These models may emerge based on core geographic/market differences such as presence of competitors, plan consolidation/power, regulation, and dozens of other market forces. Yet the primary area where this transformation would play out is with health, wellness, and the lower-acuity care points – what we're calling The Funnel Wars.

Prediction – The Rise of Health Sects
Challenges to and skepticism of the mainstream medical field and science itself have exploded in the past two years

because of the pandemic and political tribalism in the U.S. Anti-vaxxers, non-maskers, and Covid deniers are just the start of an expansion of this distrust of experts, which taken to its potential end could result in multiple "health sects" – primary "schools" of medical thought that coalesce around political/world-views. Imagine "Mainstreamers," who follow the establishment healthcare point of view, "Progressives" who follow minimal medical intervention combined with complementary and alternative medical solutions, and "Contrarians" who deny mainstream medical thought and create their own set of "alternative facts" on everything from vaccines to childbirth to end-of-life care, and everything in between. These sects will not only follow the medical thinking that best fits their worldview, they may in fact create their own reality through alternative research, diagnosis and treatment approaches, and models for the delivery of care itself.

Prediction – Disparity Dystopia
The Covid-19 pandemic shone an ugly light on the disparities that have plagued the U.S. healthcare system for decades. Unfortunately, that health gap is more likely than not to expand, as the "haves" gain access to increasingly more expensive medical treatments, health services, and personalized care, while the "have nots" face growing shortages of basic health resources, from clean water and air to physicians and clinicians, rural healthcare, and more. This shift will be compounded by the mental health crisis, which disproportionately affects systemically disadvantaged populations and groups outside traditional healthcare access channels (teens, for example). All while those entities that might address these disparities increasingly struggle financially – health systems, health plans, state and federal governments – and others lack the incentives to focus on the growing issue.

Some of these predictions will sound familiar – in fact, many of the experts we talked to shared similar views of the future. Others may feel less familiar or brand new. Our purpose wasn't to strive to find and explore only net-new thinking and predictions of the future or break entirely new ground, but rather to follow our process to see which predictions we uncovered stood out the most to us, and which might drive the greatest level of conversation.

Looking backward to look forward

So how do you come up with big, bold, and somewhat validated predictions about the future? I've laid out our specific approach in the following chapter, but when we started this process, it was difficult to get our arms around trying to predict the future 10 years out. Are we talking about house calls via drone, or urgent care clinics on Mars? A decade seems so far out it can be hard to apply practical thinking to what might take place. So it can help to start by looking back over the prior ten years to understand the level of change we've experienced in healthcare. A look back a decade helps to provide the right perspective on the level of changes we might expect in the coming 10 years, if not which trends and changes had the most effect. Of course, it matters which 10-year period is reviewed. Trying to understand economics in the U.S. by looking back a decade in 1940 would provide a very different point of view than looking back in, say, 1990. And that variance is important here, because the 10 years starting in 2011 saw a level of change in healthcare that would be hard to match in any other 10-year period. Though, interestingly, not everyone we talked to agrees that the level of change we experienced matched what we *thought* we might experience back in 2011. Sometimes the delta between expectations and reality is just as interesting as the actual pace of change.

For example, the first Joe Public book was published in 2011, which happened to coincide nearly perfectly with the passing of the ACA in 2010. The ACA was so new that by the time the book was published the following year, the law had yet to be fully formalized through actual regulations and actions, leaving its potential impact somewhat of a mystery. We addressed the potential changes the ACA might bring through what was essentially a "punt" in the book, writing:

> *What about healthcare reform? As of this writing, the true shape of reform was still being debated, as organizations across the U.S. tried to untangle the complicated guidelines of the Affordable Care Act to understand how best to adapt to the potentially significant changes. But from what I've read and from those I've talked with, healthcare reform will likely continue the trends noted above, if not accelerate them. And at the very least, reform does not change the fundamental concept that provider organizations will need to continue to compete for business. And as long as there is a need for competition, there will be a need for us to conduct effective marketing.*[1]

So in other words, the changes we were focusing on in the first Joe Public book were unlikely to be rendered moot or unnecessary by the ACA (changes such as proactively building true brand strategies, or embracing digital experiences and communications). What's interesting is hearing from those experts we talked with this time around about the ACA, who seem to recognize both that reform has had a meaningful impact on healthcare in the U.S., while at the same time not going nearly as far as many thought it might. On one hand, the legislation is credited with expanding health coverage to 20 million people, and locked-in protections for tens of millions of Americans with pre-existing conditions. On the other hand, policy goals such as reigning in rising healthcare costs have fallen short.

David Goldhill is a long-time healthcare policy expert, board member at the Leapfrog Group, and currently CEO and co-founder of Sesame, an online marketplace for discounted health services. He is a leading national voice for market-based healthcare reform, the author of the *Atlantic* cover story "How American Healthcare Killed My Father" and the follow-up book, "Catastrophic Care: Why Everything We Think We Know about Health Care Is Wrong." He calls the changes we've seen over the past decade, particularly related to the ACA, both significant and subtle at the same time. While the ACA could have been revolutionary, he says, the amount of care individuals have to pay for directly has grown tremendously, showing the limited effectiveness of the law.

Dr. Jaewon Ryu is the President and CEO of Geisinger, an integrated delivery system with more than $8 billion in combined revenue and comprised of a medical group, hospitals and clinics, a health plan, and a medical school in central and northeastern Pennsylvania, and one of the most respected health systems in the country. He was previously President of Integrated Care Delivery at Humana, and has held various leadership roles at the University of Illinois Hospital & Health Sciences System, Kaiser Permanente, the Centers for Medicare and Medicaid Services, and as a White House Fellow at the Department of Veterans Affairs. He calls the last 10 years a very important decade, but also says the level of change hasn't been what many thought it would be.

> As the old adage goes, we overestimate what can be done in a year, and underestimate what can happen in a decade. That said, it's a little surprising how incremental the change has been, or that things like value-based care haven't gone faster. We might think necessity would breed change, but I remember doing a presentation ten years ago on the need for dramatic change, and that the fee-for-service model was no longer sustainable. I thought there would be wholesale, quick adoption of value-based models and strategies, but the reality hasn't been that dramatic.

Here's Jarrett Lewis, partner at Public Opinion Strategies, a national opinion research firm. He is a former political pollster who now focuses mostly on the healthcare and health policy space.

> There was so much negativity and doomsaying about the Affordable Care Act, particularly in the early days; but as we know, none of the adverse outcomes ever really unfolded. But the biggest surprise for me is that I don't

think the law has had the positive impact that proponents thought it would. To be clear, there are good pieces of it like guaranteed issue; but has the ACA had a meaningful impact on bringing costs down or changing delivery models? It seems there was more bark than bite to the legislation.

Or Kyle Rolfing, a serial entrepreneur in the healthcare consumerism space. Rolfing was one of the founders of Definity Health, one of the first recognized consumer-driven health companies in the U.S., started in 1998 and eventually sold to UnitedHealth, and he was subsequently the founder of two other consumer-oriented health companies, RedBrick Health and Bright Health.

The biggest surprise to me looking back over the past ten years is the snail's pace in terms of model transformation. Consider value-based care and outcomes-based reimbursement. The foundational change over the last decade to better align incentives hasn't fully taken hold yet.

Russ Meyer, head of brand strategy, innovation, and design thinking at CVS Health, also has the same perspective on the level of change, saying that, while we're in a considerably different place now than we were 10 years ago, he struggles to point to any one momentous example.

The ACA was substantial in that it finally tried to break the link between employment and health insurance coverage, but it still hasn't brought a huge level of change. Far more people in the U.S. still get their health insurance through their employment than by any other means.

Wright L. Lassiter III is the President and CEO of Henry Ford Health System, overseeing the $6.6 billion integrated health system comprised of five acute care hospitals, two destination centers for cancer care, orthopedics, and sports medicine, three behavioral health facilities, a regional health plan, and a wide range of ambulatory, retail, and other health services consisting of more than 250 locations across Michigan with more than 33,000 employees. He has more than 30 years of experience working in large, complex health systems, including Dallas Methodist Health System and JPS Health Network in Fort Worth, Texas. Prior to joining Henry Ford, Lassiter was CEO of Alameda Health System in Oakland, California, where he was credited with leading the expansion and turnaround of the $865 million public health system. Finally, starting in 2022, he will assume the role of board chair for the American Hospital Association. He says his expectations might have just been too high for what the ACA might bring.

> *I'm surprised the ACA didn't have a broader impact. Some think it has had a monumental influence on healthcare in this country, but I disagree. Eleven years later and we're still debating it in a fundamental way, which shows me it wasn't as transformative as it could have been.*

Finally, we hear from Wendell Potter, a former health insurance executive, *New York Times* bestselling author, health care and campaign finance reform advocate, and authority on corporate and special interest propaganda. He leads two health care reform advocacy nonprofits: the Center for Health and Democracy and Business Leaders for Health Care Transformation, and is the founder of Tarbell.org, a nonprofit journalism organization that investigates corporate and political corruption. He is perhaps best known as a whistleblower on the adverse activities of health insurers, captured in his best-selling book from 2010, *Deadly Spin: An Insurance Company Insider Speaks Out on How Corporate PR Is Killing Health Care and Deceiving Americans.* When we spoke for this book, the Supreme Court had just rejected a lawsuit brought by Republican attorneys general from a number of states to invalidate the ACA, perhaps the last gasp of those in conservative circles hoping to kill Obamacare.

> *Yes, the ACA has brought coverage to many people in the U.S., but it was supposed to have far greater impact than it has. Lawmakers were cowed by private insurers*

and took the public-option off the table far too soon in the process, and the law kept getting whittled-down from there to keep the support of those insurers. Supporters trusted private insurers to be consumer-focused, but not surprisingly that has not turned out to be the case. In some ways, the ACA has actually further entrenched the power of private health insurance companies and solidified their role. The value of health insurance to Americans has decreased, through lower levels of coverage, even as we pay more and more. Private insurers are still fighting a public option today, tooth and nail. And they have more money than ever before, thanks to vertical integration, to influence the public, legislators, and policy makers.

Another area of expected dramatic change back in 2011 was the rise of consumerism. In *Joe Public Doesn't Care About Your Hospital,* we thought the Great Recession of 2008 might be the tipping point for finally moving consumerism forward in a meaningful way. For the first time in the modern era of healthcare, the industry felt elasticity in demand due to economic strife. Millions had lost their homes, their jobs, and their health insurance. There was a dramatic cutback in healthcare spending, with consumers avoiding non-emergent care and cutting their pills in half to get by. Some of our predictions related to consumerism from that book have proven accurate, such as consumer demand for a better experience, especially in terms of convenience and service, and that competition in the healthcare market would heat up. In other ways, our predictions didn't pan out, such as the claim that "price shopping will become the norm" or that the current drop in healthcare service and drug utilization at the time might turn into a permanent reduction in volumes and spending.

Some of the experts we spoke with felt that there has been meaningful movement in consumerism. Bryan Hamilton, Assistant Vice President of Marketing Communications at Cincinnati Children's Hospital Medical Center, a non-profit, pediatric academic medical center established in 1883, which is one of the top three recipients of pediatric research grants from the National Institutes of Health, ranked third in the nation among all Honor Roll hospitals in *U.S. News and World Report's* Best Children's Hospitals, and a research and teaching affiliate of the University of Cincinnati's College of Medicine. Prior to his current role, Bryan spent 18 years as a Global Brand Director at The Procter & Gamble Company. He says one of the biggest shifts is how the industry is finally focusing on "consumers" rather than "patients." It wasn't always the case that use of the word "consumer" was accepted within healthcare, but now there is widespread recognition of the value of thinking of those we serve as consumers. Some of those we talked to felt that the concept of consumerism hadn't gone far enough. Here's Dr. Ryu again:

> We lag behind other industries in consumer engagement and adoption. The trends are there, but for example people often make an analogy between banking and healthcare, yet those ideas were around a decade ago, and financial institutions have gotten there in ways we haven't. For example, we're trying to fully engage consumers digitally, but we could be doing so much more. Covid-19 obviously accelerated this, but we're still behind other industries in this way.

Kristen Hall Wevers, Chief Marketing and Communications Officer at UC Health in Cincinnati, and also a former executive at The Procter & Gamble Company, concurs:

> Healthcare is still out of touch with the consumer. There's a whole notion of the shared experiential world of commerce, where we'll say, "oh yes, the person who walks into Nordstrom's is the same person who walks into our clinic." But are we really close to matching a headset of unmatched consumer experience? Clinical care alone can no longer supersede patient experience in attracting consumers, and more leaders are finally embracing this. We must be obsessed with both the functional and emotional aspects of the healthcare experience; these

are contemporary expectations of human beings. The experiences consumers/patients seek and choose are fundamentally rooted in the same desires, wants, and needs.

And this from Sandra Mackey, Chief Marketing Officer of Bon Secours Mercy Health, one of the nation's largest Catholic health systems with 60,000 associates, 50 hospitals, and more than 1,200 points of care spanning seven states and two countries. Her experience also includes stints as marketing executive at the Arthritis Foundation and Emory Healthcare in Atlanta.

If we look inside of health care organizations as an industry, I'm still surprised at the general lack of understanding about the importance of consumer engagement. So much progress has been made in this regard in other industries, yet health care is constantly having to advocate for and reinforce what consumers want. Forward thinking marketers have an opportunity to flip the model on its head. If you look across health care organizations, the old guard still rules to a large degree, thinking all they need to do is tell consumers how great they are and they will come. It's taken so long for healthcare organizations to catch up in areas like shaping the digital experience, where other industries have made great inroads. It's a bit like turning the Titanic – a lot of what we're doing today others have been doing for years. The more progressive organizations listen to consumers and achieve a better outcome when there's a true partnership and alignment on a "consumer-first" approach between people delivering care and those driving consumer engagement.

Finally, Matt Gove, currently Chief Marketing Officer at Summit Health, a merger bringing together New York's largest urgent care provider (CityMD) with one of the largest independent physician practices in the country (Summit Medical Group). Prior to joining

Summit Health, Matt served as Chief Consumer Officer for Atlanta-based Piedmont Healthcare, Georgia's largest health system, and was Senior Vice President of Marketing and External Affairs at Grady Health System, based in Atlanta.

Prior to his current role, Gove was one of the most innovative thinkers in the health system space, acting as one of the first movers in the areas of online physician ratings, chat-bots, data-driven marketing, and marketing's role in shaping the consumer experience. He sees both the progress and the lack of it when it comes to consumerism over the past decade:

> As someone who is a big proponent of consumerism over the past seven to eight years, it's been great to see some of the smarter marketing and consumer platforms applied with some success. While the rush to consumerism also led to a lot of bad tactics, we've learned a lot from successes – and people – from outside the healthcare industry. That said, I am surprised we haven't gotten further. Even at the best health systems and healthcare organizations, where there is 100% buy-in on consumerism, we're still not 100% delivering on it. The dream is a relationship with consumers that other brands have. Consider Amazon and its digital platform, with all the interactions and experiences that are customized for the individual, which keeps us as consumers tied to them for our lifetimes. While not many other organizations actually do this well, it's rare for other organizations to have as much information on our consumers and patients as we do. Yet we're still struggling to really totally leverage it.

Adam Brase is the Executive Director of Strategic Intelligence at Mayo Clinic, where he is extensively involved in Mayo Clinic's strategic planning efforts and was one of the key authors of its 2030 strategy. Prior to his current role, he served as the senior marketing executive for Mayo Clinic and held various other senior leadership roles in Public Affairs during his 20-year Mayo Clinic career. Adam's sole job is to make predictions about the future to help guide the vision and strategies at the organization (best job ever?). It helps to have someone who is a professional at prediction-making to put the past in context in terms of how it relates to what's coming in the future.

> As humans, we're so adaptable, and we don't always see the true nature of change until we look backwards. Think back to the release of the iPhone in 2007 – a lot of critics dismissed the device as "not Blackberry enough." And then the iPhone went on to disrupt not only the mobile phone category, but also the camera industry and the video industry. It's hard to look back and see game-changing events, because usually it's an evolution. We just don't know until it happens. Obviously 2020 was a different story. For example, we conduct 10-year forecasts, and much of what we predicted for 2030 actually has already happened because of the pandemic – it literally accelerated our 10-year forecast by seven years! So it's true that a lot of what we might look at ten years from now could go either way. But the last ten years in healthcare were really all about building to the **next** ten years. We've teed up a lot that should lead to great transformation.

So with that, let's dive in. We'll start with an overview of how we developed our five predictions in Chapter Two, then provide a quick recap of the 20 healthcare trends that served as the foundation for our thinking. Finally, we'll dive into the deep end of our five predictions.

And hope there's enough water in the pool.

Chapter 2

Our Process, Caveats, and Whatnot

As soon as we hit on the idea of making predictions for the next decade of healthcare on the 10-year anniversary of the first Joe Public book, we knew we had a solid idea. And then we immediately smacked face-first into a brick wall: how in the world do you do that? I mean, other than shaking a Magic-8 ball or just spewing a bunch of hair-brained prophesies and prognostications, how do we thoughtfully develop insights that we can feel good about for that far out in the future? Fortunately, a former colleague had recommended to me the "Non Obvious" books by Rohit Bhargava, a best-selling author, national speaker, Adjunct Professor of Marketing and Storytelling at Georgetown University, and founder and leader of his company, Non Obvious. Bhargava has spoken in 32 countries and has consulted with organizations and brands such as the World Bank, NASA, Disney, Intel, Coca-Cola, and American Express. Since 2011, Bhargava has put out annual books on trends and predictions, winning nine international book awards in the process. His latest book, *Non Obvious Mega Trends*, was released in 2020 and includes a breakdown of the process Bhargava uses to make predictions, what he calls "The Haystack Method for Curating Non-Obvious Ideas." Lacking any other proven approach to deriving predictions in an organized way, we decided to apply the Haystack Method to our process. And thank goodness we did, for it was instrumental in driving the right kind of thinking, and ultimately, the five "non-obvious" predictions found in this book.

The haystack method

I would encourage anyone to read *Non Obvious Mega Trends*, if only for the bold predictions Bhargava makes throughout the book. While we didn't use his predictions explicitly to drive our thinking, the content was one of hundreds of points of intel that were in the mix. More importantly, though, was the process Bhargava laid out for successfully identifying trends and developing predictions. The Haystack Method is defined as "a process for curating trends that starts with gathering stories and ideas and sorting them into groups that make sense (the hay), then analyzing each of the groups to see whether they reveal an underlying trend (the needle)."[2] There are five steps to The Haystack Method, and we committed to following each of them as prescribed. But first, we needed some "hay makers." Thus was born Team 2030, a group of 15 leaders and thinkers from Revive, the agency I joined in 2014. The expertise we brought together spanned different ages, genders, and race to ensure diversity of thought, as well as expertise from both within and outside healthcare, not to mention from across the business spectrum. As I mentioned in the prior chapter, it included some of the smartest people I know. Everyone was sworn to dutifully follow the Haystack Method, which was important, because as you may have experienced, some really smart people often want to jump right to the answer. Instead, in a process spanning roughly two months, this group of thinkers took time during their evenings and weekends to dive deep into the future. (You can find the bios of all the Team 2030 participants in the Appendix).

We started by collecting everything we could about current and projected trends in healthcare. Team 2030 members were encouraged to read whatever they could and contribute whatever research and literature they could find to ensure we covered ample ground in our thinking. That's because the first phase of The Haystack Method is the Gathering Phase: bringing forward as many useful, interesting, or relevant ideas and facts as humanly possible. Inputs came from the personal POVs and experience of Team 2030 members, as well as the net new research we were doing at the time. (If you want to build your own do-it-yourself MBA focused on the future, just read all of the resources cited in this book.) Additionally, we had interviewed 21 healthcare experts of all shapes and sizes – health system CEOs, venture capitalists, entrepreneurs, physicians, consultants, researchers, and marketing and branding experts. Again we sought to summon a diversity of voices. In the end, we heard from some of the most respected leaders and brands in the space. Their diverse perspectives and experiences proved invaluable in shaping our five predictions. (You can find bios for the 21 participants in the Appendix).

Given restrictions from Covid-19, we were forced to work virtually, so we used three-hour Zoom sessions and the digital whiteboard tool Miro throughout the process. Over the course of a month and two Gathering sessions, Team 2030 members shared and discussed their ideas and facts in small groups, followed by large-group report-outs. To help organize our thoughts, we categorized all inputs in one of six ways:

1. Hospital and health system marketing (meaning marketing, communications, branding all other related disciplines)
2. Marketing discipline overall (remember, we initially set out to predict trends related to marketing overall before switching to higher-level concepts)
3. Hospital and health system industry
4. Health (overall)
5. Consumer behavior (overall)
6. Society (overall)

Keys to a successful Gathering phase, according to Bhargava, include stressing quantity over quality, and not leaping ahead to final thoughts or conclusions. By the end of the Gathering phase, the team had collected dozens and dozens of relevant inputs of import. That brought us to the next phase, Aggregating, which Bhargava defines as curating information clusters. The goal here was to pore over and discuss all of the intel we had collected, seeking to convert potential intersections, connections, trends, and insights into different themes. Bhargava recommends focusing on human needs, identifying the obvious, and looking for unusual ideas during this stage.

Once again, the team worked over a few weeks and two, three-hour sessions to organize all of our inputs into potential trends and predictions. The dozens and dozens of inputs, quotes, facts, and ideas were culled, debated, and curated, resulting in 18 possible predictions about healthcare in 2030.

From there, a smaller subset of Team 2030 took on phase three of The Haystack Method, Elevating, where according to Bhargava, it's time to find the broader themes that will become the final trend predictions. This group whittled the 18 potential concepts down to six for final consideration, which eventually turned into the final five found in this book. The final two stages in The Haystack Method – Naming (where predictions are given memorable labels) and Validation (where ideas are analyzed without bias), have taken place during the writing of the book itself. And in fact, we see the publishing of the book as the continuation of the Validation phase, where you as a reader of the predictions will evaluate for yourself which you agree with, which sound reasonable, and which sound whack.

Without Bhargava's book and his offer for others to learn and leverage The Haystack Method, there's no way we would have ended up with what we believe are insightful, provocative, and *possible* predictions you'll find here.

A few important points and caveats about these predictions

While we're extraordinarily proud of the predictions we've developed and are excited for the conversation to begin, there is some important context readers should have before they dive in.

- As is hopefully clear from the description of process we followed, the final five predictions were not singular predictions made by any one person, but rather an organic building of concepts from research, insights, and sub-trends, as well as collective contributions from the group. No one participant from Team 2030, including me, can claim to be the sole owner of any of these ideas. Further, as you'll see, each of the predictions is supported directly by a number of the experts we interviewed, and all have ample data, research, and insights supporting the premise behind each. At the same time, there are clear variants of each final prediction, as well as strong arguments against them, and we've tried to bring those forward as well.

- While quotes and input from interviewed experts are used throughout the book to support the predictions at hand, that is not to say that those we interviewed were asked to sign off on any of the predictions once they were formed. In fact, none of the interviewees knew what the predictions would be when we talked to them, so the inclusion of their contributions in this book should in no way equate to their endorsement of those predictions or how they are articulated and supported here. (In some cases, interviewees made predictions of their own that are close to the final predictions found here, but again, that does not mean they would advocate for how we've portrayed our ideas here). All interviewees were given a chance to review any content attributed to them, including the context in which that content was used, to ensure the meaning and spirit of their contributions were captured accurately.

- The final five predictions are not meant to portray a comprehensive picture of the future, nor are we trying to cover all aspects of the healthcare space. Further, these predictions are not dependent on one another. While none of the predictions are necessarily 180 degrees in opposition to another, they also don't necessarily fit neatly together. Each should be considered on its own, not as a collection of dependent trends. Trying to create that kind of interdependency would have made the task much more difficult, and/or diluted the types of predictions we could make. That said, as you'll see, there is plenty of cross-referencing between the predictions, and it is certainly true that in some cases, the more one prediction becomes reality, the more likely one or more of the others would also come to fruition.

- As noted in Chapter One, our work here is focused primarily on the healthcare provider sector and how consumers will engage with it. While we do touch on other components of the healthcare industry, such as health insurers, there is far less content devoted to areas such as health IT/technology, pharma, medical devices, long-term care, or wellness products such as supplements. That's primarily a result of the area of focus and expertise for most of the members of Team 2030, as well as the fact that the primary sector our firm engages with is the healthcare provider sector (though not exclusively). So while we hit on the science of medicine throughout the book, for example, we're not *predicting* the future of medical science and innovation, but rather how consumers will engage in the healthcare system in the U.S. overall.

- In the same vein, this is not the place to do a deep dive on the specific issues or dynamics found in this book. For example, while we consider how Artificial Intelligence will play a role in the future, we have not gone deep into all the aspects of AI. Or in another example, there are entire library sections devoted to genomics in healthcare (well, at least, entire sections at a *medical* library). We've barely scratched the surface on this topic, and likely in a way that might cause frustration for those who understand genomics at a far deeper level than I or our team does. We've only included insights on areas like AI or genomics to the degree necessary to help convey how we see these issues intersecting with the overall prediction at hand.

- A note about writing style and humor. Those of you who have read my prior books know I enjoy using humor, pop culture references, and sometimes cynical sarcasm to punctuate my points. That's simply a writing style I enjoy reading myself, and so have grown to employ in my own writing (it's good to be the author). You'll find the same style throughout this book. That said, there's nothing at all funny about some of the topics we cover, such as racism, health disparities, or the rise of political tribalism. As the predictions go forward, they start as more positive and optimistic, then turn more serious and, well, dark. I've tried to match my style to fit, so hopefully some of the lighter writing at the outset of the book doesn't diminish the import of the issues as you go farther in.

One more important point to make. While we were obviously unable to talk with the late Clayton Christensen for this book, his thoughts and ideas influenced the thinking here in numerous ways. A number of the interviewees referenced his thinking, particularly his ideas found in his 2009 book, *The Innovator's Prescription*. Christensen's ideas and concepts have always had an enormous influence on me personally as well, and some of our predictions reflect some of his own predictions made way back 12 years ago. In many respects, Christensen was far ahead of his time, so if any of our thoughts sound like a reflection of his groundbreaking ideas about healthcare, then his influence should be duly noted and celebrated.

Now, with all that out of the way, let's look at the 20 foundational trends that formed the framework of our five predictions.

Chapter 3

Twenty Questions

One of our favorite games during long family car rides was Twenty Questions. All the kids could play no matter their age, and it usually chewed up a good 20-30 minutes a game, which of course was the ultimate objective. One game still holds a sacred place in family lore, when my oldest daughter, Amber, who is super smart and can be a super smart-ass, stumped the entire family by choosing the word "dot." No matter how hard the rest of us tried, I'm not sure what questions we could have asked to get to that completely ethereal answer. (Just let it sink in and you'll see the impossibility of it).

The same might be said of this exercise – predicting the state of healthcare a decade into the future. You could almost hear what the game of Twenty Questions might sound like: "Will value-based care dominate? Will everyone have a medication dispensary in their home? Is it bigger than a breadbox?" Fortunately, the Haystack Method provided us a more ordered way forward, starting with insights, ideas, and more standard trends to find unique ways of looking at the future. In fact, with all the Team 2030 members grounded in healthcare to different degrees, there were a set of foundational trends that shaped our thinking and, ultimately, the building blocks for the final five predictions. These are trends that anyone affiliated with healthcare will recognize, and which undoubtedly will shape the future of the field one way or the other.

Rather than focus solely on the future of these foundational trends on their own, however, the Haystack Method allowed us to consider how they might shape one another over the years, the intersections and influences among them. Of the final five predictions, all but one (which is a spin on Consumerism), is a reflection of three, four, or sometimes far more of these foundational trends. And even the prediction focused on Consumerism is itself influenced by many of the other foundational trends.

So to help illustrate the background behind the final five predictions, this chapter provides, in no particular order, a quick overview of 20 foundational trends that shaped where we ultimately landed. Again, this is not the place to dive deeply into these trends, but rather to understand what influenced Team 2030's thinking to one degree or another. Think of these as the platter of tuna tartare and spring rolls before the beef tenderloin entrée with a side of chive mashed potatoes and sautéed brussels sprouts that are the main five predictions. And in the spirit of my long family car rides, we've posed a question at the end of each to create our own unique form of 20 Questions.

1 – Consumerism

You heard consumerism mentioned in the retrospective of the past decade in Chapter One, and it's a foundational trend that closely equates in a final prediction, laid out in Chapter Five. And if you've been around healthcare for more than a hot minute, you know about consumerism (or at least all the talk about consumerism). In its simplest form, consumerism is defined as the force healthcare consumers increasingly wield to change the delivery of healthcare for the better.

In some cases, consumerism is a strategy – for decades, some politicians, economists, healthcare experts, and others have called for "more consumerism" to help address the healthcare industries' various woes, most explicitly, costs. The theory goes that if consumers are given more skin in the game – that is, they are asked to spend more of their own money – market dynamics that were missing before will come into play, with greater consumer demands leading to greater innovation, more competition, better experiences, and lower prices. This happens in other sectors, such as automotive or consumer packaged goods, so why not healthcare? (Pauses here for muffled chuckle). The former governor of my state, Minnesota, and failed vice-presidential candidate Tim Pawlenty summed up this "free-market" strategy best in 2011 in his aversion to Obamacare:

> Healthcare needs to look a lot more like a cash bar than an open bar.[3]

The other way to think about the advance of consumerism is more naturally-occurring. Over the past three decades, consumers have gained access to more choices in every area of their lives, and certainly in their healthcare, from medical tourism to mall-kiosk retail clinics to free-standing EDs to virtual care. At the same time, thanks to the Internet, social media, and a cottage industry of rankings and reviews resources, consumers have more information about those choices than ever before. Finally, the fuel on the fire is that consumers are spending far more out-of-pocket on healthcare than ever before. These forces, the theory goes, combine to drive healthcare transformation in the areas of consumer preference, such as transparency, access, pricing, convenience, and experience.

Using this perspective, there's no arguing that the forces driving consumerism – more choices, more access to information, and more skin in the game – have been growing. What's less clear is to what degree it has impacted the healthcare industry. Yes, there have been changes in transparency, access, convenience, and experience, but it is unclear how much of this change has truly been driven by consumerism, a concept we'll explore in Chapter Five (the title of which, *Constricted Consumerism*, may tip our hand a bit).

QUESTION: **Whether it's a cause, an effect, or both, will we see consumerism finally upend the healthcare space in the coming decade?**

2 – Artificial intelligence

During the Q&A session following a presentation I gave a couple of years back on the contents of my book, *Joe Public III,* someone asked what my next book would be about. I said flat out there would be no more Joe Public books. So much for predicting the future. Then an older gentleman chimed in, "I know what you'll write about – AI." My response was, to say the least, skeptical. My understanding of Artificial Intelligence (AI) at the time was shaped by the rather limited use of AI to write sports recaps for news services like The Associated Press.

Of course, that was waaayyyyy back in 2019, and now it seems that AI is poised to take over the world, albeit not in many of the ways that were predicted five or 10 years ago. No, really – Elon Musk has predicted humans could be overtaken by AI by 2025[4]. If that actually happens, the predictions in this book could come out *slightly* different, I would imagine. Instead of a Cyberdyne Systems-like calamity, AI will most likely have a deep, and hopefully positive, effect on healthcare. According to a 2019 industry survey by Deloitte, 75% of organizations over $10 billion in annual revenue had spent at least $50 million on AI initiatives, and 73% of all respondents said they expected to increase spending on AI in the coming year.[5] In an article highlighting those numbers, a few dozen examples were given of AI in use, with a particularly interesting case featuring the use of AI at Mount Sinai health system in New York City to better diagnose COVID-19, which helped find Covid-19 in 68% of cases that were interpreted by radiologists as negative[6]. And of course, AI chat-bots are all the rage with health systems today.

We'll reference AI related to the field of radiology a bit in Chapter Four, as well as the ethical challenges wrought by AI bias in Chapter Eight. But the influence of AI, machine learning, and other related advancements cuts across a number of our other predictions as well. The expansion of AI in healthcare, as well as the deepening of challenges that go with it, seems obvious. So it's not a question of if…

QUESTION: **When will AI actually make large-scale transformative changes in healthcare that go beyond radiology reads and administrative efficiency,** transforming clinical medicine and the consumer experience at scale?

3 – Blockchain

If there's a race to be the "next big thing" in healthcare, blockchain is running neck and neck with AI. Blockchain has made the biggest splash to date in the world of cryptocurrency – Bitcoin, Ethereum, Dogecoin, and others have been making headlines over the past few years for their volatility, threat to traditional currencies, and, again, Elon Musk. But blockchain has applications far beyond cryptocurrency, not the least of which is in healthcare.

What exactly is blockchain? Maybe the best definition I could find comes from Deloitte, which is notable because they claim their definition is valuable because it's "less than 100 words." If describing something in less than 100 words is considered achievement, then the complexity of that thing seems assured. And the truth is, this isn't even a definition, but rather a simple way to describe how it works *and* its value:

> You (a "node") have a file of transactions on your computer (a "ledger"). Two government accountants (let's call them "miners") have the same file on theirs (so it's "distributed"). As you make a transaction, your computer sends an e-mail to each accountant to inform them. Each accountant rushes to be the first to check whether you can afford it (and be paid their salary "Bitcoins"). The first to check and validate hits "REPLY ALL", attaching their logic for verifying the transaction ("proof of work"). If the other accountant agrees, everyone updates their file. This concept is enabled by "Blockchain" technology.[7]

Rather than getting deeper into how blockchain technology actually works or its structure, it's more important for our purposes to understand its potential role in the world, as well as in healthcare. Here's how the smart people at Andreessen Horowitz, the famous Silicon Valley venture capital firm, frame the potential of blockchain:

> *Historically, new models of computing have tended to emerge every 10–15 years: mainframes in the 60s, PCs in the late 70s, the internet in the early 90s, and smartphones in the late 2000s. Each computing model enabled new classes of applications that built on the unique strengths of the platform. For example, smartphones were the first truly personal computers with built-in sensors like GPS and high-resolution cameras. Applications like Instagram, Snapchat, and Uber/Lyft took advantage of these unique capabilities and are now used by billions of people. Blockchain computers are new types of computers where the unique capability is trust between users, developers, and the platform itself.*[8]

For these authors and many others, blockchain is the next disruption. What about in healthcare? Consider all the ways and places healthcare data is stored for one individual – in their hospital's EMR, in the EMR of the urgent care clinic they use down the street, in the database of their pharmacist, in their Apple Watch, in their Peloton app, in their CPAP machine, in their diabetes monitor, in a national research study, etc. All of it unconnected, disparate, or redundant. Now imagine all that data as part of a singular, secure, digital record that was automatically updated across all databases, EMRs, or other digital nodes — instantly — whenever a new piece of data was input. That begins to help illustrate the potential power of a blockchain-enabled healthcare system, and the significance for consumers, hospitals and health systems, and all other players is monumental. This is new-school interoperability. Blockchain technology promises to be the foundation on which interoperability doesn't just mean different health systems can share information – it means information will be safe, well-validated, and even properly owned by consumers on enterprise and consumer platforms alike. Like AI, the question isn't if, but when.

QUESTION: **What will the sequence of blockchain's impact look like in healthcare, and who will gain the most from it first?**

4 - Industry consolidation

Go big or go home was the rallying cry in the wake of the launch of the ACA in the early 2010s, as hospitals and health systems sought to make up for shrinking reimbursement and the value-based care evolution through "volume, volume, volume." And go big they have. According to data from NIHCM, the average number of announced hospital/health system mergers or acquisitions averaged 56 per year in the years between 2006 – 2009. For the same four-year period between 2014 – 2017, that average had nearly doubled to 108 per year, with a high of 115 in 2017.[9] The numbers since then have slowed somewhat, and the pandemic definitely dampened the churn, but only incrementally, and maybe only for the short term. A May 2021 article in *The New York Times* claimed that the big got bigger in 2020 thanks to the use of Covid-19 relief funds to support mergers and acquisitions[10]. And many experts believe the growth in health system consolidation is bound to continue.

Provider consolidation wasn't restricted to hospitals and health systems, but also included the ongoing absorption of independent physician groups. According to a *Health Affairs* article, more than half of US physicians and 72% of hospitals were affiliated with a larger system in 2018. For physicians, that represented a 20% jump from levels just two years earlier.[11] The health plan sector also saw mega-mergers over the prior decade, including CVS/Aetna, Optum/DaVita, Cigna/Express Scripts, and the failed Aetna/Humana merger. Additionally, the digital health space set a record for consolidation in one year in just the first half of 2021, with more than $46.1 billion spent on deals for 136 transactions through the second quarter.[12]

Of course, as we now know, bigger isn't always better. There has been much press on how large health system mergers have failed to realize any meaningful improvements in quality, experience, or cost savings. In fact, there has been a noticeable trend of announced consolidation moves unwinding, some before the deal is closed, such as Intermountain and Sanford Health, Geisinger and AtlantiCare, and Beaumont Health twice, once with Summa Health, and then again later in 2020 with Advocate Aurora. And in rare cases, a separation after an earlier consolidation, such as Hoag suing to separate from Providence eight years after their merger. The wave of mergers and acquisitions in the provider space has caught the eye of national politicians, such as Minnesota senator and former presidential candidate Amy Klobuchar, who called for more regulatory action to stem the "vicious cycle" of hospital consolidation.[13]

> QUESTION: **Will scale continue to offer a safe, if temporary, haven for hospitals and health systems seeking to protect themselves from changing business models?**

5 – The shift to value-based care

Back in the early 2010s, the move from the fee-for-service model that dominated healthcare in the U.S. to a value-based care model, pushed by the advent of the ACA, was often described by speakers, consultants, and other illuminati using a boating analogy. Health systems were told that they had one foot on the pier (fee-for-service based revenue) and one foot in the boat (value-based care revenue) and that in a few years, the boat would be far enough away that they would have to jump feet first into the boat and embrace a full-on value-based care world. More than a decade after the ACA became law, however, health systems *still* have one foot on that pier and one in the boat, making for a rather uncomfortable image of doing some serious splits as the boat continues to go out to sea. In 2018, Moody's claimed only 1.9% of net patient revenue for non-profit hospitals came from risk-based payments.[14] Revive's own Trust Index research reveals that the percentage of hospitals' commercial revenue tied to value has stalled at 13% for the last four years – and that includes a broad definition of value that includes upside-only pay for performance incentives. According to a survey conducted by Coverys in the fall of 2020, less than 20% of Medicare spending was value-based.[15]

There are also plenty of stout opponents to the value-based care model, many who argue that "risk-sharing" is more about shifting risk to providers who stand to gain little or nothing from the deal. "Population health and value-based care are still answers looking for problems," claims Nate Kaufman, managing director at Kaufman Strategic Advisors, a long-tenured healthcare financial expert and outspoken critic of the move to value-based care.[16] He notes that many believe that Medicare Advantage is an example of value-based care, yet in their March 2021 Report to Congress, the Medicare Payment Advisory Committee concludes that it costs Medicare over 3% more than fee-for-service to have a beneficiary enrolled in Medicare Advantage. Kaufman asks: How can this be a value-based program when it raises the cost of care?

But nearly all the experts we talked to believe the shift to value-based care would continue. Many in the industry point to the Covid-19 pandemic serving as an accelerator for value-based payment structures, much as it was for the adoption of virtual care:

"As it crushes the finances of physician practices and hospitals, the COVID-19 pandemic is making the most compelling argument yet for a fundamental shift in how our healthcare is funded and prioritized," stated the lead in a December 2020 article in *Fierce Healthcare*, with the primary argument being that the drop in patient volumes from the shutdown of elective procedures in the spring of 2020 and subsequent reluctance of many patients to seek care during the pandemic left physicians and hospitals financially vulnerable under the fee-for-service model. [17] There's also good reason to believe the Biden administration will support the continued push for value-based care contracts. So no matter how slow that boat moves out to sea, it's likely that value-based care will only grow in the coming decade.

> QUESTION: **At what point in the decade, if ever, will the shift to value-based care induce the desired transformation of how healthcare is delivered in the U.S.?**

6 – The growth of new provider entrants

When it was announced in January 2021 that Haven, the three-year-old collaboration of Amazon, Berkshire, and JPMorgan was being shuttered, you could hear the cynical laughter from legacy health system leaders echo across the land. "You see, this is a complicated business, so good luck with all that 'disruption!'" And to some degree, the skeptics have a point. I first started talking about "new entrants" in the provider space back in 2005 – I remember giving a keynote presentation that opened with the theme music from the movie *Jaws* as I set out to warn legacy providers of such new competition as QuickMedx, the Minneapolis start-up that put a nurse practitioner in mall kiosks to provide "lite" urgent care; Best Buy, which has just opened the health concept "eq-life" store in the Twin Cities; and Revolution Health, a healthcare company led by former AOL founder Steve Case designed to "reinvent" healthcare. Of course, other than QuickMedx, which went on to become MinuteClinic, these ventures and many others went nowhere. Like so many other "hot trends" in the healthcare space, changes wrought by new entrants such as MinuteClinic, BestBuy, CVS/Aetna, Walmart Health, Haven, Google, Apple, and others have been slow to emerge. Of course, "slow" does not mean "never."

Savvy industry watchers didn't laugh at the dissolution of Haven. Many recognized that untethered, Amazon could wreak far more havoc on the traditional delivery of healthcare than as part of a cumbersome collaboration. As just one example, not two months after the announcement on Haven, Amazon launched Amazon Care, which will provide virtual-care services in all 50 states at some point the summer of 2021. JPMorgan itself announced in May 2021 its own healthcare business, Morgan Health, to serve its more than 150,000 employees across the U.S. Of course, MinuteClinics are now part of CVS Health, who, along with Walmart Health and Walgreens, could make substantial inroads in "top-of-the-funnel" care such as retail, virtual, or primary care, as well as disease management and specialty care. There is a plethora of relatively new ventures primed to attack that same space, from One Medical to ArchWell Health to CityMD. And let's not forget Optum, the apex predator, which continues to acquire and/or partner with physician groups, surgical centers, hospitals, and health systems at an increasing clip, and now is the largest employer of physicians in the U.S. Legacy health systems would be foolish to ignore these "new" entrants, even if the track record so far has brought limited change to date. In our 2020 report, "The End of the Runway," we showed how five meaningful and potentially long-term changes in consumer behavior caused by Covid-19 played right into the hands of new entrants, at the expense of traditional providers. The growth of these new entrants plays a major role in our first and third predictions, and with healthcare spending hitting the $4 trillion mark, making up more than 18% of our entire economy, there's no reason to expect anything but a continued expansion of new players in this space.

> QUESTION: **Will the 2020s finally be the decade that sees new entrants truly upsetting the traditional health-system apple cart?**

7 – The explosion of virtual care

Hey, have you heard? Virtual care took off in 2020 thanks to the pandemic! No really, the numbers were astounding, with hospitals and health systems showing exponential growth, such as one example going from zero virtual visits to more than 25,000 a month, seemingly overnight. (Honestly, it hard to know which of those figures is more astounding – that it ended up with 25,000 virtual visits a month, or that it started with zero!) Yes, from the journals of Captain Obvious, we call out the trend of virtual care. But even though this topic has been beaten into the ground, and virtual care volumes subsided somewhat once providers opened their doors again in the second half of 2020, we still need to cite this shift. For as obvious as the upshot may be, it's still worthwhile to reflect on how the expansion of virtual care underlies many of the predictions that follow in this book.

We start with all the ways health systems are seeking to expand the application of virtual care, from replacing in-person primary care visits or disease management check-ins to providing easier pre-op consults and post-surgical therapy sessions. But the amazing speed with which health systems employed virtual visits in the spring of 2020 when Covid-19 shut down non-essential encounters was made possible by the speed with which regulators relaxed restrictions that hamstrung prior expansion of virtual care, and the quick accommodations made by private payors on the payment side. While some insurers try to walk those payment allowances back, to a large degree there will be no going back because millions of consumers got their first taste of virtual care, and *they* will fight to keep it.

Some experts believe that most consumers prefer in-person clinical care and will forgo the option of virtual care once Covid-19 has finally been vanquished. Umm, have you met Millennials, let alone Gen Z? According to a McKinsey & Company report in July 2021, telehealth utilization has stabilized at levels 38 times higher than pre-pandemic.[18]

"The whole 'going to the doctor' phenomenon is something that's fading away from our generation. It means getting in a car [and] going to a waiting room," said a 29-year-old from San Francisco in a *Washington Post* story back in 2018, speaking for at least a couple of generations[19]. (Seriously, is there anything more hilarious than calling how healthcare has been delivered for decades 'the whole going to the doctor phenomenon'?). I mean, I'm 53, and after my first dose of virtual care during the spring of 2020, I've pushed my clinic to allow for virtual visits even if they weren't originally offered. Why sit around and read *Golf Digest* from 2012 waiting for my doctor when I can be in the comfort of my own home, doing whatever I please while I wait?

The changes in regulatory rules, reimbursement, and consumer expectations means it's inconceivable that the explosion of virtual care will be a flash in the pan. Those who don't fight to expand virtual care will definitely fall behind.

QUESTION: **How far can virtual care go in replacing traditional in-person care?**

8 – Healthcare dispersion

> *Disruption in health care entails moving the simplest*
> *procedures now performed in expensive hospitals to*
> *outpatient clinics, retail clinics, and patients' homes.*[20]

That was the late, amazingly great, Clayton Christensen in a 2011 article summarizing a key premise in his book *The Innovator's Prescription.* More than a decade ago, the great innovation expert claimed that the only way healthcare in the U.S. could stem unsustainable growing costs was pushing medicine out of expensive, inefficient hospitals to whatever downstream resource can provide those services. In the past decade, we've seen this occur in everything from outpatient joint replacement surgery to in-home infusion services to Walgreens offering diabetes consultations.

The Covid-19 pandemic will once again serve as an accelerator of this trend. In our 2020 report on consumerism in healthcare, we called out the role of Covid-19 in driving "Smaller Life Spheres," or the idea that after a year of having to stay put and experiencing everything from entertainment to food to exercise to school to work in their home, consumers would have different expectations about proximity, convenience, and willingness to travel. According to a July 2020 report from McKinsey & Company, both the use of "e-pharmacies" and "e-doctors" were pegged as "enduring" consumer trends coming out of the pandemic.[21] And of course there's the expansion of virtual care covered in the last trend. (We'll spend more time on this concept in Chapter Four.)

Scott Galloway, a popular entrepreneur, speaker, author, podcast host, and adjunct professor of marketing at New York University's Stern School of Business, calls it "The Great Dispersion," or "the greatest reshuffling of stakeholder value in recent history."[22] In Christensen and Galloway you have two of the most respected thinkers on modern business aligned on the same premise – what consumers used to seek out, travel for, or attend will now be brought to them. This trend plays a meaningful role in the first and third predictions, but can be seen behind the scenes in the others as well.

QUESTION: **How far will dispersion go in bringing healthcare to our laptops and doorsteps?**

9 – Health inequity and disparities

First, because we'll be revisiting this trend again throughout this book, let's make sure we're defining these terms accurately. A "health disparity" refers to a higher burden of illness, injury, disability, or mortality experienced by one group relative to another. A "health care disparity" typically refers to differences between groups in health insurance coverage, access to and use of care, and quality of care. A higher incidence of diabetes in Black people relative to the general population in the United States is an example of a health disparity, and the lack of access to quality healthcare facilities or providers in rural areas is a health *care* disparity. "Health inequity" represents the different societal, environmental, or institutional situations that contribute to or are causes of health and healthcare disparities, such as poverty, a lack of education, or the lack of safe or affordable housing. Health inequities and health care disparities combine to drive health disparities.

As long as there has been inequality in the U.S., there have been health inequities and resulting health disparities. Or in other words, since the founding of the country. Following the passing of the ACA in 2010 and the subsequent strategies of population health management and accountable care, the healthcare industry began paying greater attention to the root causes of many healthcare issues, or what are known as social determinants of health. These behavioral, socioeconomic, and environmental factors contribute up to 80-90% of an individual's health condition, with the remaining 10-20% of contributions coming from the individual's physical condition.[23]

The year 2020 will go down in history along with 1929, 1941, or 1968 as a year marking a fundamental upheaval in American society. Not one but two major events occurred in 2020 that change how we think about health inequality and health disparities, and likely will for years to come. First, the Covid-19 pandemic clearly demonstrated the atrocious state of health disparities in the U.S., as the coronavirus had an outsized impact on communities of color and other under-addressed populations. Second, the murder of George Floyd by police officer Derrick Chauvin in Minneapolis on May 25, 2021, created a social uprising not seen since the late 1960s, as millions of Americans protested police brutality and marched for social justice. Together, these two events make it impossible to ignore the extent of health inequity and its effect on health disparities in this country. Of course, recognizing a problem and solving for it are two very different things.

> QUESTION: **Can the U.S. muster the will and resources to meaningfully address health inequities and disparities in this country?**

10 – The spread of misinformation

In October 2020, Tim Nguyen from the World Health Organization joined our agency's podcast *The No Normal Show* to discuss how the "infodemic" was making the pandemic worse. The WHO defines an infodemic as "an overabundance of information—some accurate and some not— that occurs during an epidemic. It spreads between humans in a similar manner to an epidemic, via digital and physical information systems. It makes it hard for people to find trustworthy sources and reliable guidance when they need it."[24]

Head of Unit for High Impact Events in the Global Infectious Hazard Preparedness Department at the WHO, Nguyen explained that, thanks to social media, politicization, and other cultural factors both in the U.S. and around the globe, the ability to manage and mitigate the coronavirus was hampered both by *misinformation*, or data or insights that are wrong in nature, though not intentionally so, and by *disinformation*, propaganda that is spread intentionally to mislead. A Facebook post reading "My aunt says the vaccine has a microchip in it that will read your brain waves" could actually be one or the other, which matters because combatting the infodemic requires different strategies for misinformation and disinformation.

While the Covid-19 pandemic brought the problems of misinformation and disinformation to the forefront of a global crisis, the issue of misinformation (which we'll use to define all forms of bad information) has been growing in severity since the advent of the World Wide Web in the 1990s, and more so by the introduction of social media starting in the mid-2000s. Back then, the joke was "I read it on the Internet, so it must be true!" Somehow, that joke turned into an unironic statement leveraged by millions who have bought into QAnon, Hydroxychloroquine as a cure for Covid-19, flat-earth science, and any number of the thousands of conspiracy theories and falsehoods floating in the ether. Worse, misinformation has fueled greater political division and polarization in the U.S., leading to such dystopian concepts as "alternative facts." The violent incursion of the U.S. Capitol on January 6, 2021, was either an insurrection aimed at overthrowing a democratically elected government or just a "normal tourist visit," as one congressman from Georgia defined it.[25]

The spread of misinformation has all sorts of potential repercussions for America. Healthcare in particular may suffer potentially dangerous ramifications from this phenomenon, for everything from how vaccines can be used to stop the spread of deadly viruses and disease to how a health system might manage a reputational hit from a disgruntled employee.

QUESTION: **To what degree will the spread of misinformation slow or disable the advance of medical science and healthcare?**

11 – Push for data privacy

In 2017, after reading more deeply how Facebook was using my personal data, and after reading about Cambridge Analytica and other data abusers, I quit the platform for good. While I wasn't alone in this move, at the time I was certainly an exception.

The push for data privacy has been slowly building force, taking more formal shape with the introduction of the General Data Protection Act (GDPR) by the European Union in 2016, California's version of the GDPR, the Consumer Privacy Act (which, because it affects any organization with over $25 million in revenues that does business in California, affects the entire U.S.), and most recently, moves by Google to eliminate 3rd party "cookies" by 2022 and Apple's change forcing an opt-in for any app that wants to track users and their data. Apple has actually claimed the mantle of "data protector," touting how they never sell user data and launching ads slamming other web platforms for creating a Big Brotherish environment, landing with the slogan "Privacy. That's iPhone."[26]

The push for greater data privacy protections relates to the healthcare space as well, and rightly so given the increase in cybersecurity threats to hospitals, health systems, other providers, and patients themselves. In May 2021, respected San Diego-based health system Scripps Health was crippled by a ransomware attack, which impaired care delivery for more than a week, including the diversion of critical care patients to nearby hospitals.[27] The organization's EMR, patient portal, email systems, and website were all offline for some or all of the attack. In October 2020, the virtual behavioral health platform Vastaamo, the largest network of private mental-health providers in Finland, was hacked, with the private therapy records of more than 30,000 patients eventually released online.

For a frightening view of how susceptible our private data is to misuse, readers are strongly recommended to watch the documentary "The Great Hack" on Netflix. One industry expert we spoke to, from a prominent academic medical center, said her CIO claimed the most recent six months had seen more cyberthreats to their system than any time previously. As cyberthreats increase both within the healthcare industry and across the economy, consumers will likely push even harder for more data-protection regulation, or will begin opting out on their own. For healthcare in the U.S., that could result in everything from a hampering of public health efforts such as vaccine distribution to a limiting of precision medicine breakthroughs to a slowing of the push for a more universal sharing and leveraging of individual health data.

QUESTION: To what degree will the push for greater data privacy impede the transformation of healthcare in the U.S.?

12 – The affordability crisis

In a 2021 article, Tom Robertson, executive director of the Vizient Research Institute, uses the theory of "The Tragedy of the Commons" to help explain why healthcare costs have and will continue to rise in the U.S. In a nutshell, individual healthcare provider organizations do what they have to in order to survive financially – drive volumes, push for increased commercial insurance payment rates, grow bigger through mergers and acquisitions. While each organization can make a rational and understandable case for their own activities, the collective result is an unsustainable trend of rising healthcare costs, leading to lower disposable income for individuals paying more out-of-pocket, copious amounts of personal debt, bankruptcies, etc. Robertson says:

> We are fast approaching the point where health care spending will exceed the carrying capacity of the middle-class working family's income. We cannot slow the rate of increase in health care spending sufficiently by curbing utilization. If they haven't already done so, prices are on the verge of eclipsing the middle-class household's ability to pay; the market has failed to rein in health care prices despite forty years of trying.

Whether you agree with the analogy of The Tragedy of the Commons used for healthcare, it's hard to argue that unless something changes with rising healthcare costs, it will certainly be a tragedy for millions who won't be able to afford care, or who will go broke trying. The latest data from the federal government shows healthcare spending rose 4.6% in 2019 to reach $3.8 billion, or, on average, $11,583 per man, woman and child living in the U.S. As it has for years, healthcare represents the largest portion of the U.S. economy, hitting 17.7% of Gross Domestic Product in 2019.[28]

Compared with other countries around the world, our spending per capita in healthcare is fairly insane – of thirteen of the wealthiest countries in the world, the U.S. ranks first in costs, spending roughly twice the amount of money per capita as the average of those 13 countries.[29] And as we all know, when it comes to national healthcare spending, we *don't* get what we pay for. While the U.S. leads the world in many areas of healthcare, such as research and innovation, it trails its peers in so many fundamental categories. Compared to 36 other high-income countries, the U.S. has the lowest life expectancy, the highest suicide rate, the highest chronic disease burden, the highest rate of obesity (double that of the average), and the highest rate of avoidable deaths.[30] And those are just the "highest" stats. While there are some positives, such as having the highest survivability rate for breast cancer, the U.S. is a loser in almost all categories. As Robertson predicts, all of this is having a growing impact on American families. According to a March 2021 survey by West Health-Gallup, nearly 20% of Americans say they did not seek treatment for medical care the prior year due to cost, and just as many said that, if they needed some form of health care, they wouldn't be able to afford it.[31]

Unfortunately, there don't appear to be any obvious or hopeful ideas or changes in sight. Value-based care has failed to move the needle meaningfully. The private sector threw three of its most successful companies at the problem in Haven, which as we mentioned earlier closed up shop in early January. The Covid-19 pandemic has affected millions financially, and has hurt many hospitals and health systems financially to boot. The issue isn't going away, and will likely only get worse.

> QUESTION: **How much longer can the U.S. sustain rising healthcare costs without significantly damaging our economy, our healthcare system, and society as a whole?**

13 – The mental health crisis

Like many other things, the state of mental health and healthcare in the U.S. has come under greater scrutiny as a result of the Covid-19 pandemic. During the pandemic, 40% of Americans reported symptoms of anxiety or depression, up from just 10% pre-pandemic.[32] Given what we have had to go through collectively – the fear of Covid-19, hundreds of thousands of deaths, millions sick, the loss of jobs and economic security, political strife – perhaps it's surprising that percentage isn't even higher. Actually, the percentages *are* higher for those who have felt the pandemic in a more powerful way, such as communities of color and essential workers. Worse could be potential long-term and devastating damage to children, whether it be those who are pre-school age and were born into a society of mask-wearing and social distancing, or those who experienced virtual learning for months on end. An article in *The New York Times* in June 2021, titled "8-Year Olds in Despair: The Mental Crisis is Getting Younger," told the story of a girl on the East Coast who, after thoughts of harming herself and fears for her friends and family due to Covid-19, called a suicide hotline: She was 11 years old. A panel of pediatric experts said the Covid-19 pandemic only exacerbated an existing "epidemic in children's mental health," and that the country could be dealing with the aftermath for decades to come.[33]

Many experts will tell you that mental health crisis has been building in the U.S. for many years before the pandemic hit. Pre-Covid, one in five adults in the U.S. experienced some form of mental illness, with 5% experiencing severe mental illness, according to the National Association On Mental Illness (NAMI), yet less than half received treatment. On average, the time between the first sign of symptoms and professional treatment is 11 years.[34] There of course has always been a stigma associated with mental health. Even semantics matter, as many clinicians and experts call out the term "behavioral health," which includes mental health disorders, addiction, and other issues, because it infers the mental health problem derives somehow from the individual's behavior. Additionally, mental health services have been chronically under-funded and under-reimbursed. Whenever the federal or state governments tighten their belts, mental health funding often seems an easy target. Following the Great Recession, more than $4 billion in mental health services funding was cut by states facing financial shortfalls between 2009-2011. Despite new regulations stemming from the ACA and other laws calling for insurers to cover mental and physical health benefits equally, mental health coverage still lags in many ways, according to NAMI. For example, a 2019 study showed that an office visit for behavioral health was five times more likely to be out-of-network than a primary care appointment.[35]

Mental health and healthcare have often been afterthoughts in discussions about improving healthcare in the U.S. While overlooked for decades, there may be some hope that one silver-lining from the Covid-19 pandemic is that mental health will be given the due attention it deserves. In just one example, the American Rescue Plan, the $1.9 trillion coronavirus relief plan passed into law in March 2021, included $3 billion in funding to help combat mental health and substance abuse issues. More will undoubtedly be needed, but it's a start.

> QUESTION: **To what degree will mental health services and treatment become a larger, more consistent component of overall approaches to health, wellness, and care in the U.S. moving forward?**

14 – The growth of big data in healthcare

We've been hearing about the promise of "big data" in healthcare for quite some time. As articulated by one source, big data is defined as "the collection, analysis, and leverage of consumer, patient, physiological, and medical data that is too large or complex to be understood by conventional methods of data processing. Instead, big data is often processed by machine learning techniques and data analysts."[36] The potential benefits are numerous and transformative – far faster and more accurate disease diagnosis, identification of the best courses of treatment, real-time decision-making support, faster and broader spread and adoption of clinical best practices, predicative analytics, cost-savings, faster vaccine development, more efficient resource and healthcare staffing allocation. The list is truly impressive.

According to a number of experts we talked with, today we're still primarily in the collection and analysis phases, with the focus on gathering and processing as much data as possible, whether that comes from insurance claims, electronic medical records, genomics, public health data, pharmaceutical and medical device data, or wearables. Leveraging this data in a broad and meaningful way still may be some ways out, which can lead to confusion or even frustration in the industry. Consider the by now classic tale of the rise and fall of IBM Watson Health. IBM touted huge potential for Watson Health a decade ago, eventually spending millions on turning big data into AI-driven decision-making support for clinicians. Ginni Rometty, IBM's CEO at the time, spoke of big dreams, "Our moon shot will be the impact we have on health care," Rometty said. "I'm absolutely positive about it."[37] (Interestingly, we'll see almost the exact same sentiment from the CEO of another tech giant uttered nearly a decade later in Chapter 6). The organization ran into a number of failures in trying to support genomics and cancer research and working with some of the most prestigious health systems in the country, such as MD Anderson and Memorial Sloan Kettering. While IBM ultimately invested billions in IBM Watson Health, the future for the enterprise remains unclear, with a possible sell-off of the unit one idea under consideration.[38]

The story of the struggles of IBM Watson Health aren't really a sign of failure of the promise of big data, but rather the reflection of a common component of technological advancement – early pioneers often ending up ahead of their time in terms of thinking or approach. The promise of big data is real, despite the myriad of challenges it faces, including the hundreds or even thousands of organizations pursuing big data to one degree or another, interoperability hurdles, misaligned incentives, or regulatory and privacy concerns. It's clear the question isn't if big data can transform health and healthcare in the U.S., the question is when. More specifically:

> QUESTION: **To what degree will big data in the coming decade solve for the fundamental issues facing healthcare in the U.S., such as affordability, disparities, and runaway chronic disease?**

15 – The vertical integration of health insurers

The largest health insurer in the U.S., and the fifth-largest company overall, is receiving less and less of its revenue and profits from health insurance. UnitedHealth Group, which posted a $6 billion dollar profit on revenues of more than $71 billion in the second quarter of 2021 (a 15% year-over-year increase), saw even faster growth from its Optum unit, which includes care delivery, pharmacy benefits management, and analytics services. The unit saw a nearly 17% year-over-year jump with more than $38 billion in revenue in Q2 2021. Compare that to revenue of $55.5 billion in Q2 2021 for UnitedHealthcare, the company's health insurance arm. In 2018, health insurance represented 81% of the company's revenue.[39] Today that's down to 78%, with Optum growing at nearly twice the rate as the UnitedHealthcare plan arm. OptumHealth, the provider component of the unit, claims to have served 99 million people in the second quarter of 2021. Based on its plans for 2021, the organization is the largest employer of physicians in the country, making it theoretically the largest health system in the country.

United is just one example of health plans moving aggressively into the provider space – CVS Health's acquisition of Aetna in 2018 and Humana's acquisition of Kindred's home health services are two other examples. There has always been vertical integration in healthcare to some degree, with some of the most well-respected health providers in the U.S providing health insurance as part of their offering – Geisinger, Kaiser Permanente, and Intermountain Healthcare as examples. And since the advent of the ACA, we've seen more systems move into the space with provider-sponsored health plans (with spotty success at best). The difference here is scale. While Geisinger has roughly 600,000 health plan members in a limited geographical region, for example, UnitedHealthcare covers nearly 50 million nationwide. The growth of vertically integrated insurers raises a number of fundamental questions about healthcare delivery in this country:

- To what degree will insurers steer patients away from legacy healthcare providers to their own services, and what will the financial pain be for these legacy providers as a result?
- At what point does one of the most touted benefits of health insurance – to lower costs by slowing utilization and managing care – run face first into the drive to raise revenue and profits through the delivery of care in companies that do both?

- To what degree will patients experience less choice, more costs, or other negative effects of the verticalization of the health insurance industry, or will those dynamics improve as the system changes?

The vertical integration of health plans plays a critical role in two of our predictions, and likely would influence all of them to some degree, over the coming decade. In some ways, it's the biggest change to the business model of healthcare companies we've seen since the advent of managed care in the 1980s.

QUESTION: **With vertical integration clearly a winning play for health insurers, to what degree will traditional healthcare providers and consumers be losers?**

16 – Precision medicine

Precision medicine, genomics, personalized medicine – these interrelated fields hold enormous promise for advancing health and healthcare in the U.S. Moving from a mass approach to health and clinical care to one customized to the individual based on genetic make-up, relevant social determinants of health, and other personalized factors is already taking place in various ways. For example, researchers know that one specific drug, Gleevec, is effective in treating leukemia when a certain genetic make-up is present, but not in other situations, allowing physicians to use the drug only when a patient tests positive for that genetic profile.[40] The advancement of precision medicine is tied closely to trend 14 above, the increased use of big data in healthcare. That means that as of today, the promise of precision medicine is greater than the reality. As of June 2021, the FDA had approved 22 cellular and gene therapy treatments. But hundreds more are under evaluation, and the agency expects to approve between 10-20 products per year by 2025.[41]

Further, there are numerous moral and ethical issues tied to precision medicine and genomics. In one example, what should individuals do when genetic testing shows markers for potential diseases such as muscular dystrophy or Alzheimer's? How might that influence their decisions related to medical care or how they live their lives? How might it affect decisions on having children, who also might carry the same threat of disease? Who should have access to that data, and what happens should personal genetic data be hacked or otherwise made available for unauthorized use?

One of the greatest dilemmas presented by precision medicine is the cost of many of the targeted gene therapies. For example, in 2017, the FDA approved a drug called Luxturna used to treat a small population of people who inherit blindness at a cost of $425,000.

Per eye.

In 2019, a therapy called Zolgensma created to treat spinal muscular atrophy, a rare childhood disorder, was priced at $2.1 million for a single intravenous infusion.[42] The question of how to cover the costs of such treatments, which extend far beyond the means of nearly all Americans, plays a key role in two of the predictions found in this book. Payment for such expensive medical treatments is not guaranteed within the private insurance market, and even Medicare has struggled with this issue. For example, when the first genetic therapy approved by the FDA was released – CAR-T therapy – most oncologists were unable to leverage the drug because Medicare reimbursement only covered $35,000 – $40,000 of the medication's list price of $373,000.[43] (Of course, in some cases, the use of expensive gene therapies would reduce or even eliminate significant costs of treatment and care for the patient over their lifetime. But even in those cases, insurance companies may not recognize those potential savings until there has been ample time and evidence for the math to work in favor of payment, which would be years down the road.)

Precision medicine is of course only one example of how healthcare costs often exceed the ability to pay for those who need treatment. The question of the cost/benefit calculation of such drugs, which often are only usable by a few thousand people in total, joins other philosophical cost/benefit debates such as the value of spending hundreds of thousands of dollars on end-of-life care, or whether it makes sense to spend millions to keep a premature baby alive. In many ways, these harken back to The Tragedy of the Commons dilemma mentioned earlier in the chapter:

how can the U.S. afford to spend so much on so few, yet to the parents of that premature baby, the question is how can we afford not to?

QUESTION: **How will the exorbitant costs of genetic therapies and precision medicine overall hamstring this incredible advancement in medicine?**

17 – The top-of-funnel trend

Over the past decade, legacy health systems have awakened to the importance of the top of the funnel, and their strategies in this area are instrumental to understanding how the industry may, or may not, shift in the coming decade. By "top of the funnel," we mean the acuity funnel, where we imagine the continuum of care delivery and apply it to the shape of a funnel, with the first-encounter, easy access, often lower-acuity services at the top – urgent care, retail care, virtual care, emergency care and in some cases, primary care – followed down the line by specialty care, surgical care, tertiary care, and finally quaternary care at the bottom of the funnel. Historically, legacy hospitals and health systems have been primarily concerned with mid- and down-funnel services, both because their entire model was built around the in-patient care found there, and this is where the higher reimbursement care resides. I can remember back in the 1990s and early 2000s, when the shift to true managed care models had eroded, and some legacy providers shed their top-of-the-funnel offerings such as primary care because they weren't, on their own, a money maker. I recall one trauma center that shuttered its mobile mammography van because the scans provided as part of that service couldn't cover the cost of offering the service in the first place. In retrospect, of course, that decision seems at best short-sighted, for while a mobile mammography van or primary care clinic might not pay for itself, the critical role it plays in driving down-funnel encounters – which more than pay for themselves – seems obvious.

But it wasn't until the last decade where we saw leaders in the legacy provider space begin to aggressively expand their top-of-the-funnel offerings. As we highlighted in *Joe Public III*, released in 2018, many systems had expanded even further, changing their value proposition to reflect not just care delivery, but also a mission to help communities and individuals stay healthy in the first place. Much of this was driven, of course, by the ACA, as the move to value-based care, Accountable Care Organizations, population health management, and other industry shifts pushed providers to engage patients as far upstream – or up-funnel – as possible. At the same time, we saw new entrants in the space, such as MinuteClinic, Walmart, and Teledoc pose a new threat to legacy providers. I first started presenting about the threat of the "new competition" at healthcare conferences back in 2005. In the meantime, companies as varied as Apple and Dollar General have entered the space. And while the effect of these "new entrants" on how care is delivered and experienced in the industry has been incremental to date, few believe that won't change. We dive deep into the importance of the top of the funnel to the future of the industry in Chapter Six (appropriately called "The Funnel Wars"), though the import of this industry dynamic will be felt in all five predictions.

> QUESTION: **Will the continued expansion of top-of-the-funnel investment and offerings across the industry improve health and access for consumers, or will its legacy be a greater disintegration of care and yet another driver of higher healthcare costs in the U.S.?**

18 – Social determinants of health

While originating nearly 20 years ago, the concept of social determinants of health (SDH) has gained more traction in the U.S. recently. First defined by the World Health Organization, SDH considers factors surrounding the physical condition or individual risk factors in understanding the overall health of a person, such as living situation, work environment, schooling, upbringing, social support, access to transportation, or geographic residence. Some experts argue that 80%

of an individual's overall health situation is driven not by their genetic make-up or physician condition, but by these outside factors. Many of the strategies emanating from the ACA, such as the development of Accountable Care Organizations and population health management programs, helped bring SDH to the forefront. After all, if the ultimate goal of value-based care is to compensate providers for the outcome of treatment, rather than the services provided, it's critical for clinicians to understand and try to influence any factor affecting a patient's medical situation.

Many healthcare providers have taken steps to help address social determinants of health in their communities. Not surprisingly, the leaders in this regard are those providers who also provide health insurance as part of their offering, giving them more incentive to solve for SDH. For example, both Optum and Kaiser Permanente have invested hundreds of millions of dollars in affordable housing programs, and Geisinger has received praise for its successful Food Farmacy, where clinicians prescribe certain healthy foods that are then provided to patients as part of their care. In Optum's case, that investment has specifically targeted managed Medicaid members given the economics of those programs.

The debate in the industry isn't whether there is value in addressing SDH, but rather *who* should be responsible for it. While providers have made attempts such as those listed above, the ROI of investing in improving SDH for those organizations is unproven. Health plans have also joined the fray, once again with a clear incentive to lower the cost of healthcare from whatever angle is effective. And there are hundreds of federal, state, and non-profit programs focused on the issue. The shift to focus on SDH is the start of addressing one of the fundamental issues with the healthcare system in the U.S., which is that it is a system funded and designed primarily to *treat* medical problems, not prevent them. This is a key reason the U.S. is the most expensive healthcare system in the world, while at the same time delivering mediocre-at-best results, as highlighted in trend number 12 above. We spend exponentially more as a nation on treating medical issues than we do on preventing them in the first place, and it shows.

QUESTION: **Will the increased focus on social determinants of health continue to provide sporadic and incremental benefits, or will our health system as a whole see real, meaningful improvement in this area in the coming decade?**

19 – The aging of America

There are three inescapable truths about the aging of America related to healthcare. First, the Baby Boomers are the second-largest generation in America, and they are moving through an age phase requiring the most care, with roughly 10,000 people hitting Medicare eligibility age every day, and with all Boomers turning age 65 or over by 2030. Second, there are more advances in medicine in terms of diagnosis and treatment than ever before for those growing older, and those advances will only continue. Third, in large part because of the second truth, Americans are living longer and longer. The average life expectancy for Americans has gone from 50 in 1900 to 78 in 2019, with experts saying half those who live to be age 65 will live well beyond age 85. While Covid-19 has set life expectancy back nearly 18 months for Americans in 2020, double that for some communities of color, experts still predict average life expectancy to balloon to over 85 in 2060.[44] (Though it's important to note that longer life spans do not necessarily equate to longer, *healthier*, lives.)

Combine these three truths, and the aging of America is a runaway locomotive, one we've been watching approach for years, and one where we still are unclear on the ultimate impact of its arrival. Predictions range from overflowing hospitals and ICUs to a severe shortage of nurses and physicians to runaway healthcare costs. The Medicare trust fund is only a few years away from being insolvent, and any solution will likely require an increase in age eligibility, higher premiums, means testing, less coverage, or some combination of all four. Will improvements in clinical care management, precision medicine, or other advances stem the tide? Will there be a societal change in America around end-of-life options, with more and more individuals suffering from the physical and mental deterioration of old age and disease deciding to end life on their own terms, perhaps with the support of changing laws?

All five of our predictions are colored one way or the other by the aging of America, and depending on the trajectory of this trend, a few, such as our prediction for Disparity Dystopia, could become true far sooner or in a far greater way that we even imagined. In some ways, though, this trend is similar to the next one, climate change, in that it may have the most consequence for healthcare over the next decade, but the incremental nature of the trend has us feeling a tad like the frog in the pot of boiling water. By the time we realize the water has reached that boiling point, it will be too late.

> QUESTION: **What will be the actual outcome of the aging of our society on the healthcare industry over the coming decade – just an incremental shift, or an earthquake measuring 9.0 on the Richter Scale?**

20 – Climate change

Most don't think of climate change in terms of healthcare. Instead, we think of rising sea levels, epic droughts, monster storms, wildfires, water shortages, famine, and the slow death of an inhabitable planet. (If you're looking to argue the existence of climate change or the severity of global warming, this book isn't the place. Nearly all major businesses, consulting firms, and insurance companies accept that climate change is real, and that the import is potentially devasting. When the underwriters are including global warming in their 10-year projections, the argument for all intents and purposes is over.) But while many don't think of climate change as a healthcare trend, experts we talked to insist that we should.

At a minimum, healthcare providers need to prepare for the localized effects of catastrophic events – consider what we saw happen to hospitals in the wake of Hurricanes Katrina or Sandy, or the challenges posed to providers with no available electricity during the recent devastating ice storm in Texas. But beyond these ever-more-frequent, yet one-time, events, the threat of global warming to the poor, communities of color, and those living in densely populated and coastal areas, presents a growing chronic issue. A wildfire that wipes out small towns in Northern California is one thing. A years-long drought that threatens the water supply for much of the western U.S. is something else altogether. That means the challenge isn't just to healthcare provider organizations. It falls on anyone who develops health and healthcare policy in the U.S., as well as local, state, federal, and private entities responsible for carrying out those policies. The healthcare industry in the U.S. faces many large-scale, structural challenges, including the aging of the population, affordability, access, and health disparities. Not only does climate change dwarf all of these, it will make each of them exponentially worse depending on how bad it gets. (And this doesn't even include our health system's contribution to the problem, given hospitals and healthcare facilities are among the worst contributors to carbon emissions).

QUESTION: **Beyond the localized incidents of climate-driven disasters, when will the healthcare system as a whole begin to show demonstrable effects from climate change, and how bad will those effects be?**

So now you have a glimpse at 20 of the foundational trends and issues that were instrumental in our thinking. And where did they lead us? First stop, the Copernican Consumer.

Chapter 4

PREDICTION

The Copernican Consumer

The future of the Copernican Consumer is reflected in the small device attached to the back of my upper arm. Most of the time, it sits there, unnoticed by me, unless it snags when I take off my shirt, or, on a rare occasion, when I catch it on a door frame as I brush by. It's white, and roughly the size of two quarters if stacked one on top of the other. As someone with Type 2 diabetes, I use my Freestyle Libre Sensor, produced by Abbott, three to four times a day to measure my blood sugar level. Connected to my iPhone via Bluetooth to my LibreLink app, it lets me see my blood sugar level for the prior eight hours every time I check, which involves waving the top of my phone across the sensor. If I allow it (which I do), the data is accessible to my physician and nutritionist, the latter of whom I check with every few months to make adjustments to the medication and insulin I take if things aren't looking right. The sensor replaces the old-school way of measuring blood sugar – pricking my finger with a needle pen and using an expensive strip to catch a drop of blood. I was supposed to do this when I woke up and before and after every meal. Which means I rarely did it. Now, thanks to this unobtrusive sensor, which I replace every two weeks and which is covered by my insurance, I painlessly check my blood sugar levels whenever I need to. Not only has it made my experience easier and pain-free, it has ramped up the management of my diabetes with the ability for real-time monitoring and adjustments.

So what's the big deal about my diabetes sensor? After all, sensors, monitors, and other personal health technology have been with us for decades. The first insulin pump, the "Biostator," was introduced in 1974, and by the 2010s, "patch pumps" were available for those managing Type 1 Diabetes.[45] The implantable loop recorder, a small device that is placed in the chest to monitor cardiac activity, was first introduced in 1990.[46] Holter monitors, consisting of a small device connected to numerous sensors attached to the body, can help track heart rhythms for up to three days.[47]

In 2014, *Time* Magazine gushed about the introduction of the Apple Watch, with paradigm-shifting callouts such as "It's intoxicating and also a bit disconcerting to have this much functionality perching on your wrist, like one of Cinderella's helpful bluebirds." and "Technological progress tends to feel incremental, but this is a watershed, a frog-boiling moment." A tad over the top, to be sure. Seven years on, and the Apple Watch now allows you to monitor your heart rate, track your sleep, measure your blood oxygen level, track your activity (including "movement," "exercise," and "time standing"), along with, of course, all its non-health functionality.[48] In June 2021, Apple added new functionality to the Watch that allows users to selectively share health information with medical providers, loved ones, or others to help monitor their health, and an article in TechCrunch claimed, "viewed as a whole, Apple has built probably the most powerful and accessible suite of personal health tools available to an individual, and it shows no signs of slowing down."[49] I don't own an Apple Watch, but even with my iPhone I can do many of those same things. And none of that includes all the health management apps that are available for smartphones, including such popular tools as MyFitnessPal (tracking food and nutrition), Headspace and Calm (for meditation and sleep support) or Happify (games and activities to improve mental health).

So back to my diabetes sensor – as we used to say back in junior high, what's the big whup? My sensor, and other personal health monitoring devices, are at the heart of our prediction that consumers will become the center of their health universe more than ever before:

> *Consumers will become the center of their own health universe more than ever before, enabled by sensors, AI, and other technology, as well as services geared toward empowering them, leading to profound implications for both consumers and healthcare organizations. Potential results could include a dramatic reduction in the need for primary care clinicians, an entirely new sector devoted to personal health management, true precision medicine combined with health management, and more.*

The LibreLink is a great example of where we're at today, and the possibility of what's to come. On the one hand, the LibreLink sensor reflects a notable advancement from past personal health monitors. For example:

- Ease of use – It's extraordinarily easy to apply and use. No need for professional intervention or training, just use the prepackaged insertion tool to "pop" it on.
- Broadening of use – According to the American Diabetes Association, 1.6 million Americans have Type 1 diabetes. On the other hand, there are 32.6 million Americans with Type 2 diabetes, or roughly 10% of the U.S. population[50]. That means this diabetes sensor is applicable to 20 times more people than the original monitors which were focused on Type 1 diabetes, extending the reach exponentially.
- Connectedness – The "Internet of Things" is now the "Internet of Health," and an essential piece in bringing personal health management to the masses. No more printing out results, going into the doctor's office to download data from a device, or even plugging into your own computer to transmit data.

On the other hand, the LibreLink sensor has a number of shortcomings that point to where the future may take us, such as:

- Intrusiveness – My quarter-sized arm monitor is light years ahead of that original back-pack-sized monitor. Yet, it's still very noticeable through any shirt, protruding as an oddly-placed disc through a t-shirt or dress-shirt and raising questions for co-workers, friends, or others that often go unasked. As a fifty-something, my shirt-off beach party days are well behind me, so I don't mind the awkward attachment. But there will be many who pass on the LibreLink for that reason alone. For personal health monitoring to become widely adopted, it must feel unobtrusive to the user. Even the Apple Watch – a health monitoring device cleverly disguised as a watch – is something that needs to be put on, taken off, charged, etc. – and it must replace a fashion accessory and status symbol people may be reluctant to part with (their actual watch).

- Manual nature – While the LibreLink sensor is so simple (and painless) compared to the old finger-prick method, it's still far too manual in nature. I must remember to scan my sensor, open my phone, and use the LibreLink app, and then wave my phone across the sensor. I've mastered the ability to do this surreptitiously when out to eat at a restaurant or when on a Zoom call at work, but why do I have to master anything, let alone surreptitiously? Why can't my disk communicate *automatically* with the app via Bluetooth without my having to take any steps? Further, in that scenario, why wouldn't the app automatically alert me when my numbers are out of range, either high or low, so I can take appropriate action? Again the promise of what's to come, where I'm not guiding my personal health monitoring device, it is *automatically guiding me.*

- Myopic – The LibreLink monitoring sensor is a fantastic advancement for those with diabetes. But what about my cholesterol issue? And what if I had high blood pressure, or migraines, or heart disease, or chronic back pain, or any other of the dozens of common ailments that afflict tens of millions of people in the U.S.? Am I looking at a future where, rather than having one quarter-sized disk attached to my arm, I would have 2, or 3, or 6? Would I need to wave my phone six different times an hour, access six different apps, and hold six different check-ins with six different providers? For the future of personal health monitoring to reach its full potential, it must evolve in the same way the overall health system in the U.S. must evolve – away from being centered around various diseases, ailments, and hospital service lines to being centered around the individual.

This unassuming little device represents the crossroads of personal health monitoring, which itself sits at the center of a truly consumer-centric universe and our first prediction – the creation of the Copernican Consumer.

The individual as the center

As the Copernican Consumer, I am the center of everything related to my health and healthcare. I am the sun, and clinicians, doctors, nurses, health educators and coaches, services, health plans – they are the planets that orbit around me. Technology and data allow me to both explicitly and implicitly manage all of my health inputs, from heart rate to diet to management of my Type 2 diabetes. My health is monitored, unobtrusively, 24x7x365, reducing the need for "appointment" healthcare. And the vast majority of my interaction with healthcare managers and professionals takes place on my terms, wherever I'm at – home, work, etc. I rarely go anywhere to receive health support or care – it all comes to me, driven by me thanks to constant, data-driven intel.

We named The Copernican Consumer after Nicolaus Copernicus, the mathematician and astronomer who introduced the concept that the sun was at the center of the universe in 1543. Of course, introducing "consumer centricity" as some new, futuristic concept would be a pretty lame prediction, given this concept has been bandied around healthcare for at least the last decade, if not longer. This prediction goes much further than the traditional definition of consumer-centricity, however, which typically has referred to placing the consumer – or patient – at the center of a clinical experience. That would still be a healthcare system-centric universe, where the consumer is made to feel more special or "central" within a set healthcare environment or environments.

In this case, we're truly putting the healthcare consumer at the center of the health universe, with all healthcare services and encounters revolving around her, wherever and whenever she is at any given moment. A truly Copernican Consumer. (Using Copernican as our label here is for demonstrative purposes only, and the fact that Copernicus was eventually found wrong in his heliocentric model reminds of two important lessons: first, we're making predictions here, which, as we've admitted, can go any number of ways; and second, taken to their ultimate literal end, all metaphors hold the seeds to their own destruction. But as an author and brand strategist, I realize the power of alliteration, so the Copernican Consumer it is).

A finger on the pulse

We started this chapter with a key component of the Copernican Consumer – personal health monitoring. In its 2021 Tech Trends Report, the Future Today Institute did its best John Mayer shout-out with a short scenario titled "Your Body is a Dataland," which paints a somewhat dystopian first-person vision of where personal health monitoring could easily go:

> During the pandemic, we transitioned to telemedicine and remote patient monitoring systems, which relied on AI. At first, it was a more equitable way to distribute healthcare benefits and to manage the shortage of providers. Automation led to efficiencies and cost savings. A decade later, there are no more in-person

*doctor exams. Instead, the data from your smart devices
are continuously mined and analyzed. An AI agent
anticipates your health problems in advance and adjusts
your permissions accordingly. If you want to see a doctor,
you need a referral from an AI agent—but you won't get
one unless you comply with your optimization plan. Your
wristband knows if you're stressed, and your smart toilet
detects that you've eaten too much sugar. Your smart
garbage can see that you've thrown out Twinkie wrappers.
Sweets aren't on your health plan, so the garbage can send
a message to your AI agent. It's another negative mark on
your digital health report card.*[51]

Spooky, yet not really that far-fetched. There's a lot to unpack there, including the use of AI, which we'll explore in a bit. But here's a more down-to-earth, but no less industry-shattering, prediction on personal health monitoring from Deloitte:

*Today, wearable devices that track our steps, sleep
patterns, and even heart rate have been integrated into
our lives in ways we couldn't have imagined just a few
years ago. We expect this trend to accelerate. The next
generation of sensors, for example, will move us from
wearable devices to invisible, always-on sensors that
are embedded in the devices that surround us. Many
medtech companies are already beginning to incorporate
always-on biosensors and software into devices that can
generate, gather, and share data. Advanced cognitive
technologies could be developed to analyze a significantly
large set of parameters and create personalized insights
into a consumer's health. The availability of data and
personalized AI can enable precision well-being and
real-time micro interventions that allow us to get
ahead of sickness and far ahead of catastrophic disease.
Consumers—armed with this highly detailed personal*

information about their own health—will likely demand that their health information be portable.[52]

Many of the experts we interviewed for the book identified personal health and remote monitoring as a key trend for the future. Here's what Adam Brase, Executive Director – Strategic Intelligence at Mayo Clinic, told us about the advanced use of data combined with personal monitoring:

> *In the next five years, we'll see substantial progress in using the data we've been accumulating for the last 10 years. It's currently nonstructured, spread around, and hard to leverage, but we'll be solving those challenges. At the same time, the advent of sensors will transform things. An Apple Watch that looks at blood pressure and glucose measurement – two of the biggest issues in medicine today, diabetes and heart disease – when coupled with diagnosis and management, it will be huge.*

Kevan Mabbutt, Senior Vice President and Chief Consumer Officer at Intermountain Healthcare, sees this future. He came to the prestigious health system from his role as Global Head of Insight at The Walt Disney Company explicitly to infuse the consumer mindset at Intermountain. While at Disney, he led consumer experience development and transformation for Disney's theme park, cruise line, resort, retail, and digital businesses in the U.S., Europe, and Asia, and was instrumental in defining the guest experience at Disney's first theme park in mainland China (Shanghai Disney Resort) and driving the digital transformation of Walt Disney World in Florida (My Disney Experience portal and Magic Bands).

Mabbutt believes healthcare must deliver a level of personalization that other industries are delivering, and that one key to this is portable consumer information. In his vision, the line between "patient" and "provider" will start blurring as we move further into the personal health monitoring realm.

Call it 'consumers as providers' – patients will be able to administer diagnostics, tests, and treatments themselves. The notion of patient vs. provider will blend and maybe begin to fade altogether. Look at hospitality and travel – as a consumer, you're part of that process. Self-serve models will merge the two. And if that's true, it challenges all sorts of things. What is value, the role of the provider, expertise, trust – all of these will change or resolve themselves in some new way.

Personal sensors and monitors are the foundation of the Copernican Consumer concept, because they allow healthcare to be tracked and engaged wherever that consumer is – at work, at play, at home. Take the plans by Kernal, a medical device company, to introduce a $50,000 helmet that can monitor brain activity. While that may sound expensive, that price is minuscule compared to the multi-million-dollar price tag of traditional brain scan technology. An article in the June 2021 issue of *Bloomberg Businessweek*, titled "Know Thyself Down to the Neuron," captures the potential of this accessible technology:

The promise of a leagues-more-affordable technology that anyone can wear and walk around with is, well, mind-bending. Excited researchers anticipate using the helmets to gain insight into brain aging, mental disorders, concussions, strokes, and the mechanics behind previously metaphysical experiences such as meditation and psychedelic trips. 'To make progress on all the fronts that we need to as a society, we have to bring the brain online,' says Bryan Johnson, who's spent more than five years and raised about $110 million – half of it his own money – to develop the helmets.[53]

Personal health technology isn't always wearable, of course. We've been hearing industry experts sing the potential of voice-activated platforms such as Amazon's Alexa since it was introduced in 2014.

When the device became HIPAA compliant in the spring of 2019, the use in the healthcare space became real, showing the potential for Alexa or other voice-user interfaces (VUI), which use natural language processing – one form of AI – to become the center of an in-home healthcare experience. The Google Assistant platform could provide a similar interface. And you can't talk about Google or Alexa without talking about Siri, the voice-activated application introduced by Apple back in 2011. Consider how VUI were leveraged during the Covid-19 pandemic. As outlined in an article in *NPJ – Digital Medicine*, the WHO released a voice-driven chatbot to provide information on Covid-19 through WhatsApp, Apple released an app in conjunction with the CDC to share Covid-19 information, and Amazon's Alexa had its own voice-activated Covid-19 updates and content.[54]

Beyond Covid-19, of course, VUI has been implemented through chat-bot technology by health systems across the country, and Woe-bot, a VUI-driven chat-bot providing therapy and mental health support, claims to send millions of messages each year to users seeking help.[55] And you can't talk about Alexa, or Siri, or VUI, or chat-bots, without talking about Artificial Intelligence (AI). They are inextricably linked.

Beam me up, Scotty

Wright Lassiter, President and CEO at Henry Ford Health System, has spent more than 30 years in healthcare, and started out by building one of the earlier proprietary electronic medical records for what was then called Methodist Hospitals of Texas. So when Lassiter gets excited about the potential of new technology to reshape healthcare, it's time to lean in. And he doesn't hold back.

> *It may sound silly, but go back and look at old sci-fi movies or Star Trek – it was fake then, but of lot of what we saw then will come to life going forward. We'll be using 3D and 4D printing technology to understand the body better than we ever could before. AI and blockchain*

will also transform our industry in a way where we don't have to rely on people as much. This is happening more so now in other countries such as Asia than it is here, where they use more digital interactions such as kiosks, or using technology to replace nursing assistants. The application of technology for consumers will become far more personalized than it is today.

Part and parcel to the emergence of the Copernican Consumer is the idea of personalization. We'll spend more time on this in a bit, but AI has a huge role to play both in personalization and bringing the consumer to the center of their healthcare universe. Consider again Woebot, the AI-driven therapy application. Many of the experts we interviewed called out the growing mental health crisis as a huge issue moving forward, and of course the pandemic made things much worse. According to a study by the Kaiser Family Foundation, 4 in 10 U.S. adults reported symptoms of depression or anxiety during the pandemic, a number that remained steady throughout 2020, and that was up from 1 in 10 prior to Covid-19.[56] This crisis hits at the same time there is a reported shortage of psychiatrists and therapists to help those facing mental illness. My wife can attest to that. She opened her own therapy practice in the fall of 2019, and was just getting rolling when the Covid-19 pandemic hit the U.S. in March 2020. Initially, requests for support dried up, a dynamic other therapists shared during the summer of 2020, as organizations stepped up corporate mental health services for employees, and many people either avoided seeking care or didn't recognize the issues they were facing. Today? She is forced to turn away requests from new potential clients because she can't keep up with demand. Which leads us back to Woebot. While there has been an explosion in virtual mental health services such as Headspace, Calm, Lark, or Talkspace, we can study Woebot to understand the potential of AI in personal health.

Introduced in 2017, Woebot relies on cognitive behavioral therapy to help treat users. How does the experience feel? Here's an excerpt from a June 2021 article in *The New York Times* that shows how close to "human" the exchanges can be:

"I understand that you're experiencing a relationship problem, is that right?"

Yes.

"Okay, I'm delighted that you want to work on this K. I've good and bad news for you… Which do you want to hear first?"

Good news.

"The good news is, I have very powerful skills that I can teach you! These skills have really helped a lot of people build better relationships."

And the bad news?

"The bad news is that you would have to be willing to accept 100% of the responsibility for changing the relationship."

Why?

"Because you're only ever going to be able to have control over your part of it.[57]"

The value of an AI-driven solution like Woebot, according to founder and current company president, psychologist Dr. Alison Darcy, is the ability for the application to learn what is successful in helping treat patients and to scale those solutions to serve millions. Taking this concept further, imagine AI goes beyond traditional therapy and becomes a mental health companion, solving for social isolation, loneliness, or depression. That's the concept behind "social companion robots," defined in an article from *The Medical Futurist* as "human or animal shaped, smaller or bigger mechanic creatures are able to carry out different tasks and have interactions with humans and their environment.[58]" The article highlights a dozen such machines, ranging from Pepper, a humanoid robot that can recognize human emotions, respond to moods and questions, and dance the lambada, to PARO, an AI-driven robot in the form of a furry baby harp seal designed to leverage the benefits of animal therapy without the nuisance of allergies or litter boxes.[59]

Of course not everyone agrees the future of mental health support is an AI-driven app or robot. In the same *New York Times* article, Hannah

Zeavin, a lecturer and author, calls automated therapy a "fantasy" that is more focused on accessibility and fun than actually helping people get better over the long term.[60]

The application of AI technology to improve healthcare and help bring true centricity and personalization to consumers goes far beyond chat-bots or mental health treatment. Improvements in clinical efficacy, research and innovation, and the patient experience are all benefits assigned to AI in healthcare, some of which are already happening today. An article from Deloitte lists the potential applications of healthcare AI as content extraction, virtual agents, image recognition, natural language processing, recommendations, and sentiment analysis. The article assigns five primary values of AI, one of which, "transformed engagement," speaks directly to the transition of having consumers navigate a healthcare universe to having that universe reconstructed around the consumer:

> *Before AI: people engage with systems and organizations on machine terms (for example, filling in forms. After AI: machines engage with people on human terms (for example, natural language, gestures) and customers, employees and other key stakeholders receive a hyper-personalized and efficient multichannel experience.*

Perhaps as much or more than AI, blockchain is another technology that offers the potential to change healthcare and move the consumer to the center of their own health. That's because for the consumer to truly be able to operate independent of any one system or environment, all of her health data needs to be connected and accessible from a centralized position. With blockchain's ability to create always-accessible, always-updated digital ledgers, the Copernican Consumer wouldn't have to manage multiple sources of data – it would all be tied together seamlessly and invisibly. We remember Google Health, the tech giant's attempt to bring control of health information to the individual through a personal medical record. We also remember it failed, and one of the most common reasons cited was that keeping the portal updated was on the shoulders of the individual, who had to pull in data from wherever it lived, including the EMRs of one or more providers. I'll use myself as the example of why that would still fail today, as I would have to somehow collect, consolidate, update, and manage healthcare data from:

- My primary health system, home to my PCP and at least four specialist relationships
- My health plan
- The three or four urgent cares I've had to use outside of my primary health system over the years, for one reason or the other
- My optometrist, who is not part of my primary health system
- My dentist
- My therapist
- My chiropractor
- My massage therapist
- My Peloton
- My iPhone
- My CPAP machine
- My refrigerator

Without blockchain technology, the concept of a Copernican Consumer falls back to the world of sci-fi movies and Star Trek – a world of fiction.

Finally, one more advancement in the use of data that will help support the Copernican Consumer – digital therapeutics, or DTx. These are software platforms used to prevent, manage, or treat medical issues using evidence-based interventions, and often including behavioral science techniques. While DTx software solutions are often used in concert with human-guided care and management, the power in these tools is their ability to guide individual activities through the data. For example, the company Omada offers DTx solutions for diabetes, hypertension, and behavioral health disorders, among other issues. The company's website features an example of DTx use with American Eagle Outfitters, where the goal was to drive lasting behavioral change through diabetes prevention and management. Results from the 26-week program included 83% of all employees enrolling in the program, 70% of participants reported losing weight, 33% reporting loss of 5% of body weight or more, and an average interaction with the platform of 28 times per week per employee.[61] Digital therapeutic platforms must meet stringent requirements and receive regulatory approval before being leveraged in the market. According to a July 2021 report from the IQVIA Institute for Human Data Science, there are currently 137 DTx programs either commercially available or in the pipeline for approval.[62]

Me, my health, and I

So far, we've highlighted the central driver of the Copernican Consumer prediction – the advancement of personal health monitoring and management, and the technologies that will support that. But let's go a step further to the other major trend that will truly put the consumer at the center of her health universe – the personalization of clinical care. We're just beginning to see the realization of genomics, precision medicine, personalized pharmaceuticals and more. The predictions around precision medicine have been with us for some time. Once again, Clayton Christensen was prescient in his 2011 book *The Innovator's Prescription*, using the advancement of precision medicine as an example of what is necessary to bend the future healthcare cost curve. He describes medicine's march through intuitive and empirical stages to precision diagnoses and treatment, where "the provision of care for diseases that can be precisely diagnosed, whose causes are understood, and which consequently can be treated with rules-based therapies that are predictably effective.[63]" He goes on to note the difference between "precision medicine" and "personalized medicine," an important distinction that is often blurred:

> *The reason we decided to coin a new term is that most precisely diagnosed diseases are in fact not uniquely personal...The precise biological definition of a disease also does not incorporate 'personalization' that takes into account how an individual patient might respond to a particular treatment. Unlike precision medicine, personalization refers to both biological and nonbiological*

issues that can affect an individual's response to a treatment.[64]

Here Christensen hints at the role of social determinants of health (SDH) in moving from the concept of precision medicine to personalization, with where an individual was born, grew up, lives, works, received education, and a number of other factors having a substantial effect on their health conditions. The role of SDH in an individual's health has become more understood since Christiansen published his book (the term does not show up in the text), but the point is the same – approaching the clinical diagnosis and treatment of an issue custom to an individual is where the future lies. Here's how Edward Abrahams, PhD, President of the Personalized Medicine Coalition, more recently defined personalized medicine in a 2020 panel discussion:

> *Personalized medicine means 'marrying diagnostics and learning everything we can about the patient in order to prescribe the right therapies,' while accounting for patient values and experiences. This makes the term different from precision medicine.*[65]

Fellow panelist Bryan Loy, MD, MBA and lead for Oncology, Laboratory, and Personalized Medicine at Humana, also emphasized the role of SDH in moving beyond "precision" to "personalized":

> *It's what can we learn about our members—or your patients if you're a doctor—and how can we create a better experience? It's no help if patients go home to an empty refrigerator or have no transportation for follow-up care. Thus, the broader meaning of personalized medicine is to identify the highest-quality, least toxic, most effective, and convenient care for our members.*

The impact of personalized medicine is already being felt, which promises to only expand down the road. Just ask Suzanne Sawyer, Senior Vice President and Chief Marketing and Communications Officer at one of the world's most prestigious academic health systems, Johns Hopkins Medicine, former CMO at Penn Medicine, as well as formerly Vice President of Portfolio Marketing for IBM Watson Health. She asked top clinicians, researchers, and other experts within John Hopkins Medicine about what the next ten years will bring, and personalized medicine was a recurring theme.

> *Medicine is moving away from one-size-fits-all responses, as more data and more accurate diagnostics will allow clinicians to tailor treatment plans to individuals. The idea of precision medicine – for example, we'll be able to detect cell mutations. Artificial intelligence and machine learning will allow clinicians to compare their patients' results with thousands of other people's results to determine the best diagnosis, treatment plan, outcome etc. These technologies and advancements will be able to provide 1:1 personalized treatment, making medicine truly personalized.*

Laura Schoen, Chief Healthcare Officer for DXTRA Health Integrated Solutions and Global Healthcare President at Weber Shandwick, agrees. Born and raised in Brazil, and having spent years of her life in places like South America and Italy, as well as focusing on industries such as pharmaceuticals, she brings a global perspective on the changes she's seen in healthcare. Using that perspective, she believes personalization in healthcare is here to stay, and only going to grow in its impact.

> *It amazes me that healthcare is now so highly specialized. When you look at cancer drugs, 10 years ago they were focused on broad cancers – 'breast cancer' or 'lung cancer.' Now we talk about small, niche segments. There's a great revolution in terms of pharma companies moving their focus from broader, everyday challenges, like pain management, to more niche solutions. All of it – science, technology, our understanding of genetics, the mapping*

of genome, advent of companies like 23 and Me. There's just a huge move toward high specialization.

Finally, one last view on the growing importance of personalized medicine, this from the January 21 article "Human Molecular Genetics and Genomics – Important Advances and Exciting Possibilities" in the *New England Journal of Medicine.* The authors note both the incredible ramifications of the mapping of the human genome and the rapid decline in the cost of sequencing a complete genome, which has dropped from millions of dollars twenty years ago to just hundreds today.

The effects have been profound. The discovery of genes responsible for more than 5,000 rare mendelian diseases has facilitated genetic diagnostics for many patients, pregnancy-related counseling, new drug treatments, and in some cases, gene therapies. The discovery of more than 100,000 robust associations between genomic regions and common diseases has pointed to new biologic mechanisms, such as the role of microglia in Alzheimer's disease, autophagy in inflammatory bowel disease, and synaptic pruning in schizophrenia. It has also enabled the development of polygenic risk scores to identify patients at increased risk for heart disease, breast cancer, and other conditions, although additional rigorous testing of such scores is needed, including evaluation of clinical outcomes. Studies of cancer genomes have revealed hundreds of genes in which somatic mutations propel tumor initiation and growth, information that has fueled the development of new drugs. Genomic analysis is also helping to explain why some people have responses to certain therapies or survive certain infections, whereas others do not.[66]

Digital twinning is another scientific advancement that will add power to personalized medicine. Here's a helpful definition from IBM on digital twinning for the uninitiated (like myself before I researched this book):

A digital twin is a virtual representation of an object or system that spans its lifecycle, is updated from real-time data, and uses simulation, machine learning and reasoning to help decision-making.[67]

Of course this reference is to a manufactured product or system, and in the engineering and manufacturing fields, digital twinning has been in place for a long time. The application of digital twinning to the human body, however, is relatively new. Here's how a May 2021 article from the website *Plug and Play* captured the promise of digital twinning in the medical space:

The technology can also be used for modeling an individual's genetic makeup, physiological characteristics, and lifestyle to create personalized medicine. It has a more individualized focus than precision medicine which typically focuses on larger sample groups. The goal of digitizing the human body and creating fully functioning replicas of its internal systems is to enhance medical care and patient treatment - Dassault's Living Heart project was the first realistic virtual model of a human organ. The use of digital twins in modeling organs has multiple benefits for doctors such as discovering undeveloped illnesses, experimenting with treatments, and improving preparation for surgeries.[68]

In April 2021, Q Bio announced more than $80 million had been raised from investors such as Andreesen Horowitz and Kaiser Foundation Hospitals for its digital twin platform, called Q Bio Gemini, which it claims to be the first to capture and monitor comprehensive baseline patient health in a scalable virtual model. The company claims that the platform "collects information based on current health and personal risks, adapting in real time to changes in an individual's anatomy and biochemistry that are weighted by lifestyle, medical history, and genetic risk factors. Capable of scanning the whole body in 15 minutes or less without radiation, breath holds, or claustrophobia."[69]

Currently the technology takes up an entire room in a lab or clinic facility and retails at $3,495 for individual "membership." In what way could such comprehensive, AI-supported digital twinning allow for greater remote monitoring? At what point will the technology allow for in-home scanning, or will the price drop to make it more accessible to the masses?

Many journal articles, research papers and books have been written about the future potential of precision and personalized medicine to alter the landscape of healthcare delivery in the world. We only need to understand that combined with the enabling power of AI, blockchain, digital therapeutics, personal health monitors, and other advances, personalized medicine further moves us from an impersonal, generic, and non-specific healthcare experience much closer to our vision of a Copernican Consumer. So we have a taste of the how, and the what. The last piece of the puzzle is the where.

The real medical home

Personal health monitors. Artificial intelligence. Blockchain. Genomics. Precision medicine. It all sounds futuristic and amazing and transformative. It also sounds like a monumental challenge, bringing all of these advances in science and technology together to improve healthcare and turn our consumer Copernican. But anyone with experience within the healthcare industry knows that you could line all of these innovations up, and they might feel an equal match for another singular challenge to the vision of the Copernican Consumer – rearranging the healthcare delivery universe so the consumer truly sits at the center. That entails moving care out of giant academic medical centers, hospitals, and surgical centers into consumers' homes, places of work, or wherever they happen to be. Healthcare – especially the provider sector of healthcare – was built and has grown from the inside out, developed first to serve the clinicians, researchers, and educators who deliver healthcare in the U.S. Reorganizing this vast, entrenched ecosystem will involve herculean efforts, and to date, the legacy providers of healthcare – hospitals and health systems – have struggled mightily on this front.

"By and large, health systems have gotten mostly worse on this front, not better," says Kyle Rolfing, healthcare entrepreneur. Rolfing has a lot to say about consumers and their place in the healthcare universe. We cover more of Rolfing's thoughts in later chapters, but on the issue of legacy providers restructuring the industry around the consumer, he doesn't mince words.

> *Walk into any health system, it doesn't matter why you are there or who you are meeting – executive, patient visit, whatever – and it's anxiety-inducing to walk in. It's not warm, not inviting. It's confusing. I wish I would have taken a video of all my healthcare visits to show how often I have to stop and ask directions, how many units I had to walk through. What we experience represents how these things have been built over time, but also reflects how the system actually works today. Take any academic medical center – walking through these monstrosities – it's a symbol of our system.*

Volumes have been written about the need to upgrade the consumer experience in hospitals and health systems, and this thread is pulled through many of the chapters in this book. Yet what Rolfing is referring to here specifically is the healthcare environment – *where* care is delivered. Chapter Six will explore in depth the challenge this poses for legacy providers of care, and how the care environment would be a key factor in shaping the role health systems play in the future. To put it succinctly, listen to Matt Gove, Chief Marketing Officer at Summit Health:

> *For example, our team is organized with our Chief Medical Officer (from NY), CIO and CMO all working together to make a 'digital care model' an actual thing. It honestly feels different, unique. I really believe that once you're free from the weight of hospitals, you can do so many more things. In a typical system, hospitals are the centers of the universe, and they take up all the oxygen. Without them, we can truly build something different.*

Of course, the demand by consumers to engage healthcare on their own turf has only been heightened by the Covid-19 pandemic. In our 2020 report on the impact of the pandemic on consumerism, one of our five main trends, "Smaller Life Sphere," explores the long-term ramifications of a year of lock-down and diminished movement and travel:

> *During the COVID-19 crisis, our worlds have shrunk. Global air travel has dropped between 60 percent and 70 percent through August of 2020 compared to 2019. Millions of workers now office at home (though this skews heavily to white-collar workers–many blue collar and low-wage earners are still working on-site). We avoid public transportation. Students at all educational levels are experiencing some level of remote learning, if not 100 percent virtual learning. We shop at home. We order food delivered to our homes. We have Zoom happy hours. We work out at home or outdoors. We hoped to return to a more normal state of life over the summer as states reopened bars, restaurants, gyms, stores, and other businesses, and depending on where you live and how your state has fared with COVID-19, you may be experiencing this smaller life sphere to a lesser or greater degree.*[70]

As we've come out of the pandemic, some of these experiences may feel like distant memories. But as the report showed, many experts believe the trend of "Smaller Life Spheres" would be long-lasting, pushing consumers to seek out care options close to home, or preferably, in home. Obviously, the growth in virtual care will enable this shift. During the first quarter of 2020, telehealth visits increased 50% over the same quarter in 2019, according to the CDC,[71] though many individual health systems reported far higher growth rates than that. A study by Doximity released in the fall of 2020 reported that virtual visits accounted for more than 20% of all medical visits that year, and most experts agree the use of virtual care will only grow. A 2021 *Forbes* article cites Fortune Business Insights as projecting the global telemedicine industry to grow from roughly $80 billion in 2020 to roughly $400 billion in 2027, a five-fold increase in seven years.[72] And of course, the greater the virtual care expansion, the wider the aperture for remote monitoring opportunities and related clinical support.

Then there's home health. That same *Forbes* article says that thanks to the aging population, expanded access to Medicare and Medicaid, and a growing demand for care in the home, the home health industry is expected to see "strong and steady growth" over the next five years.[73]

As an example, Rolfing points to Nice Healthcare, a company founded in 2017, a direct primary care clinic that seeks to seamlessly blend virtual and at-home care in a primary care model. Or Los Angeles-based startup Heal, which is looking to bring at-home care to more people with its latest round of funding, which has raised $164 million in capital since its inception. Or Ready, an on-demand health care startup that delivers home and community-based services, which has raised $54 million in Series C funding and counts GV, the venture capital arm of Alphabet Inc., the parent company of Google, as one of its investors.[74]

While history and the current flow of investor capital may be against them, leaders in the legacy healthcare space aren't standing still in bringing their services out of the hospital into the homes and communities of those they serve. In 2018, Mabbutt's Intermountain Healthcare opened one of the largest "virtual hospitals" in the country, described as a hospital "without a building or walls." Dubbed Connect Care Pro, the organization says the service "brings together 35 telehealth programs and more than 500 caregivers to enable patients to receive the medical care they need, regardless of where they are. Connect Care Pro provides basic medical care as well as advanced services, such as stroke evaluation, mental health counseling, intensive care, and newborn critical care. While it doesn't replace the need for on-site caregivers, it supplements existing staff and provides specialized services in rural communities where those types of medical care usually aren't readily available."[75] Mabbutt explains that, while growth for the organization used to be defined in part by the addition of new facilities or hospitals, now they are building a smaller footprint with more flexible options:

We're moving some care out of the traditional hospital to standalone access points that are both more convenient and less expensive. This includes care at home, with pre- and post-care that will continue to evolve the role of hospitals.

Other systems are following suit. Amedisys, a home-health, hospice, and personal-care provider, signaled its continued growth into higher-acuity care through its 2021 acquisition of Contessa Health, which provides hospital-at-home and skilled-nursing-at-home services. Or Atrium Health, the 42-hospital system based in North Carolina, which opened a "hospital at home" program during the heart of the pandemic, March 2020, which served more than 10,000 patients in the subsequent 10 months. In a 2021 *HealthLeaders Media* article, chief medical officer Scott Rissmiller, MD, explained the value of a virtual hospital:

From a quality standpoint, we do not view this any differently than if these patients were within the walls of our hospital. All measures, including length of stay as well as readmission, transfer, and mortality rates, have been almost identical to inpatient stats, and patient satisfaction has been extremely high. Patients really would rather be in their home surrounded by their loved ones and support system.[76]

Or take Geisinger, one of the most respected and highly touted systems in the U.S. Their CEO, Dr. Jaewon Ryu, says pushing care out of facilities to wherever consumers need it is the single biggest driver of the organization's vision of the future. He notes that Geisinger's prominence over the past century was born of the "field of dreams" model – build it and they will come, which included investing in a lot of big, fancy buildings. Yet sticking a shovel in the ground is expensive, and not nearly as efficient or convenient as dispersing care to wherever individuals need it. Dr. Ryu says moving in this direction isn't just central to Geisinger's future, but represents one of the key means for solving the healthcare affordability crisis in the U.S.

This is the next chapter at Geisinger, and it's what excites me the most about where we're going. Capabilities and technology have advanced to the degree that now maybe one quarter or even one third of healthcare services could be delivered in the home. More specialist visits, in-home primary care management, bringing prescriptions to the doorstep. This consumes a lot of our oxygen at Geisinger – it's at the forefront of everything we do.

Hospitals and health systems aren't the only legacy players expanding into dispersed healthcare services. Oscar Health announced "Virtual Primary Care" services in the fall of 2020. Same with UnitedHealthcare, which rolled out their California Doctor's Plan one month later, which, according to a 2021 article in *HealthPayer Intelligence*, offers a "dedicated service team that provides personalized concierge support for members enrolled in the California Doctors Plan, Signature Value HMO plan and UnitedHealthcare Canopy Health Medicare Advantage plan. Plan members have zero co-pay for both primary care services and urgent care services. It includes 24/7 access to a provider through the plan's telehealth platform as well as UnitedHealthcare's app and the member's account on myuhc.com."[77]

Side effects may vary

No matter what sector – hospitals and health systems, health plans, virtual care companies, primary care companies – all players realize to one degree or another that bringing care to the consumer in fundamentally new ways is essential to future relevancy. Combined with the technology supporting personal sensors and monitoring, and the advances in personalized medicine, the world in which a Copernican Consumer emerges starts to become interesting.

In 2020, I ended an 8-year relationship with my Ameriprise financial planner. She was our primary financial counselor, and her company managed the retirement and college investments for our family. We like our individual financial planner a lot – she provided personalized financial guidance that was very helpful to us over the years. What we didn't like was the cost of using a financial services firm like Ameriprise, which included an annual financial planning fee, asset management fees as a commission on our total investments under advisement, individual fund load fees on investments, and high expense ratios on individual funds. These costs for a full-service financial planning and brokerage service may make sense for some, but it made little sense for us, especially given our belief in passive investing rather than active portfolio management, which was one of the touted benefits of a full-service firm like Ameriprise.

Instead, we moved our retirement funds to Betterment, an online financial services company focused on passive investing and lower costs (a .25% commission on assets under management, compared with 1-1.5% for Ameriprise, which can really add up). While the online experience, low cost, and self-service nature of Betterment served our financial needs perfectly, one of the added benefits was the ability to pull through all of our other financial resources so Betterment would have the full picture of our financial health. This included our 529 plans (which we kept with another investment company), my employer-based 401k account, our bank accounts, my wife's rollover IRA, and our home value and mortgage. This was all done through a direct digital connection to the other financial institutions in question, and while those other outside financial accounts weren't managed directly by Betterment, having them pulled through to one financial management platform allowed the service to consider *our entire financial profile* in shaping investment recommendations, tax planning, and overall picture of future financial health.

Now recall the laundry list of health data sources I would need to manage my overall health profile and truly live as a Copernican Consumer. Who can manage that today? My primary care provider? Hardly. He acts in almost the same way my former financial planner did, providing very personalized guidance for any number of acute healthcare issues I face. Sometimes he even tried to help with broader health issues, such as using cognitive behavioral therapy to help with some mental health strains about a decade ago. But he simply has no time to truly oversee or manage my entire health profile – even for my acute issues, such as my Type 2 diabetes or Crohn's disease. He's really only a facilitator for other specialists who provide deeper care. The cost would also be prohibitive for my primary care physician in the current reimbursement environment to help more than he is now. So the question is, where's the Betterment for health management? Here's Sawyer of Johns Hopkins Medicine again:

> *Artificial intelligence and other technology is the revolution, but right now, only as point solutions. The problem is point solution fatigue, an inundation of engagement and experience, but not all pulling in the same way at the same time. There's an ecosystem of solutions, but we would anticipate a consolidation of these – patient and provider-centric tools and algorithms around the individual. But so far, we haven't seen this system of systems.*

Sawyer points to AI as part of the solution, and along with blockchain, digital therapeutics, and other advances, a Betterment-type health management offering is there for the building. It feeds into an aspect of the Copernican Consumer many of our experts called out – the move to self-service in healthcare. We have seen this successfully employed in the travel and hospitality industries, among others, and it's one of the ways personalization emerges to "empower" consumers. I use quotes there because while I may feel more empowered by booking my own flights, checking in, changing my seat, and boarding using my personalized QR-code, or managing my miles through the app, all of these also represent ways the travel industry has offloaded their work onto the consumer using technology and personalization strategies. In healthcare, this shift would not only represent important cost-savings, it would also help address the growing shortage of healthcare workers. Recall early in the chapter Mabbutt identifying self-service as part of the shift to the consumer at the center of the healthcare universe, even labelling that shift "consumer as provider." Recall Lassiter noting the shift to using kiosks and technology to replace nursing assistants in Asia.

Add Sandra Mackey, CMO at Bon Secours Mercy Health, to that list. For her, the concept of personalized health and self-service are interlocked.

> *Self-service will be the name of the game. All healthcare organizations will move to this – the pace will vary. The lessons learned from cutting-edge organizations will be replicated and enhanced by the next industry and at the center of it all is consumer behavior. Like other industries, consumers want to have some control of when, where and how they receive services.*

While this trend was already in place, says Mackey, the pandemic has accelerated the shift to self-service type offerings, particularly through the expansion of virtual care. In her mind, if consumers don't find this level of self-service from traditional legacy providers of healthcare, they will seek it from new entrants who are getting smarter, faster, at delivering consumer care.

> *Consumers will demand this. We don't have to talk to a person to book an airline ticket, order a pizza, or book a hotel room. Healthcare has to catch up.*

While self-service health is definitely a trend taking hold, maybe AI will save us from having to do all the heavy lifting. In a 2020 report projecting trends in the coming decade by the global data agency Essence, two thirds of the experts they spoke with expected most brand interactions would take place bot-to-bot, meaning, "personal digital assistants like Google, Siri, and Alexa will interface directly with brand chatbots and virtual customer service agents."[78] If Alexa can connect with the AI bot at Dominos about the status of your pizza order (obviously delivered by drone in 2030), then why wouldn't Siri work directly with your online health management platform bot to update vital health data or issues?

So we can see how ideas like the "Betterment of healthcare" and self-service would help shape the Copernican Consumer. But where does that leave our current healthcare workforce? For example, how might the delivery of primary care change based on this projection? A former client of ours from the ophthalmology industry said that advances in "LASIK technology make the procedure so precise and easy that it won't be long until tech's will be licensed to do it rather than MDs." Could we see something of a "barbell effect" on the field of medicine, where clinicians and caregivers are moved to either end of the spectrum – either to broader, more personal *health* management support on one end, or deeper *clinical specialty* expertise on the other, vacating the middle where jacks of all trades – primary care physicians, radiologists, etc.– have a diminishing role? On one end of the "barbell," clinicians will become more specialized as precision medicine, genomics, and other medical advances will allow healthcare organizations to treat both diseases and individuals on a much more specific level. This reflects what Schoen highlighted earlier in the chapter about the advances in personalized medicine.

> *We will continue to emerge more specialized in areas such as prenatal care and Alzheimer's disease treatment. That will revolutionize healthcare because it will guide patients more effectively, keeping people out of the system and saving costs.*

On the other side of the "barbell," as AI, personal health monitoring, and other technologies take hold and empower consumers, we may see a shift toward the more "human" side of caregiving, away from specialized clinical care. This discussion has been taking place for some time actually, starting with an ongoing debate in the radiology field about the existing use of AI in interpreting images and what that foretells for the profession. A 2020 article in *Radiology Business* cites Robert Schier, MD, a neuroradiologist with RadNet Northern California, who considers himself on the "alarmist" end of the spectrum.

> *There are vastly differing opinions [on AI in radiology], from the apocalyptic claim that AI will make all*

radiologists extinct to the delusional assertion that
computers will always merely assist—and never replace—
radiologists. Both extremes are mistaken, but the truth
is in the direction of the first. ... Unless radiologists do
things other than interpret imaging studies, there will be
need for far fewer of them.[79]

With "The Barbell Effect," AI may push clinicians to the more human end of care, providing that supplemental support as part of a Betterment-type platform, or even just devoting more time to overall health management in our current model. The question is, does it require an "MD" to provide overall health management? After all, if an individual's health – her whole health – is being constantly monitored and managed, would we even need doctor's appointments anymore, at least at a primary care level? The industry is already seeing a long-term drop in primary care relationships – a reduction of more than 25% in primary care visits between 2008 and 2006, according to one study[80] – and many experts point to Millennials and Gen Z as forgoing primary care at a higher rate as well. In a May 2021 article in *The Medical Futurist* titled "7 Futuristic Professions in Healthcare You Can Still Prepare For," the author sets the stage with this not-so-far-from-Star-Trek depiction of the future:

With drones delivering medical supplies; an ever-
increasing wealth of data from personal health sensors;
and patients turning to telemedicine, the medical
workplace will decidedly look different ... While the likes
of artificial intelligence and robotics will indeed replace
existing professions, it cannot be stressed enough that
those same technologies will create new jobs.

The article goes on to describe potential professions such as "Lifestyle strategist: to guide patients with their health data," "Patient assistant: helping patients navigate the healthcare jungle," and "VR therapist: treating patients with new realities."[81]

Challenges to the Copernican Consumer

While we're already on the path to some form of Copernican Consumer, having individuals truly sit at the center of their own healthcare universe faces many obstacles. Take interoperability, which would be required to connect all of the healthcare dots and allow consumers to leverage technologies like personal health monitoring, digital therapeutics, virtual care, and other "remote" health data points effectively. Perhaps blockchain will solve for this, but interoperability is still a huge issue within the healthcare space. As an example, many of our experts point to the existing EMR landscape as maybe the biggest inhibitor to interoperability, where one vendor, EPIC, has a near monopoly. Here's Summit Health's Gove:

> *Big EHR vendors create walled gardens where you have to work in their world, and they are limited in creating great digital experiences. These vendors in many ways hold us hostage, and their financial success is not dependent on delivering a great experience for patients, as vendor selection decisions are made on other variables – clinical, financial, and operational.*

This won't be an easy problem to fix, according to David Goldhill, current CEO and co-founder of Sesame, and board member at Leapfrog. Goldhill says the issue of interoperability was entrenched with the 2009 American Recovery and Reinvestment Act, legislation designed to serve as a stimulus for the Great Recession that started in 2008 and included $19 billion in funding for healthcare IT, designated primarily to drive investment in electronic medical records.

> *The Federal Government rolled out a massive amount of aid to support the adoption of electronic health records and then made the almost inconceivable decision to make records essentially the property of the EMR vendors instead of individuals. Something that could have led to an absolute flowering of consumer-directed care and*

*intelligent use of data through interoperability across the
entire navigation of care, instead does the exact opposite.*

Goldhill also points out what others we interviewed expressed as
a primary concern for any advancement in the healthcare industry –
Copernican Consumer or otherwise. And that's the readiness of the
primary players in delivering healthcare – legacy hospitals and health
systems – to transform in significant ways. He states that the industry
always seems to be reacting to yester-year's problems, ensuring it's
constantly behind on today's. As one example, he says the "era of chronic
care" is coming to an end, with more than 80% of care now considered
chronic. Many cancers are now treated as chronic, not episodic, he says,
which demands a different industrial structure. Goldhill says one of the
biggest disconnects today is the industry's new emphasis on population
health and social determinants of health. Not that these aren't worthy
focal points, he says, it's just that they're square-peg strategies for today's
round hole issues.

> *The traditional healthcare industry is busy with this new
> population approach while science is going to precision,
> individual approaches. So in 20 years we will have a new
> system focused on populations – designed to the needs
> of the late 20th and early 21st century – that will be once
> again behind the medical approach we need.*

And of course, hospitals and health systems themselves aren't
known for their speedy adaption of innovation and technology. The
Covid-19 pandemic *did* see a meaningful acceleration of technology
adaption in the space, and as we've read, leaders in the field are moving
forward as quickly as they can with virtual visits, virtual hospitals,
the expansion of top-of-the-funnel access points, and personalized
medicine. But will they be able to adapt fast enough for consumers, or in
the face of growing competition from outside the legacy space? Chapter
Six explores the ramifications for those who don't.

There are also ethical issues to consider. A full-on Copernican
Consumer world sounds fantastic, if you have the education, money,

and technology access to benefit from it. Many of the breakthroughs in precision medicine, especially on the pharmaceutical side, involve treatments that can run into the millions of dollars. Who will pay for that, and who decides who can access high-cost treatments and who can't? Artificial intelligence holds promise for much of the future of health, not just in terms of consumer centricity, but the technology has already shown to bake in gender, racial, and other biases that already plague healthcare. The question of who owns your healthcare data will need to be sorted out, as alluded to by Goldhill and Gove above, and that will be a difficult knot to untie. Many of these ethical challenges are explored more in Chapter 8, where we predict health inequities and disparities over the next decade are actually likely to increase, not improve, without radical (and unlikely) change in the U.S. And of course, any future that depends so heavily on the open and ongoing transfer of private health data will need a solution to the growing cyber-threats organizations and individuals are facing. At the same time, government regulators will have to craft laws and policies that allow for a world of the Copernican Consumer, and individuals themselves will have to be comfortable allowing their health data to be shared and leveraged in a far greater way. The headline of this 2016 *Forbes* article may say it the best: "Welcome To 2030: I Own Nothing, Have No Privacy And Life Has Never Been Better.[82]"

An inevitable shift

With that set of challenges, building a world where we see the Copernican Consumer may seem daunting, at least by 2030. But for many of the experts we interviewed – especially those who have spent time in the legacy health system space – the move toward personalization is inevitable.

Kevan Mabbutt from Intermountain:

> *We have to deliver on personalization as other industries do. We're seeing the opportunity with more portable consumer information. How informed do people*

feel in managing that? Can we ask them to take full responsibility? Those may be the biggest questions.

Matt Gove from Summit Health:

Personalizing along the way to each individual's experience and needs – that's where the biggest trends will take place. Can we personalize it, but also at scale? Right now, still humans calling other humans – not the most efficient model. How do we take care of a million people with a broad set of clinical circumstances through a digital care model, and where they are at, not where we are at? Not just the experience, but full care model.

Wright Lassiter from Henry Ford Health System:

It's still a fairly rudimentary approach. We have an approach, but not a Chris approach, or a Lucy approach, or a Wright approach. We still struggle with this. But with the application of technology for consumers, healthcare will become more personalized than it is today. Think of what Amazon has done with a personalized approach – imagine if you could apply the same power to health and healthcare.

Personalization. Precision medicine. AI. Blockchain. Digital twinning. Personalized monitoring and sensors. The dispersion of care. New roles and responsibilities for healthcare providers. All of these are part of the prediction of a Copernican Consumer, a world where the individual is at the center of her own health universe, rather than navigating all the distant reaches of the current fragmented space in which we live today. The promise of such a world is invigorating, but also intimidating. One thing is for sure, it's a good bet that come 2030, we'll look back at my rudimentary example of the Copernican Consumer – my lonely little LibreLink sensor, and smile, asking "So what was the big whup?"

Chapter 5

PREDICTION

Constricted Consumerism

The Copernican Consumer will rule her healthcare universe, sitting at the center of all her health data and resources. Providers, payors, health coaches, fitness instructors, dieticians, AI bots – all of these players will orbit around her, providing her whatever she needs, wherever and whenever she needs it. She will have a plethora of healthcare choices to serve her individualized health needs, the master of her domain.

Unless she isn't.

We warned you in Chapter Two that these predictions weren't interlocking, painting a singular mosaic of the future, but instead should be taken individually. Going further, at least at first glance, the premise for this prediction seems to be diametrically opposed to the idea of a Copernican Consumer. While it's possible these two predictions would portray alternate future universes, it's just as likely that the two would, for the most part, both be possible at the same time. For while the Copernican Consumer may become a reality, she may *also* find restrictions in her choices, particularly where it matters most.

We defined consumerism in Chapter Three, but it's worth revisiting briefly here. Whether it's an outcome of government or industry policy, an organic result of industry change, or some combination of both, consumerism in general refers to the growing power of individuals to own their own health and health care decisions, and as a result, drive change in the industry that better meets their needs. There are many ways consumerism is changing the healthcare industry, and for the provider sector, the primary pressure points for consumerism are:

- Access – Consumers prefer more options for their care, whether that's multiple hospitals, surgical centers, or clinics in their town to choose from, "destination" healthcare, such as medical tourism, virtual options, or alternative or "new entrants" into the provider space, such as Walgreens, Optum or Walmart Health or One Medical.
- Convenience – Consumers want their care where they want it, when they want it, and how they want it, which impacts everything from what types of physician visit options are offered (in-person, phone, or video visit) to how many retail clinics a system has in a market to the hours of their urgent care facilities.
- Transparency – Consumers want to understand everything from how your facility is rated for comfort and accessibility to the quality outcomes for your heart surgeons to the ratings for your service and compassion of your nurses to the cost of your care, and not just your charge master price or a general range, but the cost for them individually, based on whatever their specific insurance plan entails.
- Price – In any other consumer industry, price is a major factor in decision-making, and nearly all industries have brands that intentionally span the price spectrum, from the Gap at one end to Nordstrom's at the other, from Walmart to Tiffany's. When it comes to hospitals and health systems, however, no real price-oriented branding exists. But as consumers gain power in healthcare, they will demand pricing choice. Not everyone will be after the lowest cost – just like in any other industry, some

consumers are value-driven while others are willing to pay more for greater quality or brand cachet.

- Experience – A holder for many of the attributes above, the consumer experience is a focal transformational point for many hospitals and health systems. As it is often pointed out, an organization can't use their peer hospitals as a benchmark, as consumers demand a better, more personalized experience based on the other products and services in their lives, from Amazon to Uber to Apple (the holy trinity of healthcare experience comparison brands). The biggest emphasis today is on the *digital* experience, and additionally, many health systems have focused on creating a more personalized experience (as noted in Chapter Four).

Note the above list does not include the product or service at the heart of all healthcare delivery – the clinical care itself. Consumers for the most part *assume* strong clinical quality, even if those of us in the industry know there are vast differences in the actual level of clinical quality from organization to organization, sector to sector. Further, many chronic patients will spend a great deal of effort to suss out those key differences when they research facilities or physicians for their specific ailment. But for the most part, consumers don't use clinical quality or outcomes as a primary driver of choice, both because they assume a minimal-level clinical quality and because most have a hard time actually discerning the difference in clinical quality amidst all of the report cards, rankings, reviews, and awards (more on that later).

To hear from many of the experts we interviewed, as well as many in the healthcare field, consumerism is not only here to stay, it will be the most powerful force shaping healthcare in the future. Here's Scott Weber, Chief Marketing and Design Officer at M Health Fairview, a Minnesota academic health system with twelve hospitals and more than 34,000 employees. Prior to his role at M Health Fairview, Weber was a managing partner at Accenture, and has worked in the past with brands such as Walmart, Ikea, Samsung, and Capital One.

Ten years ago, providers were paternalistic in relationships with patients. Today it is more of an even playing field. We're at information parity in healthcare – buying a house, buying a car – it's the same deal, and we've seen how those industries have changed. The driver moving forward will be injecting the consumer sensibility in everything we do. The global economy has created a 24x7, on-demand consumer experience, which is often very personalized. We have to figure out how to compete in that world.

Here's Wright Lassiter, President and CEO at Henry Ford Health System:

Over the prior 10 years, the consumer's role was more insular, more about taking the reins for their own care. The consumer is now becoming more of a driver in what we do, how we respond. Today, the consumer is telling us what they want, where they want it, and when they want it. Our white coat expertise is no longer enough to compel loyalty. They won't tolerate answering the same questions 10 different times.

Here's Sandra Mackey, CMO at Bon Secours Mercy:

What will it take for consumers to finally say 'we've had enough?' Consumers are fatigued by lack of accountability, all the finger pointing. It will take further evolution of consumerism to really raise the alarms: Covid may have been the tipping point. Consumers will seek options elsewhere if they don't get what they want from traditional hospitals and health systems.

Or Bryan Hamilton, Assistant Vice President Marketing Communications at Cincinnati Children's, one of the top pediatric systems in the country, who reflects on a similar rationale for increased consumerism:

There's been real shift in power, as educated patients make empowered patients. We used to not use the word "consumerism" because the power was with the provider. My parents would always defer fully to a provider's recommendation, for example. But there has been a democratization of knowledge – as people gained more information, more knowledge, consumerism grew. As more information is disseminated over time, the more patients can be advocates for their care. That shift will continue.

At conferences, in trade publications, in blog posts and podcasts, consumerism is a dominant – maybe *the* dominant – trend tied to the transformation of healthcare in the future. And the events of 2020 didn't change that dominance. In a December 2020 article in *Fierce Healthcare* titled "Healthcare consumerism will be the driving force post-Covid-19." author Bret Schiller, head of healthcare, corporate client banking, and specialized industries at J.P. Morgan Commercial Banking, cited digital innovation as a key solution for addressing consumerism, noting that 41% of Gen Z and 33% of Millennials prefer virtual care options over in-person, and adding "while older generations are more likely to prefer in-person, younger generations' expectations will define the future of healthcare. (Side note: a member of Generation X, I guess I constitute an "older generation" by this categorization, but I think most of my peers *also* prefer virtual over in-person encounters, whether that's seeing a doctor or ordering a pizza. That may have less to do with our age and rather our generation's overall "just give me some space" mentality.) The article concludes:

From digital reimbursements and telehealth accessibility to banking technology solutions that scale and grow as they do, organizations must understand that consumerism of healthcare is no longer just an aspirational expectation of tomorrow – it is here today. [83]

And finally, of course, there's us, here at Revive. We've produced numerous blog posts, podcasts, and papers, all dedicated to using consumerism as a cudgel to advocate for change in the health system space. There was the last book in this series, *Joe Public III: The End of Hospital Marketing*, where consumerism was cited as an instigator of change multiple times. There was our 2019 paper, *The Case for Building a Post Health System Brand*, again advocating for dramatic change in the industry, with the following opening salvo:

> *We've heard a million times about the impact of growing consumerism and new competition from players like Apple, Amazon, and CVS. The combination of these two forces shines a harsh light on health system brands. What's worked in the past for health system branding will likely not be enough moving forward. For example, the point has repeatedly been made that consumers are not just comparing your health system brand to other health systems, they are comparing it to Uber, Amazon, and Starbucks. If that's true, then why are health systems still using the same old health system brands?*[84]

And there's our November 2020 paper, *The End of the Runway: How Covid-19 and consumerism could accelerate the rise of new competitors and the decline of traditional providers*. In the paper, we review five key changes in consumer behavior driven by Covid-19 that could have long-lasting ramifications for where consumers turn for their healthcare.

At this point, you may be wondering what gives. Because the prediction in this chapter isn't about the growing power of consumerism and how it will completely and utterly upend the healthcare space. No, the title of this prediction is "Constricted Consumerism."

> *While consumers will become increasingly responsible for their own health and use of healthcare services, they will actually become less and less empowered in the choices they have for care, especially in higher-acuity, higher-cost situations. While many in the industry will continue to sing the praises of choice, the reality is most consumers*

will have far fewer choices moving forward, often in ways
they might never ever consider or see.

In some ways, we can look at the long (and we mean loooooongggg) runway consumerism has had in this industry – somewhere between 20 and 30 years, or at most since the advent of consumer-driven health plans in the 1990s. It's taken us a long time to get to where we are today, which as we've heard repeatedly, isn't quite as far as many thought we might have come. Taken one step further, there are actually many forces that are aligning to not just continue the slow roll of consumerism, but actually restrict it in the coming decade. *Especially* in the areas where it could prove the most beneficial – the high-acuity, high-cost realm of hospital care.

Hurry up and wait

When I first started presenting at industry conferences on the trend of consumerism, I used a picture of my daughter Callie to help portray the healthcare consumer. It was a classic toddler-in-a-high-chair-with-food-smeared-all-over-her-face type photo, and Callie's facial expression seemed to be saying "seriously, this is all you got?" It was the perfect way to both endear myself to the audience ("look, cute baby!") and accurately portray the mindset of healthcare consumers at the time, who were becoming more outwardly expressive of their discontent with the healthcare experience. I use this example because as I sit here and write this sentence, Callie is 24 hours away from graduating high school. Which means that picture of her when she was two was sixteen years ago, or roughly 2005. *That's* how long I've been talking about consumerism as a serious force in this industry, and I was definitely late to the game by that point.

Back then, the rate of adoption for consumer-driven health plans was low – roughly 10% of employers offered at least one high-deductible health plan option, and the average individual deductible for commercial plans was $221.[85] Retail healthcare was in its infancy – Minneapolis-based start-up QuickMedx, with its mall-based kiosk offering, had changed its name to MinuteClinic in 2003. And while the internet had established a new frontier for consumers to find information on their healthcare choices, the social media revolution had not yet begun (Facebook had just launched in 2004, Twitter in 2006). So while we knew the three drivers of consumerism were in play – more information, more choices, and more financial skin in the game for consumers – we had yet to see any kind of truly major change of the healthcare space as a result. Yet the question back then wasn't *whether* consumerism would change the industry, it was *when*.

During my presentations back then, to help explain the potential power of consumerism, I would use a hurricane analogy. I still have a clear memory of watching CNN in the fall of 2005 – Hurricane Katrina had just hit New Orleans and the Gulf Coast in August of that year, causing incredible devastation. Now, another monster storm, Hurricane Rita, was threating the gulf, and Anderson Cooper stood on the shoreline near Corpus Christi, Texas, one foot in the surf, one on the beach, pointing out into the ocean and conveying to viewers the monster that was out there, ready to strike. But from the visual of the scene – waves gently lapping at Anderson's feet, some fluffy clouds on the horizon – there was no way to actually *see* any evidence of the forming hurricane. As far as one could tell, it could have been any day on the beach in Texas. To me, that was an apt metaphor for consumerism back in 2005. It was a storm forming off the coast of healthcare, and it would undoubtedly strike. But where would it strike first, and who would it hit hardest – hospitals and health systems? Insurance companies? Individuals themselves? And when would it strike – later that year? 2010? 2020? And would it be a Category One hurricane, causing some damage here and there, but in general leaving the healthcare coastline intact? Or a Category Five, completely altering the landscape moving forward in industry-transforming ways? The truth was, back in 2005, we were like Anderson Cooper, looking out into an otherwise peaceful horizon and guessing when, where, and how hard the storm would hit.

Fast forward a few years to 2011, when we released the first Joe Public book, and consumerism was a primary point of emphasis in discussing why hospitals and health systems needed to transform in critical ways. According to a Rand study released in 2011, 20% of employees enrolled in commercial insurance plans had a high-deductible plan.[86] MinuteClinics and other retail outlets were everywhere, and medical tourism was on the rise. And the social media party was in full swing, giving consumers even more information on their healthcare choices (not to mention the launch of such online services as Hospital Compare from CMS in 2005, Healthcare Blue Book in 2007, and the addition of physician ratings on Angie's List in 2008, among dozens of other healthcare ratings and review sources). Was that then the time consumerism would finally turn things upside down, especially given the Great Recession a few years earlier? Here's how we wrote about the potential of consumerism in the introduction of *Joe Public Doesn't Care About Your Hospital*.[87]:

> *With their own money on the line, consumers are beginning to use the same value criteria for healthcare decisions – service, price, experience, brand equity and more – as they do with other purchasing decisions. To date, however, the new healthcare "consumerism" has not led to a widespread change in consumer behavior. But this nation's current economic crisis may well be the tipping point; the driver of fundamental change in how and when consumers engage hospitals and health systems.*

Now, here we are, a decade later, and, for many of the experts we interviewed for this book, Hurricane Consumerism is still a way offshore, taking its sweet time to form.

Here's Matt Gove from Summit Health:

> *As someone who is a big proponent of consumerism over last 7-8 years, it's been great to see some of the smarter consumer platforms applied with some success. But the biggest surprise is we haven't gotten farther. Even at the best health systems, where we have the best marketing teams, our approach to consumerism is still not 100%. The dream is a relationship with customers that equals what other brands have. Using digital platforms like Amazon does, with all interactions and experiences*

customized for the individual, that keeps them tied to us for their lifetimes. Not many organizations do this well, but it's also rare for organizations to have as much information on people as we do. And we're still struggling to really totally leverage it.

Dr. Ryu, CEO at Geisinger:

We've really just gotten started, and it will accelerate. But we lag behind other industries in consumer engagement and adoption. The trends are there, but take the analogy between banking and healthcare in terms of consumerism, which have been around for 10+ years – they've gotten there in ways we haven't. If we could fully engage consumers digitally, the experience could be so much better. And Covid-19 has accelerated this, but we still lag.

Kevan Mabbutt, Senior Vice President and Chief Consumer Officer at Intermountain Healthcare:

Empowerment should be further along than it is. If I think about choice today, and why consumerism has been slow to take off, it's because there is a lack of competition. There is local or regional competition, but it's not as intense as in other industries. We haven't enabled consumerism really. Why don't consumers demand more? There is a lot of industry inertia against consumerism. It's hard to truly exercise choice – not as easy to just switch to a different healthcare brand. Healthcare is not an everyday interaction. And many times you're in a situation, such as emergency care, where you don't have a choice.

Bryan Hamilton, Assistant Vice President of Marketing Communications at Cincinnati Children's Hospital Medical Center:

We still haven't gotten to the point we should have on consumerism. The right content at the right time in the

right place for the right care from the right provider –
we're not there yet. We've heard a lot about Patient 360,
an idea that is often pursued in the consumer-packaged
goods industry. But we're not there in healthcare. Hope
that's where we get, however we want to define it.

And finally Dr. Erica Taylor, Associate Chief Medical Officer of
Diversity, Equity, and Inclusion for the Duke Health physician organization,
and the first Black female orthopedic surgeon at Duke Health:

It will take another 15 years to have an impact! The
medical professionals who entered healthcare didn't
really expect to have to think about consumerism. It's
not taught or discussed in medical school. So many of
us were not prepared for this. For a simple example:
following up with patients after surgery – some patients
like receiving a phone call the next day, some don't want
to be bothered. You get reviews that drive the day to day
decisions on what standardized care should look like .
However, consumers have an experience expectation, and
it's individualized. We haven't done a very good job of
understanding this concept, but we'll have to.

So it's clear that while the potential for consumerism is still present,
many in the industry are wary of expecting too much, too soon, given
the glacial advancement of consumerism over the past few decades, and
where we still find ourselves today. It's not that consumerism *hasn't*
changed the industry, it's more that the change has been limited. The
history of consumerism is working against it. Additionally, however,
many see consumerism not only taking longer to change the industry,
but actually shrinking in its power. There are three reasons we can
identify for why consumerism may constrict over the next decade, and
it all starts with how we define it in the first place.

Reason One – Who *is* the consumer?

All the talk of consumerism relies on the agreed definition of the term, which earlier we stated as "the growing power of individuals to own their own health and health care decisions, and as a result, drive change in the industry that better meets their needs." In this widely accepted depiction of consumerism, the consumer is the individual, the patient, the person who is receiving care. That's based on the model from nearly all other consumer-facing industries – companies driving more personalized, *customer*-centric offerings focused on the person who pays the bill – the customer.

Yet as we all know, the healthcare industry isn't like other industries in many fundamental ways. The business of healthcare delivery is a competitive, market-based industry, but it's the only industry where, for example, supply (add more imaging centers in a market) drives demand (you get more patients needing images). The rules of economics don't apply the same in healthcare as they do in other industries, and that goes for all the dynamics related to customer power. Because in this industry, many would argue, the customer *isn't* the patient, the individual, the consumer. And if that's true, it calls into question the power of consumerism overall.

As we mentioned before, few have been more involved in trying to leverage the power of consumer driven healthcare than innovator and entrepreneur Kyle Rolfing. Yet experience has taught him the power of the individual in healthcare is limited.

> *The ideal of consumerism is misplaced. Because it assumes patients are the consumers. They're not - payors are the real consumers. It is their demands that are shaping the industry most, not individuals. Consumers have been disintermediated.*

David Goldhill, founder and CEO of Sesame, agrees. He notes that all other industries evolve over time to meet the demand of customers, yet healthcare is still stuck in the past in many ways because consumers don't have the power they do in other markets.

Intermediary demand is what rules health care as an industry, not patient demand. When Medicare and Medicaid were introduced in the 1960s, America was a totally different country. Physically taxing manufacturing and mining employment were still a major share of the primarily male workforce, women got married at an average age of under 21, less than 10% of the population were college graduates, and patients had minimal access to any health information. Our world is so different now, and the rest of economy has evolved – organically but massively – to serve today's citizens. But not in healthcare, because individuals are not the real customer – the true "customers" are CMS and private insurers, and their institutional needs drive the industry.

Paul Matsen, CMO at Cleveland Clinic, makes a similar point about the likelihood of an expansion of federal and state healthcare funding. While he believes we will likely always have a private market for healthcare, his belief is that we're going to move closer to a single-payor or Medicare-for-all model in the coming decade, which would only enhance this dynamic.

Today the government funds the majority of the health system in the U.S., making them the single largest "purchaser" of healthcare services.

Finally, here's Jarrett Lewis, partner at Public Opinion Strategies:

I kind of laugh when I hear people in the political world talking about how the way to solve healthcare issues is to empower the consumer in a fully market-based system. Yet the majority of provider revenue is coming from the Federal Government, which is then not truly a market-based system. I just don't know if it will ever be a consumer centric industry.

How might defining public and private payors as the actual

consumers of healthcare, rather than individuals, change how we expect consumerism to show up? One example of this dynamic can be found in virtual care. As we all know, 2020 saw an explosion in the use of virtual visits and hospitals and health systems shut down their on-site elective services during the height of the Covid-19 crisis, forcing providers and patients alike to adapt quickly to a new channel for care delivery. Historically, both these audiences can be identified as blockers to earlier adoption of virtual care: providers because of their general slowness in adopting new technologies and their lower comfort-level with delivering remote care, and patients for not knowing where or how virtual care was available, and also for a perceived discomfort with remote care.

When Covid-19 shut down in-person care, both audiences had no choice but to put aside their discomfort and try something new, and for the most part, both audiences adapted well, with a likely expansion of virtual care in the future. Yet something else changed in the spring of 2020 – two other blockers of earlier adoption of virtual care were removed nearly overnight. First, federal regulators removed restrictions that made delivering virtual care extremely complex, such as lowering HIPAA and technology restrictions and allowing for telehealth encounters across state lines.

Second, both CMS and private insurers changed payment guidelines to make virtual visits available and affordable. For years, many health plans had been slow to embrace virtual visits, under the premise that encouraging virtual visits would drive up the number of healthcare encounters, thereby increasing overall costs. Many resisted offering parity in virtual visit payments compared to an equivalent in-person visit, or sometimes to pay at all, which forced many states to take action. According to a study by Foley & Lardner, 22 states have laws explicitly addressing telemedicine reimbursement, up from 16 in 2019, and 14 require true payment parity, up from 10 in 2019.[88] In many ways, Medicare, the largest payor of all, was the most restrictive when it came to virtual visits. For example, up until Covid-19, CMS restricted e-visits to rural areas or areas with less access to on-site care, and prevented e-visits from taking place in a patient's *home*. That was only *one year ago* – and seems almost unfathomable post-Covid.

Many people might argue that encouraging greater healthcare access would be a good thing, and had individuals been encouraged – rather than discouraged through regulation and restrictive payments – to try virtual visits, many would have preferred that method to in-person visits where possible (I know I sure do). So in a truly individual-driven market, where consumer demands drive innovation and a better customer experience, we might have seen adoption of virtual care happen on a greater scale much sooner. But because insurers are the bigger "customer" of healthcare, this innovation was held back to protect their interests. It took a once-in-a-century health crisis to shake up the market, and the question remains whether health plans will allow virtual visits to grow unfettered. In a development that doesn't bode well for individual "consumerism," many insurers are forcing patients to use their own proprietary virtual care offerings rather than their doctor's or hospital's, using financial incentives and penalties to drive that behavior. Once again, is this better for the individual or for the health plan? More on this in a bit.

Here's another quick example: Based on a 2019 survey by the Kaiser Family Foundation, 78% of Americans favor allowing U.S. residents to buy prescription medication from Canada, where drug prices are often substantially lower than the U.S. because of Canada's price controls on pharmaceuticals.[89] Yet it remains illegal (in the vast majority of cases) to import drugs from Canada thanks to federal law. In other words, the largest "consumer" of healthcare in the U.S., the federal government, prevents the import and resulting cost-savings of drugs from Canada, despite the fact the vast majority of individual "consumers" desire this option.

So the notion of payors as the ultimate consumer, and thus the ultimate driver of change in healthcare, definitely fits what we see in the market. But what about over the next decade? Is there any reason this dynamic might shift, moving power away from public and private payors, into the hands of individuals? Barring a radical overhaul like the implementation of full-on Medicare-for-all or some other single-payor option (which seems extraordinarily unlikely in the next ten years), it's unlikely we'll see the private payor sector's grip on healthcare wane. It is certainly possible their power grows, however, and while we may not see a complete overhaul at the level of a single-payor system, it *is* certainly possible to see the reach of Medicare and Medicaid grow depending on how the political winds blow. And any expansion of government-funded healthcare will only increase the power of payors as consumer, diminishing the power of the individual at the same time, especially the power of those dependent on government-sponsored care.

Of course, while payors – both public and private – *are* the dominant "consumer" in healthcare, if that is defined by who actually spends money on the product, that doesn't mean individual consumers are completely out of the picture when it comes to their power to demand change. Back when most everyone had traditional "indemnity" health insurance, with lower premiums, low copays and no deductibles, there was little incentive to demand more from healthcare providers. With a $10 copay for everything from a doctor's visit to having a baby, expectations were understandably lower, and there was little on the line financially from a poor healthcare experience. Now, with families regularly facing high premiums, copays, coinsurance, AND annual deductibles ranging from $1,000 to $10,000, it makes sense that consumers are demanding more. But even if consumers demand more, will they necessarily get what they're asking for? This leads us to reason number two for a future with constricted consumerism. While there is a lot of talk and hand waving about consumerism driving change, as we hinted at with the virtual care example, there are many forces at work that are actually counteracting those potential changes, especially when it comes to consumer *choice*.

Reason Two – Payors will be payors

Choice is an interesting component of consumerism. On one hand, it serves as one of the three primary drivers of consumerism – increased options for care along with access to more information on those options, and more financial skin in the game, which combine to empower individuals to demand more for their healthcare dollars. Yet choice is also an outcome of consumerism – as consumers demand more, more options emerge to meet their demands, creating a theoretical ongoing cycle of greater innovation, lower prices, and more personalized/

appropriate choices for care. As we've alluded to, choice seems to have grown as a driver of consumerism over the past years, with new entrants in the retail, primary care, and virtual care areas, and, at least until Covid-19 curbed travel, increased options through medical tourism, both domestic and international. Even with Covid-19, according to one study, the global medical tourism market is poised to nearly triple from $105 billion in 2019 to $274 billion in 2027.[90]

But just because there are more choices doesn't mean individuals can access them all, or would want to. In fact, in many ways, choice will continue to become more limited as the next decade unfolds, curbing the power of individuals to drive change on their own behalf. The number of ways choice is being restricted is somewhat surprising.

We start of course with the health insurance industry, which seeks to restrict payments, and thereby restrict choice, by its very nature. The ways in which payors restrict choice are many, and only growing in their strength. The bluntest tool used to restrict choice of those with private insurances is the use of networks. Everyone is familiar with the financial penalties involved with receiving care out-of-network, where co-pays, deductibles, and co-insurance can all be higher, or there may be less favorable annual or lifetime limits. *Narrow networks* – where a plan may limit members to a lower number or even one provider organization – have exploded in growth over the past decade. According to a 2019 study, 72% of ACA plans were narrow networks. My father, an 81-year-old on fixed income, recently seeking a cheaper plan than his high-premium retiree health insurance plan, found he qualified for 24 potential Medicare-Advantage plans through the ACA exchanges. Only two included his physicians, who are employed by one of the five large health systems in the Twin Cities.

Payors also use *steering* and *tiering* to financially incent members to use specific providers, typically based on stated quality qualifications, but often for care at a lower cost. This typically takes the form of using lower expenses such as co-pays or co-insurance for different levels, or *tiers*, of healthcare providers based on their cost of services. While this may seem like a reasonable way to curb costs, it ultimately restricts the choice of the consumer. And what about when insurers steer members to their own providers? This is an increasing threat to legacy healthcare providers, especially as we see continued aggressive expansion into care delivery from players like Optum. A 2020 story in *The Wall Street Journal* shows how this trend is growing, stating for example:

> *Blue Cross & Blue Shield of Texas launched a plan this year that includes free primary-care visits at clinics it recently opened with a partner company in the Houston and Dallas areas. It priced the coverage 12% to 18% below a different product it offers statewide. The new plan includes some independent doctors and clinics, but members who use them would have a co-pay for primary-care visits.*[91]

Optum is also cited, with their new Harmony network in Los Angeles, built around their own physicians. CVS Health/Aetna dropped co-pays for their insurance network members who use the organization's own MinuteClinic network. And Humana has been expanding into home health and hospice care, with its most recent deal the June 2021 announced acquisition of One Homecare Health ("onehome").

The story notes that there have been integrated organizations, offering both care delivery and insurance, for decades, with some of the most recognized and lauded health systems in the country leveraging this model, including Intermountain Healthcare, Geisinger, and Kaiser Permanente. These organizations have been "steering" by definition for years, though in nearly all cases, members of these organization's insurance plans do have choices to see other providers in-network. There has also been the adoption of provider-sponsored health plans in the past decade by health systems, though most of those have struggled to gain real growth or have been closed down. The difference with large payors is the scale of those organizations to steer care on a much broader level. For example, Geisinger's insurance plan has 600,000 members, while Aetna's health insurance covers an estimated 39 million people.[92] Optum, part of UnitedHealthcare (49.7 million members) now employs more physicians than any other organization in the U.S.[93].

We can also go to what critics see as the true dark side of restricting consumer choice – the budding trend of payors retroactively rejecting claims for inappropriate ED visits. The horror stories have circulated for a number of years now about patients having their claims rejected following what they deemed an appropriate visit to the ED. This relatively new strategy – Anthem was the first major payor to institute such policies – is seen as particularly disturbing given hospitals and health systems by law have to treat emergency patients regardless of ability to pay. In August 2020, California fined Aetna $500,000 (or .0008% of the company's annual premium revenue) for this practice, and in June 2021, UnitedHealthcare suspended its policy a few days after publicly announcing it based on backlash from industry groups like the American Hospital Association, as well as fierce fire on social media.

We could go on and on about how the growth of health plans will continue to inhibit choice for individual consumers of healthcare, but we shouldn't be surprised by this dynamic. It's what we would expect. But what about healthcare providers? The value of consolidation among healthcare providers in terms of improved clinical quality, consumer experience, or healthcare costs is still hotly debated. But what's not typically up for argument is how industry consolidation has limited choice – best case, it keeps healthcare options relatively at the same level, but worse case, it limits care options for individual consumers. This happens in a number of ways. For starters, consolidation can reduce competition, which is never a good thing for consumers in any industry. Here's Sesame's Goldhill:

> Instead of consumerism driving change, the system fought back and has dampened any impact consumerism could have had. Most of this has happened seemingly under the guise of value-based care, bundles, population health – all the rage academically, but in terms of industrial structure this just a means of cementing the status quo. Without competition around price, quality, and coordination at the core of the healthcare industry - hospitals, pharma, or physician services – consumerism will continue to be stunted. At this core level, there is still not a real commitment to drive the competition necessary to support consumerism.

Rolfing sees it in a similar way. He points to work earlier in his career around reference-based pricing, which was supposed to be an example of a consumer-driven innovation to help manage costs. With reference-based pricing, consumers would be presented with different options for a clinical encounter, say hip replacement surgery, at different price levels from different providers, say $20,000, $25,000 or $30,000. That consumer would then be given financial incentive to choose the lower cost option by their employer or insurer (similar to the steering discussion above). The consumer could still choose the more expensive option for whatever reason (brand preference, proximity, choice of surgeon, etc.), but they would be on the hook for the difference in price. For this to work, there needed to be enough bundled care options with set pricing at a local level. But the idea broke down for a couple of reasons. For one, self-insured employers who were big enough to benefit from this approach typically were regional or national in size, requiring bundled payment options from multiple providers in various markets. That highlighted the second problem – getting providers on board. Here's Rolfing:

> In a true market, you'd have reference pricing all day long. But with all the health system consolidation, they had more power to fight reference pricing, which most didn't want. So you need to have a coalition of large employers in a single market, or a government entity at a state or federal level, for this to work. But then we're back to something that's not true consumerism at an individual level. It's not truly demand-side driven. It's more of the same – intermediaries making the rules.

Another way consolidation is reducing individual choice, and in a way that may not be noticeable to patients, is through increased insider referrals. One of the best ways for provider organizations to reap financial gains from a merger or acquisition is to lock in more referrals from their own physicians to down-funnel specialty and surgical care. Most systems already have strategic initiatives to reduce referral "leakage" to outside providers, and the pressure to keep referrals in-house grows following M&A activity. Ironically, health systems report that the average employed physician still sends 50% of their referrals to physicians outside the very network that employs them.

Laura Schoen, Chief Healthcare Officer for DXTRA Health Integrated Solutions and Global Healthcare President at Weber Shandwick, isn't optimistic that things will improve for consumers in terms of choice.

> *Consumer choice will be limited and pricey. Most patients will have financial incentives to follow their health plan's recommendations. Thirty years ago, all the doctors I wanted to see were independent, and most of them didn't take insurance. But ten years from now, there will be no more independent doctors. They'll be like Blockbuster - a thing of the past. Big systems will continue to acquire practices, and all docs will end up part of some network. So what before was a personal decision for a doctor is now moving to what's best for a larger organization, the health system. Choices will be limited as they keep referrals in network, and most people still trust that referral more than any other input.*

Growing financial pressures are causing the loss of healthcare providers in rural communities and urban centers. The idea of a "rural healthcare crisis" has been documented for a number of years. In the past decade, more than 130 rural hospitals have closed, including 20 in 2020 alone,[94] and according to a February 2020 *Forbes* article, one in four rural hospitals are in danger of shuttering thanks to financial stress. Many pundits blame industry consolidation on the shrinking presence of rural healthcare access points. For example, in his June 2021 executive order pushing for more competition across industries, President Biden points the finger at hospital consolidation as a primary cause of rural hospital closings. The truth, however, is far more complicated, and it is often provider consolidation that *saves* rural hospitals and physician groups from going under.

Compared to the situation in rural healthcare, urban hospitals are closing at a much less frequent clip. But the consequences can be just as devastating, if not greater, given the size and make-up of the populations these urban hospitals serve and the safety-net protections they provide. As just one example, a September 2020 article in *Modern Healthcare* told the story of Mercy Hospital & Medical Center in Chicago (owned by Trinity Health) which after 168 years of service – surviving among other things the Great Chicago Fire of 1871 –announced in July 2020 it was closing its doors due to financial failure. The story notes that 55% of Chicagoans who live in poverty and 62% of the city's Black residents reside within Mercy's service area.[95] (After a plan to have the state of Illinois step in to support the hospital failed in the state legislature, a non-profit group stepped in to save the hospital in the spring of 2021.[96])

So the healthcare industry itself, in many ways, is stifling choice at the very same time it purports to prioritize transformation in response to consumerism. Which leads us to the third and final reason consumerism is likely to be constricted in the coming decade – consumers themselves. We have seen the enemy, and she is us.

Choice – HUH! What is it good for...

During the final year of my MBA at the University of St. Thomas back in 2006, my team selected my idea for a new business that would be the focus of our final project: we called it "Third Opinion." The premise was that consumerism was coming in healthcare, but most consumers were ill-prepared to leverage their power. The situation was not unlike consumers managing investing for their own retirement, which of course had become the responsibility of consumers as classic pension plans were replaced by save-it-yourself 401ks and IRAs. (The idea of consumer-driven healthcare is not dissimilar from consumer-driven retirement – "let's shift the burden from employers to individuals. It will be great!" How's that working out for retirement savings? For Americans aged 55-64, those on the cusp of retirement, the average retirement savings level was $107,000.[97] But I digress.) There are few people who have the time, smarts, and resources to manage their own retirement savings, which entails staying abreast of the latest in the economy, the markets, tax law, etc. So we hire financial planners, or brokers, or use Betterment, or whoever or whatever understands and manages retirement investing full time. From our MBA team's perspective, healthcare was not much different. Who would be equipped to understand clinical quality metrics, differences in brand experiences, differences in individual clinicians, cost differences, etc.? What if there was a Charles Schwab of healthcare decision making, someone who could help you make an educated decision about a surgery or chronic disease management based on choices in the market, your preferences, and your budget? Someone who knew all the providers in the market, who was the best for what, who had the longest wait times? An expert that understood the ins and outs of individual insurance plans to help consumers make both the best medical *and* financial choice. Perhaps you paid an annual membership fee for the service, or paid on an as-need basis – say $500 to find the best knee guy in town based on all of these variables. Voila - Third Opinion!

Any number of businesses have come along (and gone along) that are similar in nature, though usually as an employer-based service rather than consumer-facing retail outlet – Redbrick, Carol.com (look it up – wayyy ahead of its time) and, who can forget, the Don Quixote of them all, Castlight Health. Health insurers play this role to a large degree, but they are typically focused first and foremost (or solely) on cost comparisons. Who's on the side of the little guy?

It seemed like a great idea then, but we didn't have the guts to really go for it and launch the company. Unfortunately, it *still* seems like a good idea, because 15 years on, individual consumers are still for the most part really unequipped to deal with the healthcare choices they face. For all the talk of consumerism and empowerment, you only have power if you can wield it.

Wendell Potter knows something about consumerism. Potter is famous for turning whistleblower on the health insurance industry with his book *Deadly Spin*, which shared how his former employer, Cigna, and other health insurance companies put profits before patient care. Since the book's release in 2010, Potter continues to be an outspoken voice on the trespasses of health insurers, and he jokes that he was "in the room" when the euphemism "consumer-driven health care" was invented by insurers to mask the true nature of the strategy – shifting costs from employers and insurers to individuals. Given his experience in the industry, he's, let us say, *skeptical* of the power of consumerism.

> *Look, it's been 20 years plus since we first started talking about the power of consumerism, and guess what – it ain't gonna happen. Healthcare doesn't work like other parts of the economy, where consumers can drive demand, innovation, or lower pricing. It's way too complex and confusing for consumers to navigate. Look around your neighborhood – how many people could truly figure out this system? Even I wouldn't know how to pick the best hospital if I had a heart issue, and I have a deep understanding of how healthcare works. Trying to figure out my options for Medicare Part D is crazy. Most of what we hear on consumerism, quite frankly, is still marketing bullshit.*

Consider the ultimate result of any consumer-driven power in any industry – pricing. If consumers were truly in control, were truly driving change, we'd see consumer-driven pricing pressure. Yes, there are some examples of price reduction over time as competition has increased – LASIK surgery, for example, has seen *some* pricing improvement over time. Though of course LASIK is a 100% elective procedure not covered by insurance, so not the most representative example. Not only are we *not* seeing this dynamic across the board, consumers actually choose their care based on price at a far lower rate than most would believe.

Oh, we'll *talk* about driving pricing changes. Hell yeah!!! According to a survey released by Advisory Board in 2017, "cost" was the number one factor listed by respondents in deciding where to receive surgical care, at 53%, more than perceived surgeon quality, brand affiliation, referral and proximity *combined*.[98] Consumer research we've done has shown how patients are willing to switch primary care providers for a lower price, all other things being equal. Oh yeah, get us in a focus group or on a survey, and we *talk* BIG about our price sensitivity.

But how do we act about pricing in healthcare? Most insured

consumers will opt for in-network care options over out-of-network if they can. But after that? Meh. Do we see patients switching primary care docs like they switch their toilet paper choices on whichever is offering the lowest cost that week? Nope. In a survey published in 2017 and featured in *Health Affairs*, only 13 percent of respondents who had some out-of-pocket spending in their last health care encounter had sought information about their expected spending before receiving care, and just 3 percent had compared costs across providers before receiving care.[99] According to a 2018 paper released by the National Bureau of Economic Research, researchers observed the behavior of (rather than asked the opinion of) 50,000 people who were told to find an MRI option in their market. Less than 1% of the participants used a pricing tool to shop for their MRI,[100] which, given its perceived commodity status, is a perfect candidate for price shopping. Compare that to typical retail shopping, where according to one study, 80% of retail shoppers compare pricing online before shopping in a store.[101]

So what's the deal? As everyday consumers of everything from milk to shoes to cars, we tend to research and compare prices, and often respond to price incentives such as sales, discounts, and coupons. Why not in healthcare? It's more complex, more personal, and still, despite movement toward transparency, opaque. Yumin Choi is partner and head of the healthcare group at Bain Capital Ventures. Before his current role, he was General Partner at HLM Venture Partners, a healthcare-focused venture fund, and has served as board director and board observer for numerous companies, as well as lecturer on entrepreneurial finance in the Gordon Institute at Tufts University. Here's his take:

> Until we get to point where consumers have perfect information, it will be hard to realize the power of consumerism. Right now, decisions are driven essentially by hearsay - word of mouth. That's still the number one way. As consumers we're still blind on making educated decisions - we don't know enough to really make a decision, so we just rely on others.

Adam Brase, Executive Director – Strategic Intelligence at Mayo Clinic, concurs:

> *Many consumers believe healthcare is like airline travel – they expect a certain level of quality and safety. They can't parse actual differences, and ratings and rankings are too confusing. Everyone seems like they're the best at something. Very few consumers will actually spend the time and have the knowledge to do this.*

And Dr. Ryu, CEO at Geisinger:

> *There are also negative aspects of consumerism– empowering individuals is good, but there is risk. Consumers will never fully understand the medical sciences. They just can't. For example, we often have patients who demand a full-body CT scan, which likely is not clinically appropriate. But they don't understand the cost, efficacy, or danger of that option. There's a place where consumerism stops and medical expertise begins, and it varies by issue, by person, by balance. We need to equip and empower consumers, but also be mindful of that balance.*

Finally, some of the experts we talked to questioned whether choice is even desirable in healthcare. Choi says we shouldn't assume choice will drive better outcomes, lower costs, or improve competition. Mabbutt raises a similar question:

> *In healthcare, consumers don't necessarily want wider choice, they want relevance and support. Most want focused choice, not wide-open choice. We need to curate that choice for them – it's very nuanced and complex with the stakes so high. We're not like other industries. The solution isn't just throwing choices at consumers, that's just another level of complexity. We need to enable the*

choices that matters most to consumers rather than just more choice.

And finally, Goldhill points out how an unfettered healthcare market, full of consumer-powered choice, can go tragically wrong.

Look at the opioid crisis in this country, the absolute human carnage, shortened lifespans, meaningful injury, immense pain. Most everyone agrees more access to care is better, and we want to ensure everyone has access to what they need. But it's a reminder that wide-open, undisciplined or unmanaged care can lead to harm as well, in this case through the extensive over prescription of medication. The choice shouldn't be seen as either markets or regulation: it's how to use market forces so that regulators can focus on regulating. We see it in other industries, such as airlines: the government is a better regulator when it's no longer the industry's business partner. In health care, the government is the industry's business partner.

Taken individually, maybe any one of these reasons that points to a future of constricted consumerism – the disintermediation of the individual, the growing restrictions placed on individual choice, and the limits of individuals in a space such as healthcare – could be mitigated over the coming decade. But taken together, and given the unlikelihood of any of them changing for the better, it becomes clear the power of consumerism won't follow an upward trajectory.

Instead, the impact of consumerism will really depend on where you stand in the healthcare world. As an individual, do you live in a rural setting or urban area where access is restricted, and options are fewer? Do you live in a market where there is healthy competition (such as my market, the Twin Cities, with five separate healthcare provider systems) or a market where a single provider dominates (such as Pittsburgh and western Pennsylvania where UPMC enjoys a 60% market share)? Are you searching for care for your daughter's likely strep throat, where you have many options, including any number of virtual care offerings or brick and mortar retail or urgent care clinics right around the corner? Or are you in need of a total hip replacement, and your health plan's narrow network limits you to one surgical center in town?

Or maybe it's a matter of differing perspectives? If you're an optimist, sure consumerism isn't the all-powerful force we thought it might be, but it will still drive change, and even if incrementally, for the good? Do you believe that the Biden's administration renewed focus on promoting "competition" in healthcare, including ramping up the financial penalties for hospitals not complying with new price transparency rules, will make a difference? Or maybe you're a pessimist, and you see the golden era of consumerism in its twilight, with the next decade bringing a net reduction in the power and promise of consumerism? Or maybe it's all tied to whether you believe in our next prediction, with consumerism showing up differently after chasms appear across the provider sector? Maybe you should read Chapter Six and then decide.

Chapter 6

PREDICTION

The Funnel Wars

FROM: PR Newsource
Big Six Becomes Big Five

DATELINE: June 30, 2030, Chicago, Illinois – Following intense negotiations, Prov-cension, the third largest health system in the U.S., with more than $50 billion in net patient revenue, has agreed to merge with East Coast Health, the sixth largest health system, with $32 billion in net patient revenue, to create Prov-East, the third largest health system in the world. The new organization will only trail OptHCA, the second largest, and Amazon Health, the largest health system with more than $100 billion in net patient revenue. That brings the vaunted Big Six group of health systems, which collectively own 70% of patient care market share in the U.S., down to five.

"This merger combines the outstanding clinical quality of Prov-cension and our commitment to individual and community health with the superior health plan offerings and home-based healthcare of East Coast," said Susan Synergy, the proposed future CEO of the new colossus.

"We look forward to improving the health of the 50 million people under our care and coverage."

Officials at both companies do not foresee any FTC challenges from the Gaetz administration, which has repeatedly signaled its intent to remove any regulatory hurdles from private business consolidation under the slogan "Everyone loves to play monopoly!" Meanwhile, leaders of the National Association for Legacy Hospitals announced that despite growth in membership of 20%, their members – primarily single hospitals or groups of hospitals focused solely on specialty and surgical care – still face financial difficulties from shrinking reimbursement and price control pressure from the Big Five.

"We all realize care needs to be pushed out of the hospital into physician offices, retail access points, the home and the cloud – we get it already," said association president Sam Shrinkage. "But how many times do we have to keep repeating it – we still need hospitals! Between continued cuts employed by the Centers for Medicare, Medicaid and Medi-Bridge Services, and the constant pressure on pricing from the Big Five, we will continue to see hospitals close across this country. As it stands now, unless you're in one of the top 20 largest metros in the country, you can expect to have to travel an average of 100 miles just to receive joint replacement surgery. While 300 million people are covered by what is now the Big Five, we shouldn't have to remind everyone that it's our members that actually deliver the vast majority of specialty and surgical care as downstream vendors of these behemoths."

OK, we exaggerate to make our point. But only a little? Well, probably more than a little. But based on our research and the input of experts we talked to, the next decade could see a fundamental shift in the hospital and health system spectrum. That shift is our third prediction...

> *Today we tend to consider hospitals and health systems as birds of the same feather in terms of business model, with variances based on size, scope of services, for-profit/non-profit, and other factors. Moving forward, we could see the splitting of the health system model, with some systems moving even further to the larger,*

more comprehensive "health" organizations, others retracting into solely acute-care destinations – the "giant ICU on a hill" – and others somewhere in the middle. These models may emerge based on core geographic/ market differences such as presence of competitors, plan consolidation/power, regulation, and dozens of other market forces. Yet the primary area where this transformation would play out is with health, wellness, and the lower-acuity care points – what we're calling The Funnel Wars.

Let's talk funnels

My first exposure to the concept of the acuity funnel – and the related importance of the top of that funnel – was through my connection to Matt Gove, currently Chief Marketing Officer at Summit Health. The idea of an acuity funnel is not new, but when I interviewed Gove for the last Joe Public book in 2017, his perspective on the import of the funnel felt unique. As we explained in Chapter 3, the acuity funnel takes the continuum of care delivery and applies it to the shape of a funnel, with the first-encounter, easy access, often lower-acuity services at the top – urgent care, retail care, virtual care, emergency care and in some cases, primary care – followed down the line by specialty care, surgical care, tertiary care, and finally quaternary care at the bottom of the funnel. Gove's unique perspective was based on data he uncovered at Piedmont that showed how much the acuity funnel acted, like, well a funnel. While most health systems focus on trying to drive growth through marketing at a mid-funnel level – where the higher-margin services such as specialty and surgical care live – Gove's data showed why the focus should actually be at the top of the funnel. Here's how we articulated Gove's point in *Joe Public III*, released in 2018:

We ran our inpatient numbers, and overall, 55% of all encounters by volume are ED encounters, the rest, 45%

*we call non-ED or service-line encounters. We found
that of these inpatient, service-line encounters, 83% had
a low-acuity visit within the Piedmont system in the
prior 12 months. And that means that only 17% of our
service-line-oriented encounters came to us directly from
outside the system. So why in the world would we spend
so much money and effort to try and attract only 17%
of the patients? Look, it's a funnel, right? Service-line
marketing is like trying to force people into the side of the
funnel. That's not how funnels work.*[102]

The point of this story in *Joe Public III* was to highlight the
contrarian nature of Gove's strategy of focusing marketing on top-
of-the-funnel patients rather than those needing specialty or surgical
care. (Not that health systems shouldn't market to that down-funnel
audience, it's more that the way they traditionally have – through
mass advertising – was wasted effort. Search-engine marketing, direct
marketing, and physician-targeted marketing are all examples of
perfectly effective ways of engaging specialty and service-line patients
who need care. Big advertising campaigns, however, should focus on the
top-of-the-funnel. But I once again digress.)

For this book, however, Gove's perspective holds the essence of why
we care so much about the top-of-the-acuity funnel, and why it is here
a war is forming in the healthcare industry. Because based on Gove's
findings and other research that verifies it, health systems gain the
vast majority of their new patients through top-of-the-funnel services.
Should they lose the competitive battle at the top of the funnel, systems
will not only lose patients for any immediate down-funnel encounters (a
woman who presents with stomach pains at an urgent care needing an
appendectomy, for example), they potentially could lose that patient *for
life*. The top of the funnel is where most of the consumer relationships
in healthcare start, but if that consumer is diverted to someone else's
funnel, the loss in lifetime value could be hundreds of thousands of
dollars, per patient.

Further, in the time since we've been advocating for TOF (top-of-
the-funnel) strategies, we've added another layer at the top – health

and wellness services, offerings, and value. More and more systems have shifted their value proposition to expand beyond providing reimbursable clinical care alone to helping individuals lead healthy, happy lives, and/or focusing on community health. That's because, in many cases, systems have recognized that potential patients could be intercepted *before* they even enter the acuity funnel, by other health systems or healthcare companies that are focused on health and wellness. This TOF landscape – health and wellness offerings, urgent care, virtual care, retail care, emergency care and primary care – is now the greatest target of new entrants in the healthcare space. Most have little interest in down-funnel, higher-acuity care, such as specialty or surgical care (let alone transplants or other complex care). Walmart Health, CVS Health, Walgreens, Apple, Amazon, One Medical, Teledoc, IoraHealth, OakStreet, Archwell, Firefly Health, Galileo, Nice Healthcare, PM Pediatrics, City MD, Concentra, GoHealth – all of these brands, and many more, are focused solely on TOF services. (The noted exception is Optum, which has expanded TOF services as well as surgical offerings, such as through the acquisition of Surgical Care Affiliates in 2017). This mix of new and not-so-new entrants includes longstanding brands that have proven to be truly consumer-focused, and new entities supported collectively by billions in venture capital. They see the healthcare sector — the largest part of the U.S. economy with $3.8 trillion in spending in 2019, or 18% of the gross domestic product[103] – as ripe for conquering, and they aren't focused on the difficult clinical challenges of down-funnel surgical, tertiary, or quaternary care. They are all cherry-picking the easier segment of the healthcare continuum – the top of the funnel.

So, you're a legacy health system, desperate to find and keep new patients, and you have 99 new problems at the top-of-the funnel, all gunning to build a relationship with consumers in your market. Let's add some fuel to the fire. Because not only is the top of the funnel the hottest battleground in healthcare, it's also where the powers of consumerism, such that they are, have the most impact. Remember in Chapter Five we laid out the primary pressure points of consumerism in healthcare: access, convenience, transparency, experience, pricing. It turns out that, while these may have limited influence when it comes to traditional hospital services, they can hold tremendous sway over consumer choice at the top of the funnel.

Let's take price as one such driver of consumer decision making. Theoretically, the cost of surgery should have a huge influence on where consumers receive their care – after all, costs can range from $30,000 for a hip replacement to $200,000 or more for heart valve replacement (not including all the other related costs, such as hospital stays, medication, therapy, etc.). Yet, for most insured consumers, pricing variability can go out the window with *any* surgery, because any surgery is bound to blow an existing deductible, and likely max co-insurance or annual out-of-pocket limits. Assuming in-network options, it doesn't matter where they go for their spinal fusion or gastric bypass, a consumer's cost will be the same, taking the variability out of the decision-making equation. (Out-of-network choices would obviously cost more.)

But what about urgent care? What if one urgent care is covered by insurance, so the cost of the visit is $25, versus another that is outside of a consumer's insurance network, with an expected cost of $150? Or maybe the cost of a flu shot is $50 with co-payment at your legacy system's retail clinic, but just $25 or even $0 at Walgreens? While the cost level and variable is much lower at the top of the funnel, consumers may make the decision to save $25 or $50 or $100. And in that decision, where they choose to receive care may determine where any additional care may take place down-funnel. If they've chosen your system's care, you have the opportunity to refer them within your own funnel. But if they've chosen another system, you will have lost them. And even if they've chosen a retailer like Walgreens that doesn't offer surgical care, you've lost *control* of that down-funnel referral.

Take access as yet another example. Most people will use the pharmacy that is closest to them for their prescriptions, or the closest urgent care or MinuteClinic. But patients routinely wait weeks or months to see a desired specialist or surgeon, and often travel across town, to a nearby metro, or even across the U.S., for the same reason, bypassing many other clinical options that are far closer.

So where the power of consumerism may start to dissipate as one moves down the acuity funnel, it has outsized influence at the top of the funnel. Which is where all the big retail brands, tech company brands, and new entrants are focused. So as we like to say around the office – wheeeeeeeeeee!

Market to market combat

To say there is a lot at stake for legacy hospitals and health systems at the top of the funnel certainly would be an understatement. Many in the industry believe the winners and losers in the health system space will be determined by who can thrive at the top of the funnel. Some will grow to be vast regional or national players (or "vaster" in some cases), offering the entire spectrum of value to consumers, from health and wellness to insurance coverage to the full continuum of clinical care. Others may shrink back, focused on the essential hospital services all communities will still need, dependent on others at the TOF to feed them patient referrals. Others will float somewhere in the middle. The fallout of such a shift would shake healthcare in the U.S., and over the next decade, things definitely could get ugly.

Let's start with Kyle Rolfing, the healthcare entrepreneur we've heard from previously. From Rolfing's view, those entering the top of the funnel from outside the legacy space are far better positioned to meet consumers where they are, starting with using better data to understand consumers, care utilization, and costs. He believes the advantages for these TOF-companies will lead to a change in who determines where patients go, and ultimately, who manages the relationship. This will shift from legacy hospitals and health systems to primary-care companies, other health management companies, or even health plans, potentially turning many of those legacy providers into dependent, marginalized vendors of downstream acuity, losing the patient relationship along the way.

> *There will be a war on this, but we don't know who will end up winning. We'll see microcosms where the distributed model succeeds, with lower costs and better health. In other markets, we'll see hospitals and health systems successfully keep these alternatives out, or they will buy*

them out. There will be pockets – Kaiser, Intermountain, Geisinger, maybe HealthPartners in Twin Cities – where those systems crack the nut and their integrated model will be successful. Others that can't make that move will become suppliers to other entities like primary care companies, contracting with those who own the patient relationship. In fact, we already see those two paths diverging today in some areas.

Russ Meyer, the head of brand strategy, innovation, and design thinking at CVS Health, sees healthcare's future through the past of other industries when it comes to The Funnel Wars:

The likelihood of this division is 100%. There isn't enough business or brand space at the top of the funnel for everyone. So some providers will cease being true consumer brands, and will move from out in front of the wall to behind it. Take technology – there are brands that used to have a primary relationship with consumers that had to retreat to become "infrastructure." They no longer drive choice because they don't own the consumer relationship. There's a good business in infrastructure. It's just a different business.

An August 2021 article in *Fierce Healthcare* about this year's HIMSS conferences reflects Meyer's contention that the free-for-all at the top of the funnel isn't sustainable. The story, leads with the following:

Whether it's a patient app, symptom checker, digital concierge services or a telehealth platform, there's little shortage when it comes to options for a "digital front door" in the modern healthcare landscape. Particularly with the COVID-19 pandemic still in full swing, nearly every healthcare organization is developing or adopting new digital tools to facilitate a smoother patient experience and encouraging other healthcare stakeholders to do the same.

The story states that expert panelists agreed that the deluge of near-equivalent digital tools has reached the point where it is often harming the patient—or healthcare consumer—experience. "One of the things that concerns me is the consumer gets hit up by everybody's digital front door, everybody's digital interaction," said Dennis Weaver, M.D., chief clinical officer at startup insurer Oscar Health.[104]

Yumin Choi, head of the healthcare group at Bain Capital Ventures, sees the next ten years playing out in one of three scenarios:

> *In scenario one, scale matters. Dominant regional players like Kaiser or Geisinger, they offer all the right components, components most health systems don't have. In Scenario Two, there are national dynamics, but also hyper-local dynamics that will shape this transition. For example, in Nebraska, Blue Cross owns 90% of the health insurance market, and hospitals and health systems are beholden to them. While in Ohio, we could see new entrants at the top of the funnel own the patient relationship, relegating legacy providers to downstream acute care suppliers. In the Third Scenario, systems will try to partner with others to have their cake and eat it too, but also really having no choice. We could see this all play out at a regional, state or even local market level.*

During our last Joe Public Retreat in February 2020 (jussssst missed that Covid thing), a confab of more than 50 of the top health system marketers and consumer strategists in the country, a very interesting debate broke out highlighting the tension between these scenarios. An executive from a top primary care organization was sharing with the mostly legacy health system executives how he saw their choice as "if you can't beat 'em, join 'em," and he confidently said his organization and others like them would surely "beat them" otherwise at the top of the funnel. A CMO from a very large, prestigious health system piped up and reluctantly agreed, saying her organization had failed to move fast enough in the space of urgent care and other TOF offerings and rather than giving up altogether, had agreed to partner with the first executive's primary company. There was a realization by Executive Two that in doing so, they were losing ownership of those patients, who might be diverted to other systems by Executive One's company, and you could see the resignation on her face. At that point, Executive Three, a CMO from another prominent and very prestigious health system chimed in, aghast at the idea of handing over the extraordinarily valuable TOF turf to some other company. That set of offerings was just too important to give up, or worse, cede to a brand other than his own, and his system, having seen the writing on the wall early, had invested heavily in building out their own TOF services such as urgent retail care. Executive Two could only nod, grimace, and acknowledge the battle lost. Winners and losers.

Going further, some like David Goldhill, CEO of Sesame, are actively rooting for such a change:

> There's a real chance this could happen, and it could be with primary care companies or other health management organizations, especially since fewer people today have primary care relationships. This might provide the opportunity for better continuity of care than we have today, better record keeping, better service, more convenience. This trend would be a good thing.

Some see the inevitability of such a shift in the health system space through the lens of negative repercussions. Here's Wendell Potter, author and former health plan executive:

> Absolutely this will play out market to market. We're already seeing the closing of rural hospitals, and more community hospitals will likely fail. Unless something is done, there will be real winners and losers. There's a real worry here that the main losers would be those losing

access to acute care and hospitals, such as those in rural communities. They already have few choices, both from a care and an insurance coverage perspective. Some health systems will make this transition better than others, but those that don't will shrink, fold or be gobbled up. It's almost inevitable.

And on that last point Kevan Mabbutt, Chief Consumer Officer at Intermountain Healthcare, agrees:

This trend is inevitable – the value chain will be broken up. If you don't have a broader, successful portfolio as a health system, it's dangerous. You have to own the relationship – if you do, you can provide value across the whole journey – health and care. Economies of scale start to make sense and it is viable to truly move from fee-for-service to value-based care. But if you aren't strong, your top-of-the-funnel access will be picked off, by vertically based health plans, retail, primary care companies. They will do it better, and that will hurt those systems that aren't strong. Clinical excellence is even less important than convenience, holistic care, and other components at the top of the funnel. If you're not making changes to be competitive at the top of the funnel, you will be eventually marginalized to acute care/hospital-care only.

So the Funnel Wars have already begun, and the future holds the possibility for a real shakeout. What do we see today for each side as it girds for this battle?

News from the frontlines

What do we see from the invaders, those entering the healthcare industry with the goal of establishing top-of-the-funnel dominance, owning the patient relationship, and truly redefining how consumers engage in the healthcare space? We've already provided some examples, whether it's Nice Healthcare and their virtual/in-home primary care company, Woebot offering AI-driven mental healthcare, Humana's deep dive into home health, or even the idea of a "Betterment" for healthcare. Here are just a few other examples that should paint a fuller picture. (Note in some cases, like with Walmart, we will talk to their growth and future plans, knowing many of them have hit bumps along the way. More on those bumps later in the chapter.)

Walmart and their healthcare offerings continue to expand. The retail giant opened its first foray into healthcare delivery in 2014 with a mini-clinic model, which had been started and popularized by MinuteClinic, which itself started in 2000 before being acquired by CVS in 2006. (There have even been industry rumors of Walmart acquiring Humana or Anthem, but so far nothing like that has materialized). In September 2019, the retailer made headlines by launching Walmart Health, a primary-care clinic, at a Walmart store in Dallas, Georgia. A step up from the mini-clinic model, this outlet offered scans, annual check-ups, and dental services. By 2000, Walmart had 15 such locations, with plans to add seven more, and the company reported $37.8 billion in net sales for its health and wellness division in fiscal year 2020.[105] In spring of 2021, Walmart announced the acquisition of telehealth company MeMD, its first foray into virtual care, where they plan to provide consumers access to virtual urgent care, mental health services, and primary care.[106] And finally, the Walmart board approved a plan in 2019 to scale to 4,000 primary care "super centers" by 2029, though there are reports this expansion has been slowed internally.[107] All of this while charging a flat $40 for a primary care visit for adults, $20 for children.

As we mentioned in Chapter 3, many healthcare industry insiders had a good laugh at the closing of Haven in January 2021, the joint venture between Amazon, Berkshire Hathaway, and JP Morgan Chase designed to transform healthcare delivery in the U.S. When initially announced in 2018, the venture made huge headlines and caused quite a stir – here were three corporate giants, leaders in their spaces, coming together to solve the puzzle of a U.S. healthcare system that doesn't deliver for the ever-rising costs it incurs. It attracted healthcare thought leader and physician Atul Gawande as its CEO, as well as Jack Stoddard, a long-time healthcare executive with experience at Optum, as its COO. Here's how leaders described the vision of Haven at its launch:

> The three companies, which bring their scale and complementary expertise to this long-term effort, will pursue this objective through an independent company that is free from profit-making incentives and constraints. The initial focus of the new company will be on technology solutions that will provide U.S. employees and their families with simplified, high-quality and transparent healthcare at a reasonable cost.[108]

Amazon, Berkshire Hathaway, and JP Morgan Chase – if they couldn't solve healthcare, who could? Well, hopefully someone else, because Haven didn't make it. But the *reason* Haven didn't make it should have given pause to anyone thinking these competitors were conquered. According to many experts, Haven failed because each organization put more effort and resources into their own healthcare ventures separately. Sure enough, following the closing of Haven in January 2021, JP Morgan launched Morgan Health in May, a unit charged with improving the healthcare of the organization's 165,000 employees. More ominously, Amazon also took little time to head out on its own, and not just to engage its own employees. In May 2021, Amazon announced that its newly developed telehealth offering, Amazon Care, would expand beyond its own company to be available to employees at other companies across the U.S. starting in the summer of 2021. According to the company's press release:

> Amazon Care gives instant access to a range of urgent and primary care services, including COVID-19 and flu testing, vaccinations, treatment of illnesses and injuries, preventive care, sexual health, prescription requests, refills, and delivery, and much more.

One of my favorite podcasters and business thinkers is Scott Galloway, the adjunct professor of marketing at New York University's Stern School of Business mentioned earlier. In a weird cosmic confluence, as I was writing this chapter back in June, I took my dog for a walk and listened to the latest episode of "The Prof G Pod," and lo and behold, it sounded as if Prof G had been right there with us in our Team 2030 brainstorm meetings a few months earlier:

> *Healthcare organizations have continued to raise prices over inflation, while NPS scores have actually declined... This is an industry that is sticking out the mother of all chins...So who's going to come in? You're going to see a ton of startups, but you will also see the fastest growing company in terms of healthcare dollars, and that is Amazon, surrounding healthcare with Alexa, the app on your phone, with Prime. They know the food you order, they have a fulfillment network to get you your prescriptions, they have the credibility and the skills to sit on top of datasets, and that is effectively what healthcare is – the opportunity to sit on the digital data set of your corpus. And the exciting thing from a strategy standpoint, healthcare needs to move from a defensive on your heels disease-driven industry to an offensive on your toes health-driven industry. Amazon will go vertical, find out the high margin elements of health, and then they will outsource the rest, the shitty businesses, and they will build a platform like their third-party marketplace today. Consumers can use that platform to find doctors, specialists, care. That will start a real consolidation of healthcare. If someone said there could be one company that could own 50% of share in healthcare, that company is Amazon. That is by no means unthinkable – it's very doable. Once they start showing progress with this, the market will start providing cheap capital such that they can pull away, and all these little health groups, these hospital groups, aren't going to be able to compete because they can't access the same*

cheap capital. Maybe two thirds of healthcare costs can be digitized – doctor visits, surgical consults, RX, physical therapy – and could be dispersed away from doctors and hospitals. So it definitely wouldn't be hard to take 20, 30, even 50% away from the medical industrial complex. I'm convinced the first $3 trillion company will be Amazon, and on the back of the most disreputable industry in the history of business, U.S. healthcare.[109]

If not Amazon, then how about Apple? In a 2019 interview with CNBS shock-financial-jock Jim Cramer, Tim Cook, CEO of Apple, declared that the company's greatest contribution to mankind will be in health.[110] The company has invested billions in research and development centered on health-related products and services, and has aspirations to offer Apple primary care clinics with Apple physicians sometime in the future. While recent reports have suggested this effort has struggled to get off the ground internally, the company has inserted itself headlong into the health system space with its electronic medical record (EMR) feature. Announced in 2018, this component of Apple's Health app allows partner health systems to connect their EMR to the Health app, so patients of those systems can see important information such as lab results, immunizations, and other data from their personal health record. While this is a great feature for consumers, and many health systems tout it as an innovative offering of their own, what it in fact is doing is once again disintermediating health systems by having a far savvier consumer brand take over a key component of the patient journey – access to personal health data.

And after all that, Apple's focus on health in its products and software alone make it a formidable top-of-the-funnel entrant. We already covered some of Apple's growing role in health through the Apple Watch and Siri in Chapter Four. The data Apple is able to generate from an individual's health situation is growing by the day, as is the company's exploration of how to leverage that data to help improve health. One fascinating example is the development of what Apple calls "walking steadiness," a new metric that came from the introduction of its fall detection feature, which used motion sensor data to determine user falls and automatically alert medical professionals. Using data gathered from studying falls, clinicians were able to determine warning signs in people who were susceptible to falling, leading to the preventative measurement of "walking steadiness." As described in a June 2021 *TechCrunch* article on Apple's continued advances in health, "Apple actually accomplished something with its Walking Steadiness feature that is very rare in the health and fitness industry: It created a clinically validated, meaningful new metric around individual health." The story's author went on to state:

> ...*viewed as a whole, Apple has built probably the most powerful and accessible suite of personal health tools available to an individual, and it shows no signs of slowing down.*[111]

Let's look at the largest usurper, Optum. The health services unit from UnitedHealth Group has been building the organization's vertical integration for years with continued expansion into the provider sector. As noted earlier, Optum has become as of this year the largest employer of physicians in the U.S. In 2020, Optum reported $136 billion in annual revenue, and its medical network, Optum Health, treated 98 million people that year.[112] Compare that to the top five largest health systems in the U.S., which *combined* had net patient revenue of $135 billion as of July 2020.[113]

Or consider that the largest health system in the U.S., HCA Healthcare, with 186 hospitals and 46,000 physicians, logged 35 million patient encounters in 2019, or roughly one third of Optum's in 2020. Optum has continued to expand its network of providers, with its first move to manage an entire health system coming in 2019 with the announced partnership/para-acquisition of John Muir Health, the respected health system north of San Francisco. In April 2021, Optum announced that its own national telehealth product, Optum Virtual Care, was available in all 50 states, with the company saying the goal was to integrate physical care, virtual care, home care, and behavioral care.[114]

And in maybe the most important recent venture relative to legacy health system and the Funnel Wars, Optum announced the acquisition of Change Healthcare, the data analytics technology company with a vast foothold in the legacy health system space. For example, 60% of Change's revenue comes from provider customers, and its patient engagement tool reaches 200 million people per year. The move will provide Optum line of sight into the data of hundreds of health systems, essentially inviting one of the strongest enemies of legacy health systems right into heart of their organization. In a January 2021 blog post by our own Shannon McIntyre Hooper, formerly Chief Growth Officer at Revive and now Chief Strategy and Product Officer at BehaVR, the import was laid bare:

> *Optum already has one of the most sophisticated analytical infrastructures in the industry, and they're now extending it into every aspect of care and communication. They are responding to the dispersion of healthcare by building an interoperable network that connects marketing, operational, financial, and clinical data. If they can pull this off, the value to the consumer will be significant: an easy digital patient experience and flow from virtual care, to in-person visits, to prescription management, and ongoing engagement. What if the Amazon of healthcare isn't Amazon, but Optum?*

If legacy health systems only had to worry about these four giants, not to mention others not even mentioned here such as CVS Health and Walgreens, the Funnel Wars would be hard enough. Heck, even Dollar General is getting into the game. The fastest growing retailer in the U.S., with more than 17,000 locations, hired a Chief Medical Officer and announced in July 2021 that their goal is to, "build and enhance affordable healthcare offerings for our customers, especially in the rural communities we serve."[115]

But it's not only the mega-corps lining up for battle. From an article in *Fierce Healthcare* in July 2020, here's a list of primary care companies that have raised millions in capital:[116]

- One Medical – "a membership-based, tech-integrated, and consumer-focused primary care platform" (raised $245 million in its January 2020 IPO).
- Forward – "a membership-based primary care company (raised $100 million to date).
- Aledade – "an ACO partnership organization" (most recently raised $64 million in a Series C round).
- ChenMed – "a physician-led primary care company focused on seniors."
- IoraHealth – "a primary care company focused on the Medicare population" (raised $126 million in a Series F funding round in January 2020, and was set to be acquired by One Medical in 2021).
- Crossover Health – "a primary care provider focused on the self-insured employer market (raised $113 million to date).
- Oak Street Health – "a primary care provider focused on the Medicare population" (went public in August 2020 with an initial market capitalization of $328 million, now at a market cap of more than $11 billion one year later).
- VillageMD – "a fast-growing operator of primary care clinics" (landed $100 million in a Series B funding round in October 2019).
- Privia Health – "a national physician organization partners with other providers" (went public in May 2021, now with a market capitalization of $3.4 billion).

And that's just primary care. Similar indicators include:

- According to an article in *Modern Healthcare*, there were more than 30 private equity deals involving urgent care clinics between 2010 and 2020, affecting 896 locations (of the roughly 10,000+ total urgent care sites in the U.S.). The article also notes that of all the urgent care sites in the U.S., only 40% are owned at least in part by hospitals or health systems.[117]
- A 2017 study by Grand View Research predicts the market for U.S. retail clinics will reach $7.3 billion by 2025.[118]

- A study by Frost & Sullivan predicts the virtual care market in the U.S. will grow seven-fold by 2025.[119]

We could go on and on, but here's one final example to show just how explosive growth from non-legacy provider organizations is. In June 2021, Bright Health, the health plan that targets the individual insurance market, raised $924 million in its IPO. Notably, the health plan is building its NeueHealth unit, which partners with more than 200,000 health care providers and 28 managed and affiliated risk-bearing clinics. Over the past 18 months, Bright Health has acquired two medical groups, as well as the Minnesota-based telehealth company Zipnosis.[120] What makes this one example stand out: The $924 million raised makes Bright Health's IPO the largest of any company based in Minnesota, ever, outpacing notable brands such as Ceridian, Sun Country Airlines, Best Buy, and NRG Energy.

With this impressive array of forces aligned against it, what are legacy hospitals and health systems doing to join the battle? We can start with those organizations most identified as the likely future "winners" by those we interviewed – the large regional integrated systems like Geisinger, Intermountain Healthcare, and Kaiser Permanente. By the very design of their specific business model – a long-standing combination of care delivery and health insurance – they have been the leaders to-date in building strong top-of-the-funnel offerings. For example, in having worked personally with a number of health systems on the West Coast, many simply dismiss considering Kaiser as a competitor, because they believe that once an individual is a member of Kaiser's plan, there is no hope in bringing them out of the locked system into their own acuity funnel. With nearly 12 million members in eight states, Kaiser's integrated model essentially slams the lid on the top of the funnel.

But that doesn't mean Kaiser ignores top-of-the-funnel strength. The organization has a robust system of urgent care, emergency room, virtual care, and primary care offerings, and in 2020, they launched a "virtual-first" health plan in Washington, which incents members to leverage phone, online chat, video, or email for non-urgent issues. The organization claims to be one of the first health systems to deliver a majority of care via telemedicine, with 65% of all appointments now conducted virtually.[121] Kaiser has also been a national leader in addressing issues in that first level of the acuity funnel, health, and wellness. It's Thrive campaign, now nearly 17 years old, has continued to advocate for the individual health and wellness of consumers. More recently, the organization has been investing heavily in addressing social determinants of health. In 2018, among other activities, Kaiser dedicated $200 million to add or preserve affordable housing in communities it serves. In May 2019, it announced a plan to create social health networks in 39 communities it serves, partnering with an organization called Unite Us to focus on improving social issues such as housing, food, safety, utilities, and more[122]. More recently, Kaiser launched an influencer marketing campaign using popular eSports team members and the popular video game livestreaming service Twitch to engage gaming audiences around mental health care.

Geisinger, based in northeast Pennsylvania, has similarly focused on top-of-the funnel services and community health. As we heard from the organization's CEO, Dr. Ryu, in Chapter Four, a primary focus of the organization's future sits at the top-of-the-funnel, improving access to services through expanding outpatient care, virtual care, in-home care, and more. He also believes health systems are in the best position to "own the life – the entire continuum of care."

> If care isn't well coordinated, it will cause issues. We have to integrate care, but the more players in the mix, the harder this is. Take virtual care companies as one example. Access is great, but they could run the risk of fragmenting care more. Hospitals and health systems already own most of that continuum, so we're set up better in many ways. Well-capitalized corporations like Amazon and Walmart might play a big role, but the rest of the actors are too small or only touch part of it.

To own that "whole life," Dr. Ryu believes health systems themselves must be the aggregator of all healthcare services and take on broad population health. He points to Geisinger's innovative Fresh Food

Farmacy, introduced in 2016, as an example of impacting community health. This service prescribes food as medicine, helping those with specific medical issues or just needing better nutrition, and according to the organization has provided more than 700,000 meals to nearly 5,000 families since its advent.[123] Other recent top-of-the funnel innovations at Geisinger include 65 Forward, a holistic primary care approach for those over age 65, and Neighborly, a social care response platform.

If integrated organizations like Kaiser and Geisinger are leading the way for legacy health systems in the Funnel Wars, perhaps it's more insightful to review those organizations who may stand to lose the most from a future bifurcation of the health system model – academic medical systems. These organizations are traditionally considered the crown jewels of the U.S. health system, with their focus on research and the advancement of medicine, as well as their role in the education of future generations of clinicians. Think Cleveland Clinic, Mayo Clinic, UCLA Health, Vanderbilt Health, Johns Hopkins Medicine, Mass General Brigham and many more. These organizations are often considered the source of the best clinical care in any given market, where patients want to go when the clinical shit really hits the fan. It's these organizations that thrive both clinically and financially at the bottom of the funnel in delivering tertiary and quaternary care.

Yet it's this very strength – focusing on complex, high-acuity care – that sets these organizations behind in Funnel Wars. That's because for years they have thrived on high-cost inpatient care, with most of their business focused on their academic medical center facility, and often a pediatric hospital, and/or cancer center. These organizations have been slower to adopt top-of-the-funnel offerings like urgent care, retail care, or primary care, often because their faculty model makes it difficult to expand their physician base with non-faculty doctors. Further, while these institutions are known for their research and high-acuity clinical care, they are also perceived as having among the worst patient experiences in the healthcare system. Many AMCs are centered in a vast complex of buildings, often located in a dense metropolitan area. They are notoriously hard to navigate, from finding parking to locating care sites to navigating large, confusing buildings. Access is an issue far beyond the physical location – because these organizations often employ the top specialists in their fields, it can take months for a patient to schedule an appointment. AMCs also typically rank far below other hospitals and health systems in patient satisfaction scoring – the inpatient setting is often beset by visits from multiple doctors, residents, and students, and bedside manner usually takes a back seat to clinical expertise. Often, these facilities are decades old, leaving patients with a poor overall experience. While smaller community and rural hospitals may face the first threat from losses in the Funnel Wars, these AMCs may stand to lose the most. And over the past five to ten years, they are fighting like mad to stay relevant at the top of the funnel despite delivering the best high-acuity care in the world.

In some cases, they are growing organically or through acquisition, adding urgent care, primary care, retail care, and virtual care offerings. In other cases, they are using partnerships and affiliations to extend their top-of-the-funnel presence. Many health systems partner with Walgreens to provide retail clinic offerings, for example. Our Lady of the Lake Regional Medical Center, an AMC based in Baton Rouge, Louisiana, and a part of the Franciscan Missionaries of Our Lady Health System, started a joint venture with Premier Health in 1999 to offer urgent care services. The JV grew to 17 locations in Baton Rouge and in 2021 a majority stake in the JV was sold to Trinity Health, based in Michigan and one of the largest health systems in the country.

In 2012, Vanderbilt Health started the Vanderbilt Health Affiliated Network (VHAN), a collaborative alliance of physicians, health systems, and employers combined in a multi-state clinically integrated network. While there are many stated goals for VHAN, one surely is to expand the AMC's footprint both geographically and "up funnel," generating down-funnel referrals that initiate in partner access points. Since its launch, VHAN has grown to span five states and includes 60 hospitals, more than 235 physician practices, 6,100 participating physicians and clinicians (including 1,400 primary care providers), more than 120 quick care clinics, and 13 health systems.[124]

In 2017, Penn State Health, the dominant AMC in central Pennsylvania, entered into a $1 billion shared investment with Highmark Health, the largest insurer in Pennsylvania, to expand access to care throughout the region. According to the organizations, goals for the partnership include advancing population health and development of a "value-based, community care network, including new facilities, to ensure patients and members in central and southcentral Pennsylvania are in close proximity to primary care, specialty care, and appropriate acute care hospital settings." In the most recent example of top-of-the-funnel expansion, the partners announced the opening of a new Penn State Health Medical Group – East Pennsboro practice, a primary care offering in East Pennsboro Township.

Many AMCs are expanding their continuum of care through acquisitions of community hospitals and systems, such as the acquisition of ValleyCare Health System by Stanford Health Care in 2017, VCU Health's announced acquisition of Riverside Health System in 2020, or the 2019 acquisition of two South Florida health systems by Cleveland Clinic.

Finally, one of the most widespread trends over the past decade that unifies the efforts by larger integrated systems, AMCs, and other legacy organizations is the move from delivering "sick care" to "health" in terms of brand positioning and overall value proposition. We covered this in-depth *in Joe Public III*, released in 2018, as one of the six key strategies pursued by leading health systems in the U.S. Of course, there's the roster of systems that have changed their names to reflect this change over the past decade – Northwell Health, Brigham Health, Vanderbilt Health, UNC Health, Allina Health, M Health Fairview, Wake Forest Baptist Health, Duke Health, Novant Health, Beth Israel Lahey Health, etc. etc. etc. In nearly every one of these cases, the name change was not just an external brand identity change, but a reflection of a change of strategic direction for these health systems, moving from organizations focused solely on delivering care to expanding their value proposition to helping keep people healthy. Many changed their mission and vision statements, and strategic plans to reflect this change. When announcing their name change from Allina Hospitals & Clinics to Allina Health in 2012, the organization stated the change reflected a "new mission that shifts the emphasis away from places we go when we're sick and onto disease prevention and personal vitality." Then CEO Ken Paulus was quoted, "We're never going to build another hospital."[125]

Part of this was a natural response to the ACA, and the strategies of population health and accountable care that fell out of it. Part of it was a recognition that one way to build relationships with consumers was to connect with them in a meaningful way *before they needed clinical care*, at the top of the funnel. This quote from UC Health Chief Marketing Officer Manny Rodriguez from *Joe Public III* captures the potential vision of this move to a "health brand:"

> *The Nikes and the Under Armors of the world have really done a great job of claiming the "health/fitness" brand segment. Nike has a brilliant campaign with an overweight young man who loses weight through running, and they give the credit to his shoes. They fail to mention the cardiologist and the primary care doctor and the trainer who helped him really drive this change. How do we take that space back from them?*[126]

A 2019 article in *Becker's Hospital Review* by Dan Michelson, CEO of Strata Decision Technology, captured the momentum of this shift with the headlining statement, "It's the platform, stupid." Using the J.P. Morgan Healthcare Conference as a proof point, Michelson observed what *Joe Public III* had captured the year before – there was tremendous opportunity for health systems to be more than just the place to receive clinical care.

> *So the No. 1 takeaway from the 2019 J.P. (Morgan) Healthcare Conference is this — for healthcare providers, there is a major shift taking place. They are moving from a traditional strategy of buying and building hospitals and simply providing care into a new and more dynamic strategy that focuses on leveraging the platform they have in place to create more value and growth via new and often more profitable streams of revenue. Simply stated, the healthcare delivery systems of today will increasingly leverage the platform and resources that they have in place to become a hub for both health and healthcare in the future. There is a level of urgency to move quickly.*

Many feel that if they don't expand the role that they play in both health and healthcare in their community, someone else will step in.[127]

While showing the promise of building a health platform, Michelson also captured the foreboding threat many in the field feel. So the question is, can these organizations, long the backbone of healthcare delivery in the U.S., stem the tide of new and aggressive entrants into the health system sector? Can they "own the life," the whole patient relationship, or will they cede top-of-the-funnel ground to other healthcare companies, shrinking into down-funnel vendors of high-acuity care? As we've heard, "winners" may be determined by the markets they're in, their current state, or other key factors. But based on the input of those we talked with, and the history of the legacy hospital and health system sector, it's very likely we will see "losers" emerge in the next decade.

The tidings of war grow ill

Most everyone we talked to for this project who opined on the threat to legacy health systems from new and outside-the-industry competitors claimed that threat was already here, the Funnel Wars already joined. By the look of it, it might seem these new provider entities are struggling to gain a foothold. We mentioned the dissolution of Haven earlier. A June 2021 article in *The Wall Street Journal*, titled "Apple Struggles in Push to Make Healthcare Its Greatest Legacy," noted that the long-planned development of "Apple Clinics," staffed by Apple primary-care doctors, has, "largely stalled as Apple has shifted the focus of its health unit to something it knows well: Selling devices..."[128] The company did launch test clinics for use by its own employees, which are still in operation, but has not yet found a way to take the concept broader.

There have also been reports that Walmart is slowing its planned launch of 4,000 primary care clinics by 2029.[129] And the truth of the matter is, for all the hype over the past decade about these big brands and new ventures overhauling healthcare, it hasn't happened in an industry-redefining way, at least in terms of how the vast majority of patients receive care, or in how the legacy hospital and health systems operate. As we noted in our 2020 report on consumer trends, "The End of The Runway," there has been merely incremental incursion by new entrants, in large part because the legacy providers have been "insulated from deeper change thanks to long-standing industry dynamics like opaque pricing, locked-in referral channels, government regulation, fee-for-service polices, and baked-in consumer trust and brand loyalty."

Yet the point of that paper was not to argue that legacy providers have the advantage in The Funnel Wars. In fact, in studying potential long-term consumer behavior changes that would result from the Covid-19 pandemic, our finding was that each of the five changes we identified played right into the hands of new entrants, potentially ending the built-in and seemingly insurmountable lead enjoyed by legacy health systems (thus the paper title, "The End of the Runway."). To help make our point, we referred to author Nassim Nicholas Taleb's concept of unpredicted events that could have devasting consequences – "Black Swans." Whether or not Covid-19 would be considered a Black Swan (Taleb would argue no, because it was a predictable event), this once-in-a-century catastrophe may serve to open the flood gates to change in healthcare, even more so because of those built-in advantages traditional providers of care have always had.

> Taleb argued that another attribute of Black Swan events was that a system that is propped up and insulated from risk ultimately becomes more vulnerable to catastrophic loss...Traditional providers have been trying to adapt to consumerism for nearly two decades. In many ways, hospitals and health systems have been insulated from a significant risk of consumerism – the threat of new entrants. But because of the consumer behavior changes resulting from Covid-19, we've hit the end of the runway.[130]

Covid-19 will likely accelerate the advancement of new entrants in the Funnel Wars, but there are two other foundational challenges facing legacy providers in this fight as well.

One – The innovator's dilemma

As noted in the introduction, Clayton Christensen's shadow falls over much of this book. As one interviewee said, you could re-read *The Innovator's Prescription*, released in 2009, and see many of the themes the industry is discussing today (as well as shades of some of the predictions in this book). But we can look to Christensen's seminal book on "disruptive innovation," *The Innovator's Dilemma*, released in 1997 for more insight on the struggles of legacy health systems to adapt and transform. One of the guiding principles of this business classic is that industries are eventually cut down by new entrants because the entrenched leaders can't help but reinvest in what has made them profitable in the past, making it nearly impossible for them to disrupt themselves. Eventually they fall prey to better, less expensive offerings, and the entire industry is transformed. Later, in *The Innovator's Prescription*, Christensen addresses this dynamic in relation to the healthcare system, and in particular, hospitals, who he famously called "the only factory that has to produce 100 products."

Here's how Christensen explains it, under the header, "What Will Become of Our Hospitals?",[131] along with my asides tying his statement back to what we've already covered about The Funnel Wars:

> *In nearly every instance of disruption we have studied, the survival instincts of the disruptees–the prior industry leaders who are being disrupted–set in motion defensive actions intended to slow the pace of disruption.* (**See list of industry barriers either erected or taken advantage of by legacy providers above – opaque pricing, locked-in referrals, etc.**)
>
> *In the end, however, the advantages that disruptive competitors bring to customers in terms of quality, cost, convenience, and accessibility become so apparent that the regulations are removed, and the disruption proceeds apace.* (**As we've noted, nowhere do the forces of consumerism such as cost, convenience, or accessibility have more power than at the Top of the Funnel.**)

This results in significant excess capacity among the companies whose business models are being disrupted, because there just isn't enough volume at the high end of their markets to support everyone. They respond by going bankrupt, merging, taking out cost and capacity, merging again to take out more cost and capacity, and so on." **(See rapid acceleration of industry consolidation among legacy hospitals and health systems over the past decade, along with the prediction that some will collapse into downstream vendors of high-acuity care, the ultimate outcome stemming from The Funnel Wars prediction).**

The input of many of our interviewed experts reflects this sentiment. For example, Gove has witnessed the difference between driving change at a legacy system versus a new entrant first-hand. As noted at the beginning of this chapter, he oversaw the implementation of some of the more advanced consumer-focused innovations, such as online physician star ratings and AI chat bots, when he was at a large legacy health system. Yet when he moved to his current organization, Summit Health, the ability to move faster and more forcefully with change was obvious. And one of the reasons aligns exactly with Christensen's point about the legacy entity's inability to focus meaningfully on anything that doesn't reflect their traditional, ongoing financial success, which for health systems are their hospitals. Gove, along with others we interviewed, noted the insatiable need to feed hospitals, given their fixed costs and the financial upside of their inpatient, higher-acuity encounters. Health systems live or die financially by higher-margin, inpatient care found in hospitals, which makes it extraordinarily difficult to justify investment in other areas of the operation.

I really believe that once you're free from the weight of hospitals, you can do so many more things. In a typical system, hospitals are the centers of the universe, and they take all the oxygen out of the room. Without them, we can truly build something different.

We'll talk later about how a lack of investment in, and offerings related to behavioral health lends to increased health disparities in Chapter Eight, but this dynamic helps explain why mental health care lags so far behind physical health care – it's typically not a lucrative, in-patient, hospital-oriented offering.

Kevan Mabbutt from Intermountain Healthcare sees the same negative impact of hospitals on a health system's ability to innovate:

> *The gravitational pull of traditional hospitals is just immense in a health system. They demand so much because of the fixed cost. It's like a ball and chain. We have to have them, and they are still the primary driver of revenue, but they can be a drag on innovation and change. They are both the core of our existence and the bane of our existence. If we started over, would we even create hospitals as we know them today?*

And David Goldhill, CEO of Sesame:

> *We have this weird idea that healthcare responds to some fixed demand, even though we all realize that's not the case. We built our system to deal with episodic care, the unanticipated condition, and none of it fundamentally works with chronic issues today, or will work with personalized medicine. We have the wrong system for what we're trying to do. It's shocking that we're in the most scientifically progressive field with the greatest potential impact on human well-being, but we're still tweaking a frozen-in-place industrial infrastructure from the mid-20th century. What other industry has changed so little in the past 50 years? Why do we even have general hospitals anymore, much less make them the centerpiece of a 21st century system?*

Legacy health systems aren't exactly known for their speed of innovation. Naturally, the industry is risk adverse, with lives on the line.

Advances in medicine can take years to become accepted, and following best practices is a critical strategy to ensure the application of the most advanced clinical approaches with a minimum of risk. Yet innovation by definition assumes failure – if at first you don't succeed, try, try again. That stands counter to the conservative nature of delivering care. Consider how long it took legacy hospitals and health systems to finally adopt some form of the mini-clinic. Based in Minnesota, I saw this innovative new care delivery model start from the ground up with the founding of QuickMedx in 2000, turning to MinuteClinic in 2003. Working with local hospitals at the time, I continually questioned why they didn't develop their own version of mini-clinics. The answers were universally the same – our physicians don't believe that's "real" clinical care. You can't treat people with a nurse practitioner in a mall kiosk, that's not real medicine. In 2007, in a story reporting the opening of the first mini-clinic by Mayo Clinic, an executive at another Minnesota health system was quoted as saying that while his system hadn't opened any mini-clinics, they had "recently finished a three-year study that concluded 'we must be in this marketplace.'"[132] So, it takes *three years* to study the viability of putting an NP in a kiosk in the local mall? Woof. Of course we saw rapid innovation in 2020 caused by the Covid-19 pandemic, as health systems across the U.S. quickly ramped up virtual care to levels never seen previously. The question is, without such a stark motivator, can they keep that pace of innovation moving forward?

One final example of the struggle for legacy health systems to innovate. On the heels of the ACA, many believed one path to success would be the implementation of provider sponsored health plans. Many of the systems cited as ahead of this pack in this chapter – Geisinger, Intermountain, Kaiser – were integrated systems featuring both the clinical delivery side and payor side of the equation. These organizations were often held up as examples of the model of the future during the debates around the ACA legislation, sometimes by President Obama himself. The key to bending the cost curve in the U.S. were organizations that were incented not just to deliver great care at any cost, but to deliver great care while managing costs. These types of organizations already strove for value-based care, recognizing the ever-growing costs of the fee-for-service model.

So as a result, a number of health systems set out to build their own integrated models, building provider-sponsored health plans (PSHB). But this adjacency strategy failed to truly take hold. For most organizations, moving into the insurance industry was a completely new endeavor, and they had little to no experience or expertise in what it takes to manage a population of insured. Many grew only to the point of including their own employees, never attracting any employer groups or external individual members. According to a study by the Robert Wood Johnson Foundation released in 2017, of the 37 provider-sponsored health plans formed since 2010 at that time, only four were profitable five years later.[133] Many PSHBs have since been shuttered or sold off.

To hear Dr. Ryu describe it, moving beyond the bounds of where legacy health systems had traditionally played could be a scary proposition for many healthcare leaders. He points to Covid-19 as just one example. At Geisinger, they saw the value of implementing a contact tracing program, because it helps prevent the spread of Covid-19, which obviously would have a positive effect downstream in the hospitals and ICUs. For them, it was an obvious benefit.

When I talked to others across the industry about this, many asked 'Isn't that the role of the public health department? Why spend our resources on that?' My answer always was, if we don't, who will? Personally, I'd want to see more expansion into broader health, but that's way outside the comfort zone for many hospitals, way upstream from where they're used to playing. It really calls into question the role of a traditional health system. The prevailing narrative is that 'upstream health' isn't consistent with a hospital's focus. Without hospitals and health systems, whose role should it be? The debate rages on among my colleagues, and Covid-19 has really exposed this division. What are we really about? If you're truly a community partner, shouldn't you also be about health? The answer I hear often has been a little disappointing to be sure.

Two – The moot argument for integration

The Funnel Wars are all about that prime real estate at the top of the funnel – health and wellness, urgent care, retail care, virtual care, emergency care, and primary care. That is also the focal point of a related divide in healthcare – whether or not integration in and of itself is a key component of a better healthcare system. Because when integration is thrown into question, it's typically because of the incursion of all of these new players at the top of the funnel. As we mentioned before, the idea of integration – the entire care continuum being offered and managed through one organization – was part of what was held out as the ideal during discussion around the ACA. That argument has continued over the past decade, as many industry experts, researchers, and academics continue to claim that the best way to improve the health of individuals and society overall is to ensure an individual's care is managed by one entity. This is the core concept behind the medical home, another strategy that came from the ACA, but which has generally subsided in actual practice. The argument is simple and intuitive: having one source of oversight for an individual's health and clinical issues ensures a consistent, comprehensive approach that takes into consideration all aspects of an individual's personal situation, medical history, potential social determinants of health, and more. Every time a different provider is introduced, there is a potential for missed or mistaken information, misdiagnoses, gaps in key intake or care, etc. For Dr. Ryu, integration is a fundamental truth behind improving healthcare in the U.S.:

> At some point the lanes merge between these trends and the current situation through technology, but if it's not all coordinated among all the players, it will cause issues. We have to integrate care, but the more players in the space, the harder this is. Virtual care players are just one example. In one way, expanded virtual care is a positive, helping consumers gain better access in more convenient ways, and it can help with affordability. But more accessibility comes with more options for virtual care, and we run the risk of fragmenting care more.

Every time we see these disruptors, it actually leads to
more fragmentation, more utilization, and therefore
more cost.

Not surprisingly, those on the other side of the fence see things differently. Kyle Rolfing has heard these arguments throughout his career, but he doesn't believe integration is the answer. From his perspective, the integration argument is based on the idea that all parts of the continuum care are working together seamlessly, from urgent care to primary care to surgical care to chronic care. And while that idea may prove worthwhile in an ideal situation, the vast majority of health systems currently are not delivering on that ideal.

I would challenge those that say multiple care options
are fracturing care or making care less integrated. How
is our current system doing this well? It's fractured within
existing health systems as it is.

His point, along with many others, is that the benefits that come from offering more care choices to consumers, with those choices typically bringing more convenience, a better experience, lower prices, and an overall consumer-centric approach, outweigh any idealistic vision of what integration might, someday, offer.

Taking this argument further, Danny Fell, a senior strategist at Optum and former marketing and branding agency leader in the health system space, believes that integration is dependent on building and maintaining those consumer relationships over the course of a lifetime. That's not something he believes legacy systems have historically been strong in, and are really at the ground floor of today.

The hospital industry has really struggled to manage
their customer relationships, and are not quite halfway to
really understanding and building this core competency.
Historically, the idea of a "customer" was a term rejected
by many healthcare leaders and clinicians. These
organizations have become much better at delivering

great patient care, as well acquiring new patients. But
that's different than maintaining relationships – you can
come in this month for a $100,000 cardiology procedure,
and next month, we'll forget who you are. After my wife
delivered our son, we received two newsletters and a couple
of phone calls, and that's it. Hospitals just haven't put as
much investment into maintaining relationships, which
would affect everything from medication compliance to
care management to outcomes. They're getting better,
but how are you building and retaining that relationship,
and also adding value to that? True customer relationship
management?

Goldhill also sees holes in the integration argument. He acknowledges that during Covid-19, hospitals and health systems were essential to front-line response, meaning theoretically integrated health systems might be better at dealing with something unpredictable at a broad level like a pandemic. On the flip side, vaccination in the U.S. didn't really take off until it was expanded beyond hospitals and health systems to retail health outlets like Walgreens and CVS as the primary distribution source, and even beyond to grocers and other retailers.

Hospitals and health systems have argued that the
integrated approach to the continuum of care is better for
quality and cost. But did that happen in the pandemic?
Or was it primarily success attributed to their hospitals,
where 50% of their revenue comes from. So clearly
hospitals at least were needed for public health issues.
But is fully integrated care really better, especially if it
comes more and more from consolidation?

In addition to their own flaws when it comes to integration, health systems are facing a new threat to that very model: payors. Wendell Potter points out how large health insurers have grown, and how much deeper into care delivery they've gone. For example, Cigna used to be 141st on the *Fortune* 500 list, and today it's 13th. Aetna, now part of CVS

Health, is fourth. Anthem is 25th. And of course UnitedHealth Group is now fifth itself.

> These big players are getting even bigger, and trying to control more of our lives, more and more through care delivery. These "insurers" now own PBMs, surgical centers, primary care, physician practices, and on and on. As we've discussed, United is now the largest employer of physicians in the country. Their long-term strategy is all about diversification, and away from traditional insurance, which is no longer where the majority of their revenue comes from. They now make more revenue from government-backed MA and Medicare plans than they do from commercial plans. They realize that this is where the growth trajectory is moving forward – it's a huge change.

Potter goes as far as believing some of these large payors will eventually exit the insurance business altogether, spinning off their plans to focus on the areas of growth and profitability, such as care delivery. He notes the cyclical nature of some of this, with Humana starting out initially as a nursing home company, and then at one point standing as the largest manager of hospitals in the U.S. Now with their purchase of Kindred's home health offerings, Kindred at Home, and other acquisitions, they are "coming home" to their roots (pun intended). This would in fact be a double blow to legacy healthcare providers. Not only would they face a massive competitive threat in payors focused primarily on their business of delivering care, they would be losing their most important source of revenue – payments from commercial insurance. Today legacy providers lose money on the government-funded plans of Medicare and Medicaid, and need commercial plan payments to stay viable. As health plans continue to move out of that space, or as Potter postulates, they move out altogether, legacy health systems will be up a financial creek without a paddle.

So how would the system in the U.S. be better off – with a system that delivered integrated care management, but with far few choices, and founded in the existing structure that is the legacy health system? Or with a system that offered nearly unlimited choices for health and care access at the top of the funnel, with better experiences, more convenience, and lower prices for those services? The answer is… it's a moot question. This integration battle of the Funnel Wars is likely over, and the disruptors and new entrants have won. There just simply isn't any way the toothpaste is going back in the tube. There are far too many established players, huge brands, and VC war chests for this dynamic to play out any differently. But does that mean the Funnel Wars themselves are over? Not necessarily, and certainly not in certain locales and markets, where established integrated legacy systems can still win out. For the rest of hospitals and health systems, the tidings are ill.

Closing arguments

So where will this all end up? Will we actually see 4-5 mega health systems ruling the world, as our tongue-in-cheek press release envisioned at the outset? Actually, probably not, at least according to those we spoke to, most of whom did not believe we'd ever get that far. There are essentially too many regional-sized legacy health systems that could likely survive or even thrive on their own, no matter what role they ultimately play. Additionally, it's unlikely antitrust advocates and the FTC would ever allow such extreme consolidation.

Yet it seems far more likely that we very well could see a splintering of the legacy health system sector, with a minority growing to provide more integrated care regionally or nationally, many more reverting to smaller, downstream deliverers of mid-funnel, higher acuity care, and some floating somewhere in the middle, having made peace with the enemy and partnering with retail health brands. For the final word on the potential outcome of The Funnel Wars, let's hear from a representative from both camps, who actually end up singing very close to the same tune.

First, Russ Meyer, Senior Director of Brand Strategy at CVS Health, currently the largest pure healthcare company by revenue in the country. He's spent his entire career building brands at top agencies such as Landor and Siegel + Gale, and before he joined CVS Health, was part of the agency team that helped his current company pivot to a pure-play health company, in part by dropping cigarettes from store shelves in 2014. He has helped brands make meaningful shifts, and so he understands firsthand how difficult that can really be. For him, the crux of the question on who will win The Funnel Wars is this: which will bear out, knowledge or culture?

*These legacy health systems absolutely own the medical knowledge to deliver a full continuum of care. But what most, maybe all, don't have is the culture do it. These entities were not started with the consumer at the center of everything – hospitals and health systems instead were designed with themselves, the provider, at the center. On the flip side, those of us coming in from the outside, like CVS Health and all the rest, we don't have near the knowledge these systems have, but we were built and run with a mindset that puts the consumer at the center of all that we do. And in my experience, it's far easier to gain knowledge than it is to change culture. We can buy medical knowledge now, and data capabilities makes that transaction faster than ever before. But culture is really, really hard to build new or change. You can make things look consumer-centric, but actually **being** consumer-centric is a completely different animal. That's culture. So in the end, in the race to truly own the ultimate consumer relationship, those who have to gain knowledge will get there faster than those who have to change culture. If the culture is about aligning to the consumer mindset, it will win out. And here's the deal: today, every single one of the top five Fortune 500 companies – Walmart, Amazon, Apple, CVS Health, and UnitedHealth Group are making substantial bets in this area. They are amazing brands, well-funded, and full of smart people. If just the top three non-healthcare-only brands devoted 10% of their business to healthcare, that would be an investment*

153

collectively of more than $121 billion annually. Those are just astounding numbers to combat.

And here's how Scott Weber, Chief Marketing & Design Officer at M Health Fairview, sums up the battle ahead:

> *On disruption, if we don't come to a clear point of view about how we compete in the world, we will become the department stores of the next decade. Twenty years ago, we might have laughed at the idea of going to Home Depot for appliances, or to Costco for tires. But those are the changes, along with the internet and Amazon, that pushed Sears, a first-class brand for decades, right out of business. They were left trying to sell things no one else wanted to carry. Well look at healthcare – what does no one want to deal with? Inpatient care – it's complex, variable, risky. Unless we figure it out, that's what we'll be left with while everyone else cherry picks the rest.*

Chapter 7

PREDICTION
The Rise of Health Sects

Welcome to the Liberty Land Clinics – could you just fill out this small form with your information? No, we don't need your medical history – most of that is based on false or outdated clinical practices. I mean like vaccines, right? You've never gotten any of those diseases, and you never had those vaccines, yeah? So what good are they? Our doctors know better than to worry about fake science like vaccines, or other so-called "healthy" practices. We've developed a proven healthcare regimen that lets you do pretty much whatever you want – after all, it's America, and your personal choice supersedes any kind of rules a doctor could give. We're just here to help, so you can do you. All of our medical practices are based on our own research, developed at premier institutions, and we have more than 10,000 physicians across the country who work in our 30 hospitals and 100 clinics. And best of all, you won't have to worry about any kind of woke propaganda coming from our doctors. There's no indoctrination here, because we realize woke terms like "health inequity" and "health disparities" are simply politically correct lies spread to make you feel guilty. And what's healthy about that? Yes, we can take credit cards, but we recommend Bitcoin or Ethereum, that way your spending is untraceable by the federal government. So please take a seat, and the doctor will be right with you.

Dr. Stella Immanuel stood on the steps of the Supreme Court, surrounded by other members of the self-described America's Frontline Doctors group. This "White Coat Summit," held in late July 2020, was organized by a right-leaning political group, The Tea Party Patriots, and attendees included U.S. Rep. Ralph Norman, a Republican from South Carolina, who introduced the Houston-based Dr. Immanuel. Other physician attendees at the event, all clad in white coats, included an emergency and general practice physician from California, a private-practice pediatrician, two ophthalmologists (one who was no longer licensed), a physician and clinical researcher from UCLA, and the owner of an urgent-care clinic.[134]

A licensed pediatrician in Texas, Dr. Immanuel was there to claim that masks and lockdowns were not necessary to combat Covid-19, and that instead, she has used hydroxychloroquine to effectively treat the virus in hundreds of patients. This despite prior warnings from health officials that not only was their zero evidence that hydroxychloroquine could treat Covid-19, taking the malaria drug presented the threat of harmful side effects, such as heart rhythm irregularities. The FDA, which had previously issued an emergency authorization for the use of hydroxychloroquine to treat Covid-19, had revoked the authorization the prior month. Dr. Immanuel had other ideas:

> *Hello, you don't need a mask. And today I'm here to say it, that America, there is a cure for COVID. All this foolishness does not need to happen. There is a cure for COVID. There is a cure for COVID is called hydroxychloroquine. It's called zinc. It's called Zithromax.*[135]

She also claimed that research showing that hydroxychloroquine was not effective in treating Covid-19 was "fake science" sponsored by "fake pharma" companies.

The video of the event was a viral sensation, topping an earlier video hit spreading misinformation, "The Plandemic." The event was live-streamed by right-wing media outlet Breitbart and viewed more than 16 million times,[136] with more than 13 million views on Facebook alone,[137] also trending on Twitter. Both social media platforms (as well as YouTube) scrubbed the video from their sites citing their guidelines against Covid-19 misinformation, but not before it was touted by President Trump and some of his family members. The president's son, Donald Trump Jr., tweeted the video, calling it a "must watch." Twitter suspended Don. Jr.'s account the following day for posting the misinformation, as well as Kelli Ward, the Arizona Republican Party chairwoman, who had also tweeted the video.

The President himself posted versions of the video on Twitter. At that point, the President was also an advocate for hydroxychloroquine, claiming he took the drug over a 14-day period. Trump later stated he wasn't making the same claims as Dr. Immanuel, simply passing along recommendations from doctors. But he defended her after the video was removed, stating, "For some reason the internet wanted to take them down and took them off," the president was quoted the next day. "I think they are very respected doctors. There was a woman who was spectacular in her statements about it, that she's had tremendous success with it and they took her voice off. I don't know why they took her off. Maybe they had a good reason, maybe they didn't."[138]

Not only did the hydroxychloroquine claim fit the President's personal health views, the entire message of the event, that lockdowns and masks weren't needed, fit a broader narrative from many in his administration that the country should be opening back up despite the spread of Covid-19, given the economic harm that had occurred.

Of course, this example had a somewhat notable ending. Less than a day after the "White Coat Summit" video hit the big time, reports started surfacing about the background of Dr. Immanuel. In addition to touting claims about Covid-19 cures and strategies that were debunked by most health experts, she had also in the past claimed that gynecological issues such as cysts and endometriosis experienced by women were caused by dreams in which they had sex with demons. A citation from one of her books states, ""Many women suffer from astral sex regularly. Astral sex is the ability to project one's spirit man into the victim's body and have intercourse with it. This practice is very common amongst Satanists. They leave their physical bodies in a dormant state while they project their spirits into the body of whoever they want to have sex with."[139] She has specifically called out the Harry Potter series, Pokémon, the shows "Wizards of Waverly Place" and "Hannah Montana," and has said that Magic 8 Ball toys introduce children to witches.[140] She had also stated she believes that alien DNA was in current use in the medical field, and that Covid-19 was actually a plot by the government to prevent people from being religious.[141]

Research by multiple media outlets found that, despite the claims of the self-described "God's battle axe and weapon of war," there was no evidence showing she had successfully treated hundreds of patients, and Dr. Immanuel herself has not provided the evidence.

I had quit Facebook a few years earlier, but my wife showed me her feed, filled with posts from neighbors and friends who had retweeted the video after it was first posted, touting the claims by Dr. Immanuel and others at the event as further evidence that the threat of Covid-19 was exaggerated and that masks and closing the country were unnecessary. Just like President Trump, they immediately backed claims that fit their narrative without first verifying the source of the information. After the background of Dr. Immanuel became public, my wife showed me how many of the posts we had first seen had now been deleted.

If this sounds like a rant you might find on a left-wing MSNBC show or something in *The Atlantic*, that's definitely not the point I'm trying to make. Everything described above happened as described, and I've tried to scrub any hint of editorializing on my part. I raise the crazy Houston demon doctor story as a prime example of how the field of healthcare has become more politicized than ever. It certainly wasn't the only one, of course. The act of wearing a mask had turned into a modern day "Don't Tread On Me" rallying cry. The already small but verdant anti-vaccine movement grew overnight as many refused to take the available Covid-19 vaccine, often for reasons that aligned with their political views. Dr. Scott Atlas, a controversial radiologist from Stanford University Medical Center with approximately zero experience in infectious diseases or pandemics, was named as a special advisor to

President Trump in August 2020 because his views on downplaying the virus and keeping the economy opened matched those of the President. Alternatively, Dr. Anthony Fauci, a member of Trump's own coronavirus task force, director of the National Institute of Allergy and Infectious Diseases, and the man many consider to be the nation's foremost expert on infectious diseases, became public enemy number one for those on the right of the political spectrum because his views were often counter to the President's.

But the events surrounding that memorable press conference on the steps of the Supreme Court serve as a microcosm for something much larger. The story contains within it any number of reasons why 2020 marked a turning point, one that will reverberate for the next decade, and even beyond: the politicization of nearly every facet of life, tribalism, the growth in the power of influencers, the rise of anti-science sentiment, and the loss of trust in experts.

And it wasn't just the Covid-19 pandemic that made 2020 a watershed – the murder of George Floyd in Minneapolis on May 25, 2020, unleashed a wave of social justice protests and pushback not seen since the 1960s. While not tied as directly to the field of medicine as the Covid-19 pandemic, this social awakening put organizations of all kinds on notice – they would no longer receive passes on taking a stand on the issues of DEI, social justice, police brutality, and more, at least from a large segment of the population. This held true for healthcare providers as well, who historically were above the political fray. Even more, the combination of the Covid-19 pandemic and the focus on social justice issues focused attention on the existing health disparities in the U.S., which the pandemic only exacerbated. All of these dynamics combine to give us our fourth prediction:

> Challenges to and skepticism of the mainstream medical field and science itself have exploded in the past two years because of the pandemic and political tribalism in the U.S. Anti-vaxxers, non-maskers, and Covid deniers are just the start of an expansion of this distrust of experts, which taken to its potential end could result in multiple "health sects" – primary "schools" of medical thought that coalesce

around political/world-views. Imagine "Mainstreamers," who follow the establishment healthcare point of view, "Progressives" who follow minimal medical intervention combined with complementary and alternative medical solutions, and "Contrarians" who deny mainstream medical thought and create their own set of "alternative facts" on everything from vaccines to childbirth to end-of-life care, and everything in between. These sects will not only follow the medical thinking that best fits their world-view, they may in fact create their own reality through alternative research, diagnosis and treatment approaches, and models for the delivery of care itself.

In its 2020 report, "What Comes After the Coherence Crash," global communications network Weber Shandwick (parent company of the agency I work for, Revive), referenced the tumult of 2020 by asking the frank but necessary question, "What The F*** Happened?" The answer:

People are empowered to bypass public authorities, increasingly engaged in private networks, banding together around shared interests, socially constructing their own facts, and using a new collective voice to make sense for each other.

In other words, here come the Health Sects.

The red and blue of everything

Following the passage of a mask ordinance in Pasadena, California, the city's chief of police was quoted in the local paper as saying:

This is the most unpopular law placed on the Pasadena records. We are cursed on all sides.

That quote comes from January 22, 1919, the final year of the Spanish Flu outbreak in the U.S. Which is to say, healthcare has always triggered societal and political differences, even in something as stark as a deadly pandemic. Jarrett Lewis, partner at Public Opinion Strategies, is a researcher and pollster focused primarily on healthcare. He says that while the politicization of healthcare has grown significantly over the past decade, the roots go back much further. He recalls the infamous "Harry and Louise" ads that first appeared in the early 1990s (and that one of his firm's partners was heavily involved with), funded by the Health Insurance Association of America, to combat healthcare reform pursued by President Bill Clinton and his wife, Hillary, who led the effort. ("Having choices we don't like is no choice at all. They choose... and we lose," moaned the couple in one of the first ads disparaging "a few select insurance plans selected by government bureaucrats." An ad released in 1994 to combat this effort inferred Louise had died in part from lack of health insurance, showing a spokesperson spinning the yarn while in a cemetery. Nice! Harry and Louise made a return in the early 2000s, this time supporting Democratic interests.) Yet in Lewis' mind, things changed in a notable way with the passing of the Patient Protection and Affordable Care Act, now known as the Affordable Care Act (ACA) or, of course, Obamacare. Since its inception in March 2010, *Newsweek* counted 70 Republican-led attempts to repeal the law, including the dramatic "thumbs-down" vote by John McCain in July 2017. And that doesn't include lawsuits, the last of which was an attempt backed by President Trump's administration to invalidate the law, which was rejected by the U.S. Supreme Court in June 2021.

The way the Republicans (mostly successfully) went after Obamacare for more than a decade, and then Democrats (also successfully) using the threat of repeal to drive electoral success in the 2018 midterms, it's tough. It's now almost impossible to separate healthcare from politics, and we have some big issues to face. So much gets screwed up in the politics of it and it has left us with an inability to really do things that could move the needle on, for example, expanding coverage or controlling costs. Political polarization often becomes a zero-sum game, where for my side to win, the other side must lose. How do we get anywhere on an issue like healthcare, which hits everyone equally in reality, but team red is fighting a fix because it benefits team blue, or vice versa? It's a huge problem, and we're not going to get anything done with that mindset.

The list of health issues that has been politicized is long: vaccines, women's health rights, health insurance, welfare and food stamps, Medicaid, mask wearing, mental health, consumerism, gender identity, health care costs, drug prices, end-of-life rights, hospital and health system consolidation, stem cell research, etc. etc. etc. With a few notable exceptions, most of the issues that are politicized surround, but do not include, the actual practice of medicine. But that could change, especially given the flash point that was 2020, with the elevation of political division from a lightning-rod president running for a second term, Covid-19, and the social justice movement. Lewis believes the level of politicization regarding the pandemic was unprecedented, and that now it seems, *everything* is politicized. "If you look back to March 2020, and everyone seemed to be on somewhat the same page," he said. "And then around April the wheels started to come off." He says that a number of years ago, the firm began including questions of political affiliation and ideology on every single survey, regardless of topic.

When I first rejoined our firm in 2019, one of our firm's founders made a small but important suggestion – "include political party ID in everything you do." Apart from health policy surveys, political party is not something that is standard for healthcare research. But his point, which seems increasingly true (for better or worse), was that divergence in attitudes, opinions, or behaviors can often be attributed back to what political party a person belongs to, regardless of the topic. Sometimes it's correlation and sometimes it's causation, but it's often there.

Healthcare is not the only industry that has faced increased politicization. Consider sports, which like healthcare has touched politics here and there over time. One of the more famous incidents was at the 1968 Summer Olympics in Mexico City, where two Black track medalists from the U.S., Tommie Smith and John Carlos, raised their fists on the podium during the medal ceremony to protest racism and other social issues (many people don't remember they also went shoeless, donning black socks, to reflect black poverty; Smith wore a black scarf to represent black pride; and Carlos unzipped his tracksuit top to call attention to blue-collar workers).[142]

It wasn't until Colin Kaepernick took a knee during the National Anthem at the start of an NFL football game on September 1, 2016, that sports seemed to collide head-on with politics. Kaepernick's gesture was in protest of racial injustice and police brutality, but was quickly spun as an anti-American protest against the flag, the anthem, the military, and veterans. Not uncoincidentally, the country was in the throes of a heated presidential campaign, and then candidate Donald Trump used the protest as a wedge issue, saying, "I think it's a great lack of respect and appreciation for our country and I really said they should try another country, see if they would like it better." [143] The following year, at one of his rallies as President, he spoke out again in harsher words about pro players protesting by kneeling during the anthem, "Wouldn't you love to see one of these NFL owners, when somebody disrespects our flag, to say, 'Get that son of a bitch off the field right now. Out! He's fired. He's fired!'"[144]

Since that time, political protests in sports have only grown, accelerating after the death of George Floyd in 2020, often in support of the Black Lives Matter movement. Athletes from four sports leagues – Major League Baseball, Major League Soccer, the WNBA, and the NBA – boycotted games in August 2020 following the police shooting of Jacob Blake in Kenosha, WI. More recently, Major League Baseball moved the 2021 All Star Game out of Atlanta following new voting restriction laws passed in Georgia, which many believe are designed to suppress the vote of Black people, among others. Conservatives responded by running advertising during the game bashing the league's decision, and calling "woke" those companies who spoke out about the changes to the election laws. It's unlikely the heated debate on how social protests are handled in sports and what they mean will end anytime soon, and the division of opinion is defined nearly universally by political affiliation.

It's not only sports – following the events of recent years, it seems everything has been politicized: the car you drive (Hybrid on the left, Ford F-150 on the right), police brutality (Black Lives Matter on the left, Blue Lives Matter on the right), music (Bruce Springsteen on the left, Ted Nugent on the right), the food you eat (vegan on the left, red meat on the right), and even the light bulbs you use (fluorescent bulbs on the left, incandescent bulbs on the right). Every issue facing the country has sides. Even the weather forecast may be succumbing to politicization. Climate change has for years been the driving force for disagreement among political parties, with many on the right claiming climate change science was wrong, overblown, or even a "Chinese hoax." In December 2020, Fox News Media announced the network would launch a 24-hour weather channel in late 2021, causing many on the left side of the aisle to worry about a counter-narrative on climate science.

But perhaps no area of life in the United States became more politicized during 2020 than health. The Covid-19 pandemic, along with the social justice protests, were game-changers. During an episode of one of his The Prof G Pods, host Scott Galloway talked with Andy Slavitt, the former head of the Department of Health and Human Services under President Obama and a senior advisor to President Biden's pandemic team, who provided his view of what went wrong with the U.S. response to Covid-19 in 2020. He listed what he called the "three deadly sins" of our country's response, all tied to President Trump and his administration's plan, or lack thereof: the first was fighting hard in the beginning of the outbreak to try and downplay or even deny the existence of the crisis. The second deadly sin was actively preventing dissent from within the government to his own beliefs and biases, including from scientists, health experts, and others who saw the error of many of the aspects of the government's response. And finally, the third deadly sin, was Trump intentionally using a deadly pandemic as a wedge issue, politicizing everything from mask-wearing to reopening the country to the value of science.

> *He (Trump) over-politicized something that didn't need to be politicized. A populist and a pandemic are not a good combination. A pandemic requires tough decisions, and instead he played to his own crowd.*

Of course, given Andy Slavitt worked primarily under President Obama, it might not be surprising that he pins the blame 100% on a conservative President, or that there are plenty of people who disagree with that take.

Or consider the latest political battleground related to Covid-19 – vaccine adherence. Like so many other aspects of the pandemic, belief in the value of taking the Covid-19 vaccines, let alone believing in the safety or social responsibility of getting the vaccine, breaks down along political party lines. A survey done by the Kaiser Family Foundation in June 2021 found that Americans who say they will definitely not get the Covid-19 vaccination are "overwhelmingly white and Republican."[145] Similarly, a *Washington Post-ABC News* poll released in early July 2021 showed that the number one correlation with anti-vaccine views was political affiliation.[146] The spread of the even more contagious Delta variant of Covid-19 in the U.S. can also be traced geographically to political leanings. The day I'm writing this chapter, July 12, 2021, cases of Covid-19 have increased 47% nationally compared to the prior week, and 1/3 of those cases come from five states: Florida, Louisiana, Arkansas, Missouri, and Nevada.[147] All five have historically been "red" states, with four of them voting for Donald Trump in the 2020 election (with Nevada the exception, in a close win for Biden). An editorial on CNN.com in mid-July captures the unfortunate and mind-bending implications of something as important and relatively straightforward as vaccine adherence in the face of a deadly virus becoming twisted by politics.

> Consistent efforts to wring political advantage from the pandemic by leaders like ex-President Donald Trump are continuing while he is out of office and are tarnishing the critical late-stage push to beat Covid-19. The idea that anyone would perish because they listened to a politician playing into Covid-19 skepticism for their own career advancement, or a conservative media host chasing ratings, is nauseating. But it's happening — as opportunists cite misinformation or play into preexisting US skepticism of authority. Even the act of publicizing life-saving vaccines can founder on political divides.

Tennessee's vaccine chief, for instance, says she was fired after she merely shared a memo explaining state law allowing health care providers to decide whether minors have the capacity to consent to a vaccine themselves.[148]

That last statement refers to the firing of Tennessee's top vaccine official, Dr. Michelle Fiscus, after conservatives in that state complained about a memo stating a decade's old statute in the state allowed minors aged 14 and over to receive a vaccine without their parent's permission. "It is just astounding to me how absolutely political and self-centered our elected people are here and how very little they care for the people of Tennessee," Fiscus said in an interview. "The people of Tennessee are going to pay a price."

Whether one agrees with her take on her firing or the underlying issue of minors' ability to receive vaccines on their own, there is no doubting politics was the driving force behind this episode.

Laura Schoen, Chief Healthcare Officer for DXTRA Health Integrated Solutions and Global Healthcare President at Weber Shandwick who brings experience from around the globe, bemoans the further politicization of healthcare:

We have so many other important things to worry about, and now we have to include how highly politicized the healthcare environment has become. Health is a top priority for people around the world, and politicians are becoming more heavily involved. Consider just one ramification: we're developing more effective, specialized drugs, but they are more expensive, and not everyone can deliver or pay for them. So who will decide who gets them? And how might politics warp that?

Eight factors reshaping the politicization of health

Our prediction here is not just that healthcare will become more and more politicized, though that is certain to be the case. More so, we see the potential for this politicization to lead to the formation of two or more health *sects* – a word that is defined both as "a dissenting or schismatic religious body, often regarded as extreme or heretical" and "a group adhering to a distinctive doctrine or leader."[149] This moves us past the current situation where those with a common political view share certain common views on health issues, to a future where organizations and populations are oriented and organized *around* a shared view of health that varies from others, similar to how the Catholic religion has leadership, doctrines, places of worship and followers distinct from those of the Lutheran religion. In this world, we might see entire populations act in concert related to health issues, such as vaccine adherence, supported by the emergence of healthcare providers whose mission is to target and serve one of the health sects.

This is not to be confused with the existence of faith-based healthcare providers today. There are health systems based in Catholic, Jewish, Baptist, and Adventist faiths throughout the U.S., among others, and while their overall approach to care and the services they offer to one degree or another reflect those faiths, they are not intentionally targeting *only* those who follow their faith. In fact, in most cases, the degree to which faith plays a role in care delivery is often minimized publicly, both in an effort to appeal to those who might not be of that faith, but also because research has shown the faith orientation of a hospital or health system typically has little impact on how consumers choose where they receive care. Which in some ways shows the power of identity politics and its effect on consumers. While most will not use their own religious affiliation or the religious affiliation of a healthcare provider in deciding where to go for care, many will use their *political affiliation* to dictate everything from which car they drive to what music they listen to, and potentially, which doctor or hospital they choose. In this way, at least, identity politics has a stronger influence than even religious affiliation (though of course the two are often correlated).

To see how these health sects might take shape over the coming decade, it's helpful to consider eight core factors that would drive such a transformation. Many of these will be very familiar in terms of concerns raised in other areas of society, so we've tried to show in each case how the dynamic would play a role in shaping a world where two, three, or more health sects would emerge.

Factor One – Tribalism

The concept of tribalism often goes hand in hand with the rising tide of politicization. It may be best defined as individuals shaping their beliefs and behaviors to conform to a selected group. This adherence, driven by a base human need to belong and be accepted, can be so powerful as to overcome facts, reality, or an individual's pre-existing sense of self and values. Going further, a powerful dynamic of tribalism is the belief that one's own group is right, or good, or valued, and by definition, all others are wrong, or bad, or of no value. In a *New York Times* article titled "Belonging is Stronger Than Facts," about the power of tribalism to lead people astray in the Covid-19 pandemic, author Max Fisher lays out a number of reasons people may buy into false or misleading information. The first is that primal urge to belong, which drives individuals to accept whatever the group accepts, facts or no facts, often with little or no consideration or critical thinking. Fisher notes the power of the tribe can be especially overwhelming in times of crisis, such as a global pandemic.

> *...most important, is when conditions in society make people feel a greater need for what social scientists call ingrouping — a belief that their social identity is a source of strength and superiority, and that other groups can be blamed for their problems. As much as we like to think of ourselves as rational beings who put truth-seeking above all else, we are social animals wired for survival. In times of perceived conflict or social change, we seek security in groups. And that makes us eager to consume information, true or not, that lets us see the world as a conflict putting our righteous ingroup against a nefarious outgroup... Framing everything as a grand conflict against scheming enemies can feel enormously reassuring. And that's why perhaps the greatest culprit of our era of misinformation*

may be, more than any one particular misinformer, the
era-defining rise in social polarization.[150]

The most basic level of tribalism related to politics is the Red Blue divide, Democrats vs. Republicans, Liberals vs. Conservatives. With Covid-19, the dramatic divide in vaccine adherence led to the idea of "Two Americas" – one vaccinated, one not, divided in general along political party lines. But it can certainly be more nuanced than that. In a story for *The Atlantic*, author George Packer identifies how America has morphed into four core political tribes.[151]

- One – "Free America" – those with more libertarian views who believe in the power of the individual and that the less government, the better.
- Two – "Smart America" – typically successful, wealthy, "elite" Americans who thrive in the knowledge-based economy and seek modernity, diversity, and progress.
- Three – "Real America" – traditionalists with conservative views, often blue-collar, religious, nationalist, and populist with anti-intellectual, anti-progressive views.
- Four – "Just America" – progressives who are cynical about capitalism, meritocracy, and the power structure in U.S., who want to tear down what they see as a broken society and rebuild in the vision of a better, more just, and more equal society.

In the article, Packer conveys the following:

They rise from a single society, and even in one as polarized as ours they continually shape, absorb, and morph into one another. But their tendency is also to divide us, pitting tribe against tribe. All four narratives are also driven by a competition for status that generates fierce anxiety and resentment. They all anoint winners and losers.

One can imagine how a health sect might coalesce around, say, Real America, where there are already commonly shared views around vaccine skepticism, the value of science, and an anti-elite/intellectual bias that can easily be applied to modern medicine.

Schoen sees how tribalism is a growing power not just in the U.S., but throughout the world:

> *There has been a shift from global perspectives to tribal perspective. If media and politics have further tribalized our society, when will healthcare go there? This isn't just in the U.S., or about Trump's nativism – we see it all over the world, particularly in Europe where there is such negative perception of the 'other.' It's very negative and potentially harmful – how bad will it be?*

Kristen Hall Wevers is Senior Vice President, Chief Marketing and Communications Officer at UC Health in Cincinnati. From her view, Covid-19 had the effect of shrinking everyone's world, leading to more fracture and segmentation in society. She believes that tribalism could have a huge influence on healthcare, given that one result is the emergence of "alternative facts" and different realities.

> *What is truth, if everyone can define it in their own way? As people become more and more comfortable in their tribes, they will create their own realities. It's very much like religion – what do you want to believe in? The idea of multiple truths will collide with so much of what's happening in society. Consider the move to strengthen diversity and inclusion following the social justice movement of last year. The idea of different truths and realities collides directly with the idea of inclusion, so in many ways we're going the opposite direction with this issue. It is more divide and conquer, not dissimilar to religious wars. Those have been going on for centuries. Aren't we smart enough to learn from them? Covid-19 should not be a political issue, but that's what it became, and that's where we went off the rails. We just take any issue and create our own platform and our own truths.*

In our discussion for this book, Wevers and I wondered aloud what, if anything, could everyone agree to in our current age of tribalization and politicization? After all, if a global pandemic driven by a mindless, voiceless virus couldn't do it, what could? An invasion by another country? What used to be considered foreign enemies we all agreed upon, such as Russia and North Korea, were now considered differently by different political tribes. We knew it couldn't be the potential for global catastrophe driven by climate change. The arrival of aliens from another planet? We ended up without a real answer.

Factor Two – Social media

Social media has been blamed for many of the ills in today's society, and often rightly so. The positive power to connect people and give voice to all is undeniable. The flip side is social media tends to bring out the worst in people, giving license to confront and shame and lie and attack in ways most people would never adopt in a face-to-face situation. And if tribalism is a fire raging across the countryside, dividing neighbors and entrenching political acrimony, then social media is the gasoline. Social media allows for the dissemination of thought and information from anywhere and anybody, and the very nature of its network structure allows for that dissemination to spread far and wide at an extraordinarily rapid rate. Further, social media amplifies the likes and predilections of the participant, further cementing her world view and tribal association by only showing her information and opinions that conform to her perspectives. Social media can create an alternate reality framed by a curated set of facts and input shared by others of like mind. Schoen sees these alternate realities happening on both a global and personal level.

> *Why does misinformation spread? The penetration of social media – worldwide. People get their news from social media. There are of course potential benefits of greater access to information. The major drawback is the ability of groups that aren't well-informed to pass judgment and influence others. With journalism, there are policies,*

*standards, editors. With some websites and social media,
people say whatever they want, and other people believe it. I
see it even among my friends – they will requote politicized
comments they see on social media, as if they are facts.*

A great example of this was the lightning quick spread of the video
of Dr. Immanuel's press conference highlighted at the top of this chapter,
which occurred primarily through Facebook. Social media, and Facebook
in particular, is designed both to cement the beliefs of tribes, while at
the same time expanding their numbers. According to Facebook's own
internal research, 64% of those people who join extremist groups on
their network were prompted by Facebook's recommendation tools.[152]
Many point to this aspect of Facebook as a key driver behind the QAnon
conspiracy (definitely fitting the definition of a tribe) and the attack on the
U.S. Capitol on January 6, 2021. Some feel the power social media wields
to inflame groups in this way is an existential threat to democracy in the
U.S. – a headline in the *Washington Post* in April 2021 read: "Congress
must decide: Will it protect social media profits, or democracy?"[153]

Back to the rise of health sects — it's clear to see how social media
as it's currently construed would be a key component of any new,
separatist school of healthcare. We saw it support alternative medical
beliefs throughout the Covid-19 pandemic, including the current divide
among those taking the vaccine. Healthcare experts blame Facebook and
other social media platforms for allowing the spread of misinformation
about the vaccine, despite their stated attempts to remove false or
misleading information from the network. Millions of people cite lies
and disinformation and hoaxes found on Facebook as their rationale for
avoiding the Covid-19 vaccine – the vaccine causes infertility in women,
doesn't work or isn't necessary, contains a computer chip to allow Bill
Gates to follow your whereabouts, or is part of a government plot to
control the masses. "It's scary," says Kaleese Williams, who is one of
the subjects of a *Bloomberg Businessweek* article titled "Facebook Built
the Perfect Platform for Covid Vaccine Conspiracies." "I believe in the
immune system. I do not believe in vaccine-induced herd immunity."[154]

Just how powerful could social media be in spreading
misinformation and feeding the alternate realities of new health sects?

According to research published in May 2021, just 12 people, named the "Disinformation Dozen," were found to be responsible for 65% of shares of vaccine misinformation on social media.[155] In July 2021 remarks concerning the growing spread of the Delta variant of Covid-19, President Joseph Biden reflected his growing frustration with the influence social media had on those avoiding the vaccines, stating, when asked about his message to platforms like Facebook, "They're killing people. Look, the only pandemic we have is among the unvaccinated. And they're killing people." (After backlash from Facebook and others, he walked that statement back.)

Factor Three – Advancement of technology and personal data

Not to stretch an already cliched analogy to the breaking point, if social media is the fuel to the tribalism fire, then personal data and advanced technologies are the sparks that continually ignite that fuel. Facebook can't feed you the incredibly relevant, thought-conforming content it does without knowing a lot about you. A. Lot. According to one source, back in 2018, Facebook was collecting 52,000 points of data about each user.[156] One researcher claimed that when he accessed the option to download all the data Google had collected on him, the file was 5.5 Gigabytes, enough data to fill three million Microsoft word documents. (A similar download of Facebook's data on this individual was a piddling 600MB file, or enough to fill "only" 400,000 Word docs.)[157]

What does all this personal data collection mean? According to one study, a person's Facebook data can reveal more about a user's psychological profile than friends, family, or even a spouse could identify.[158] It was upon learning the degree to which Facebook collects information on users, combined with scandals like the 2016 Cambridge Analytica fiasco showing how Facebook used and let others use that data, that led me to leave the platform for good in March of 2018. In the movie *The Great Hack*, a must-see for anyone who wants to understand the power being wielded – for good and for bad – from personal data, Professor David Carroll asks one of his classes the following question:

173

Who has seen an advertisement that has convinced you that your microphone is listening to your conversations? All of the students raise their hands. And we've all had that feeling, whether it's from the Alexa in our kitchen or the way ads follow us around the internet. But Parson's point isn't that Google or Facebook or Apple are listening to us, it's that those phenomena we experience actually are due to the vast amounts of personal data that exist for purchase and use. So it's not that Alexa is listening, it's that your personal data is so complete that advertisers and others *know* you need a new umbrella for your patio set.

It's this personal data that will define who belongs to which health sect, and further, who would be a ripe target for persuasion for a given sect. And social media platforms, AI, and recommendation engines are all technologies designed to leverage personal data. As outlined in an article from SEMrush, "Recommendation engines can help marketers and organizations increase the likelihood of arriving at recommendations tailored to a user's past online activity or behavior using in-depth knowledge based on big data analysis."[159] This is what powers the personalized experience at Amazon, Facebook, Netflix and so many other successful companies. Imagine a health system powered by such technology and algorithms. So if you like Snickers, the Oscar-winning moving *The Unforgiven* starring Clint Eastwood, and the New England Patriots, then you might be a perfect target for a promotional mailer from Liberty Clinics. If instead you're partial to kale smoothies, a follower of Gwyneth Paltrow's Goop, and drive a Prius, you may prefer to see a holistic healer at Green Leaf Clinics. Of course, hospitals and health systems, like nearly all other types of companies, use technology and personal data to target potential customers/patients. That activity is just not centered on a political view or tribal allegiance today. But there's no reason it couldn't be.

Factor Four – Distrust of experts

I start each day thinking about the terrible burden you
bear. I don't know what I would actually do, if in your
position, but I do know what I wish I would do. The first

thing would be to face the truth. You and I both know that: 1) Despite the White House spin attempts, this will go down as a colossal failure of the public health system of this country. The biggest challenge of the century and we let the country down. The public health texts of the future will use this as a lesson on how not to handle an infectious disease pandemic.

Thus began a letter written on September 23, 2020, from former CDC director Bill Foege to the then current CDC director Robert Redfield. The exchange is captured in the Michael Lewis book, *The Premonition: A Pandemic Story*, and that private letter was eventually leaked publicly.[160] As Lewis portrays in the book, the damage to the reputation of the CDC had been building for years before this letter came to light. In an October 2020 speech, Dr. Anthony Fauci said, "We've got to admit it, those of us in government, all of us, you and I and all the people that work for me, and all the people that work for you, that there is a building distrust now in the transparency of what we do. It's the elephant in the room."[161]

This list of missteps and fumbles by the CDC and other government entities, some self-inflicted, some wrought by the political influence of the Trump administration, is brutal. It started with the development of a failed Covid-19 test by the CDC that delayed critical testing at the outset of the pandemic in the U.S., and only grew from there. The agency was painfully slow and conservative in issuing guidance, leaving many who depend on that guidance, such as hospital and local public health officials, scrambling. For example, the CDC didn't acknowledge that the virus is airborne and can be spread through airborne particles, something that was taken as scientific fact from the outset of the pandemic, until May...*of 2021.*[162] There was flip flopping on mask guidance, including from Dr. Fauci, who said early on that there was "no reason to be walking around with a mask." While there were valid reasons for suppressing the use of masks early on – to preserve the limited supply for healthcare workers – the back and forth only served to confuse the public and lower their trust in public health messaging coming from the government. Research released in October 2020 by *Ipsos/Axios* showed that only 68% of Americans trust the CDC to provide accurate information, and that further: "Levels of trust in the federal government, the White House, and Donald Trump to provide Americans with accurate coronavirus-related information are at an all-time low. Fewer than one-third of Americans place a great deal or a fair amount of trust in these institutions/actors."[163]

In our 2020 report, "The End of the Runway," one of the five key trends we cited that would change how consumers engage in healthcare coming out of Covid-19 was the loss of trust in government health institutions. This loss of trust in official, government health experts opens the doors for others to step into the void, particularly those with an alternative view that can have tremendous appeal to those in tribes who find that view conforming to their own. In March 2020, an epidemiologist from Stanford named John Ioannidis was outspoken on what he considered the overblown danger from the emerging Covid-19 virus. "We're falling into a trap of sensationalism," Ioannidis said at the time. "We have gone into a complete panic state." As stated in a *Washington Post* article, his frequent appearances on cable news networks such as Fox were "seized on by right-wing firebrands seeking to discredit public-health officials and reopen the economy." The article cited, as one case in point, this example from right-wing provocateur and Fox News host Laura Ingraham in April 2020, when Ioannidis appeared on her show:

> *'I'm so excited about this next interview,' Fox News host Laura Ingraham said on April 21. Her upcoming guest, she said, would explain that the coronavirus's prevalence in the population 'may be 55 times higher than previously thought by the, quote, 'experts,' — here Ingraham raised her hands in a pair of mocking air quotes — 'meaning the true fatality of the virus is somewhere below that of seasonal influenza.'[164]*

Dr. Immanuel, Dr. Ioannidis, Dr. Atlas – all are "alternative" experts providing "alternative facts" or opinions that were seized upon by a huge swath of the population, primarily because their views conformed to those of the tribe. Dr. Carter Mecher, a figure who is credited with helping develop some of the most critical insights on Covid-19 and how to manage it, and one of the protagonists in Lewis' book, is cited expressing extreme disappointment in Ioannidis as someone who should have known better:

> *Ioannidis predicted that no more than ten thousand Americans would die. He condemned social distancing policies as a hysterical overreaction. That was all those who wished to deny the reality needed to be able to say, look, we have experts, too. To say: See, all the experts are fake.*[165]

While most of this section has focused on the loss in trust in government health experts, who's more expert in health than doctors, hospitals, academic medical centers? If people are willing to move away from the head of the CDC or a county health supervisor, then moving away from clinical experts in the hospital and health world is an easy leap.

Factor Five – Anti-science sentiment

A corollary to the loss of trust in government and other health officials is the growing rise of what's been labeled an "anti-science" movement. That is, a rejection of scientifically proven aspects of our universe, and just as importantly, a rejection of the discipline of science itself. Take for example the growth in "flat-earthers," or those who believe the earth is in fact flat, rather than round. In 2018, a national survey found that as many as 1 in 6 Americans aren't completely convinced the earth is round, as has been the accepted scientific belief for thousands of years.[166] Scientists, who by definition are supposed to be objective in their approach to work, have been dumped in with other experts, as noted previously, as well as "elites" – two groups that invite the scorn of many Americans (particularly the group known as "Real America" from Packer's categorization cited earlier). The anti-science perspective is a critical component of views on everything from climate change to federal government nutrition standards.

According to an article in *Scientific American*, anti-science is defined as "the rejection of mainstream scientific views and methods or their replacement with unproven or deliberately misleading theories, often for nefarious and political gains." Going on, the article states that the modern anti-science movement was fully realized by Joseph Stalin in the Soviet Union, who, in the 1930s and 40s, dismissed accredited scientists of the era and instead followed the views of Trofim Lysenko. Those views "promoted catastrophic wheat and other harvest failures" that resulted in millions of Russians dying from starvation and famine. From the article:

> *Soviet scientists who did not share Lysenko's "vernalization" theories lost their positions, or like the plant geneticist, Nikolai Vavilov, starved to death in a gulag.*[167]

The Covid-19 pandemic became a further breeding ground for anti-science sentiment, especially as it helped support the minimization of strategies to manage the pandemic, such as keeping the economy open. (Of course most experts argued this was not an either/or proposition, that the best way to keep the economy open *was* to mitigate the spread of the virus as quickly as possible through efforts such as lockdowns, social distancing, and mask wearing. But political divisiveness doesn't love nuance.) Further, those who would traditionally be seen as trustworthy advocates for following the science, such as government leaders, themselves fought the scientific establishment. For example, in a July 2020 op-ed piece in *USA Today*, Peter Navarro, then President Trump's trade advisor, ripped into Dr. Fauci, claiming "Anthony Fauci has been wrong about everything I have interacted with him on." (The media outlet ended up retracting the piece due to numerous misleading comments.) President Trump himself ignored scientific research when touting hydroxychloroquine as a cure for Covid-19, or in the infamous press conference where he suggested bleach could be injected into patients to fight Covid-19 (one could argue that was not only anti-science, but anti-obvious).

Trump wasn't alone in using anti-science rhetoric to bolster his own views and appeal to his base – leaders in Brazil, Mexico, and the Philippines, among others, used similar strategies. In maybe the best example, Brazil's President Jair Bolsonaro (also known for his vehement denial of climate change in regard to the threat to the Amazon rain forest), has consistently attacked science in his strategy to downplay Covid-19. "Being a scientist in Brazil is so frustrating," says an epidemiologist working in Manus. "Half of our deaths were preventable. It's a total disaster."[168]

The growth of anti-science sentiment is bad news for medical providers. First, these views often align neatly with political views, once again forming the basis for an emerging health sect that disputes accepted medical practices. Second, anti-science sentiment strikes at the heart of medicine itself – the idea of following a doctor's advice because she is the expert becomes anathema to those who dismiss the value of science. How will providers manage patients who fight the very expertise that is offered, on the basis of something as fundamental as the science that underlies medicine? We already see this dynamic play out in the expression, often found throughout Facebook, of those who dismiss medical science when it comes to vaccines: "I'm not going to trust them on whether I should use this vaccine, I do my own research." The problem is made infinitely more difficult when considering the more complex levels of healthcare, where most consumers have little understanding of medical history or best practices. For example, says Wevers, one might think Academic Medical Centers, with their advanced research and clinical approaches, might be immune to political adversity. But an anti-science worldview knocks that elevated status off its pedestal.

There is a general lack of understanding about how healthcare is advanced and delivered to communities. People should hold up AMCs and others as untouchable places of value. We wouldn't have vaccines or transplants without AMCs. But today, you can choose your own story. There are no stories without data, and no data without stories. You must have both, but today, those with certain political views can create either or both on

their own. Truth then becomes ambiguous. If we can't
retain a shared set of values and principles, then truth
becomes whatever one decides it should be.

Factor Six – The power of influencers

If many in the U.S. have lost trust in national health experts and scientists in general, where are they finding it? In many cases, from influencers from outside these fields, and in particular, social media influencers. For example, take Dr. Drew Pinsky, the celebrity therapist known for his stints on realty television, who said early in the pandemic that Covid-19 was "way less serious than influenza," called it a "press-induced panic," said "the flu virus in this country is vastly more consequential," and that the odds of dying from the virus were the same as being "hit by an asteroid."[169] (Pinsky later apologized for his statements, and caught Covid-19 himself and was categorized as a "long hauler" for suffering symptoms for months after his diagnosis). Or Dr. Phil, the popular pop psychologist who said of the pandemic in April 2020, "The fact of the matter is we have people dying, 45,000 people die a year from automobile accidents, 480,000 from cigarettes, 360,000 a year from swimming pools, but we don't shut the country down for that, but we're doing it for this?"[170] (There's no way of verifying these numbers, in particular the drowning figure which seems absurd, but of course none of these causes of death are *contagious* nor preventable by measures such as social distancing or closing down businesses.) What makes these two great examples of the power of influencers is that neither Dr. Drew or Dr. Phil are *medical* doctors, let alone experts in infectious disease or pandemic management. Yet the millions who follow them will take their word as gospel.

The sheer scale of social media influencers is somewhat mindboggling. According to a June 2021 report, soccer legend Cristiano Ronaldo has 517 million online followers, making him the most followed person on both Facebook and Instagram. Justin Bieber has 455 million followers; Kim Kardashian, 319 million; Ellen DeGeneres, 260 million; LeBron James, 157 million. (Donald Trump had more than 140 million followers before he was banned from multiple networks in 2020 for breaking platform policies).[171] Joe Rogan, an influencer with the most popular podcast in 2020 and more than 10 million YouTube subscribers, made headlines in April of 2021 by saying, "If you're like 21 years old, and you say to me, should I get vaccinated? I'll go no."[172] That was counter to the CDC's recommendation that anyone 16 years of age or older should receive the vaccine, not for their own health, but to help stop the spread of the virus. The fact that Rogan later apologized, reversed his opinion, and admitted, "I'm not a doctor, I'm a bleeping moron," somewhat misses the point of the power non-medical experts can have in influencing their followers. When we think of the potential emergence of health sects, the leverage of personalities to shape the views of the group is undeniable. In fact, one of the primary foundations of tribalism is the adherence to one or more individual leaders or influencers. Take for example the QAnon conspiracy, where millions of followers hung on the every word of an anonymous online poster.

There are a number of ways the power of influencers intersects with healthcare and the idea of health sects. For one, influencers will have the ability to override advice of medical professionals with their followers, with obvious repercussions for public and individual health. But there's also the potential for a new class of influencers from within the medical community itself. For if Dr. Phil and Dr. Drew can build followers in the millions and dole out medical advice, why couldn't actual medical doctors? We've seen this already with celebrity doctors such as Dr. Mehmet Oz, Dr. Sanjay Gupta, or even Dr. Ruth Westheimer. But social media is changing the game, democratizing the ability for physicians to grow into online influencers. Bryan Hamilton, Assistant Vice President of Marketing Communications at Cincinnati Children's Hospital Medical Center, notes that both Harvard and Stanford offer fellowships in medical media, helping train physicians on how to use media effectively.

> *We'll go from 'I want a billboard' to 'how can I leverage my fellowship in medical media to build a greater panel of patients, to build my brand?' Our providers, especially the younger ones, are more educated on the business of healthcare, including marketing and media. Individual*

doctors being their own brands could be explosive.
Everybody can be a social media maven. Anyone can
play in this game. I mean, I was invited to Clubhouse
(the social media speaking network) by a physician who
was in Clubhouse.

Factor Seven – Individualism

Individualism – the belief that one's lot in life is dictated not by society, or government, or other people, as much as it is by the individual themselves – has been a cornerstone of American culture since the country's inception. Many point to a unique and powerful strain of individualism in Americans as the primary reason for the country's growth into a world power, driving everything from personal and societal wealth to powerful industry, military success, and scientific advancement. Individualism has always played a role in health in this country as well, as heroic doctors are celebrated, and some of the most powerful stories in our culture are those that highlight how individuals have overcome extreme adversity, whether the loss of limb in a car accident or a highly deadly form of cancer.

Every strength has a flip side, and for the trait of individualism, that often takes the form of selfishness, egotism, and putting one's own well-being in front of all others. This raises particular difficulties in combating infectious diseases, where the collective efforts of a society can make or break its success in combating a virus such as Covid-19. Indeed, many who have resisted pandemic strategies such as lockdowns, social distancing, wearing masks, or taking vaccines have done so under the banner of "Don't Tread On Me," stating rhetorically, and often audibly, "I'm going to do what I want to do, what's best for me." Research conducted at the outset of the coronavirus outbreak in 2020 at the University of Virginia studied the effect of individualism on adherence to Covid-19 measures. They found that "higher levels of individualism reduced compliance with state lockdown orders by 41% and reduced pandemic-related fundraising by 48%.[173] The group pointed out that America ranks as the most individualistic country in the world, which, while generating huge benefits for the country, can also cause difficult challenges. Here's lead researcher Ting Xu:

> *The costs and benefits of individualism vary with economic conditions. In good times, individualism encourages effort and innovation. But in bad times, it can be very costly, because it disincentivizes collective actions that are particularly important when facing challenges.*

Since the outset of Covid-19, those espousing individualistic views in objecting to Covid-19 measures have, not surprisingly, adhered to political divisions, with those on the right-wing of the aisle far more likely to claim their personal liberty outweighs calls from government or health experts to sacrifice in some way to combat the spread of the virus. In many cases, the argument goes beyond a personal choice – YouTube and TikTok are full of videos of those in masks being accosted by someone in a Walmart or at a gas station for being "sheep" for following mask guidelines. In a July 2020 editorial, economist Paul Krugman calls out individualism as a key culprit in the country's inability to manage the pandemic. Using push back on such banal regulations regarding phosphates and light-bulbs as examples, he claims, "Many on the right are enraged at any suggestion that their actions should take other people's welfare into account. What the coronavirus has revealed is the power of America's cult of selfishness. And this cult is killing us."[174]

The point here is not to lambast one political party over another, or to state that individualism is right or wrong. Most would believe, as I do, that individualism has pros and cons, benefits and drawbacks. And that research and observation has shown that applied to a public health crisis, individualism is more of a challenge than an attribute. Instead, the point here is to demonstrate that America's powerful trait of individualism has a huge impact on health and healthcare, and might feed directly into the rise of health sects. At first blush, that may seem oxymoronic. The very power of a sect is in its deeply held group beliefs, in the conformity to a group identity and personality. Isn't that diametrically opposed to the belief in individualism, that an individual's rights and beliefs and actions should be independent of any outside force?

Theoretically, yes. In real human interaction, not as much, particularly if a group's identity is based on opposition to the norm, to the status quo, to the establishment. With health sects, we are likely to see just that, the rise of at least one collective with common views on health and healthcare that are in part, and intentionally, opposed to the healthcare establishment. Consider the opposition to mask-wearing, which was, like so many other things, tied to political persuasion. Research shows that it was those on the conservative side of politics who were anti-mask more than the left. It was *also* that same political persuasion that called out the individualistic trait of "personal liberty" as one of the primary reasons for opposing mask mandates – "it's *my* choice whether I wear a mask." Yet that individualistic song was sung by a chorus of millions, all singing in tune and in unison. And, even more interestingly, singing under the orchestration of a single choral director – President Trump. So even when the fundamental argument is individualism, it can fit neatly into a tribalistic, political grouping, particularly around health.

This factor becomes very important in considering its place in fueling the rise of health sects when combined with others, such as anti-science sentiment and loss of trust in experts. Together, these take on accelerated weight when we consider the eighth and final factor, consumer health empowerment.

Factor Eight – Consumer health empowerment

One of the many definitions for "Dr. Google" found in the satirical website "Urban Dictionary" says, "A 'Doctor' who largely reduced the prestige of licensed medical professionals in the intelligent public's mind between 1998 and 2009."[175] Physicians might quibble with some of that – the use of the word "intelligent" for example, or the idea that the phenomenon that is Dr. Google ended in 2009. What most would likely agree with is the idea that the use of the Internet by patients to self-prescribe diagnoses and treatments *has* in many ways dinged the prestige of actual medical professionals. There are fewer encounters as frustrating to a doctor who has spent years in a field of study, preceded by a decade of schooling, as when they see a patient walk in with print outs and an opinion. Most clinicians *would* agree that an educated patient is a better patient, and we've been hearing for years how patients need to advocate for themselves. Chapter Four, focused on the prediction of the "Copernican Consumer," takes this concept even further.

But we don't have to realize a full-on Copernican Consumer future to see how emboldened health consumers will help fuel the rise of health sects. The more power taken away from mainstream medicine and claimed by others – in this case consumers themselves – the easier it is to accept alternative takes on health and health care. We've already seen how a stronger focus on consumer preference in the clinical field has influenced care – take the "patient-driven outcomes" (PRO) movement. With PROs, healthcare professionals consider those outcomes identified by patients themselves as equally important to medical or provider defined outcomes. For example, a doctor who guides a patient in treatment for cancer and sees the cancer driven into remission may see that clinical outcome as success. However, if the patient desired an outcome that minimized pain, and instead experienced increased levels of pain throughout the treatment, she may label the outcome as a partial failure. There's a long way to go with such an approach. A report cited in 2019 showed that, "less than two percent (32) of the 1,958 quality indicators in the National Quality Measures Clearinghouse are PROs."[176] Nevertheless, movements such as PROs, while oriented in admirable perspectives on patient empowerment, will also provide agency to those who want to define clinical efficacy on their own terms.

The growth of empowered patients came from access to medical information through the Internet and social media, alongside a greater understanding in the industry that an educated patient, whose desired outcomes are taken seriously, leads to better healthcare outcomes. For the most part, the trend toward empowered health consumers had been apolitical, at least until Covid-19 spurred protests against everything from mask mandates to school closures to social distancing. Now, consumer views on health and healthcare are warped by political views, and it's doubtful the genie can be put back in the bottle. Moving forward, clinicians will have to grapple with an ever-more irrational, subjective take on health from their patients. It was one thing to deal with minimal and often misleading interpretations patients could get from Dr. Google. It will become something completely different as Dr. Google starts pontificating from a political pulpit.

The future is now

It's not hard to imagine – consumers who are more and more empowered in their own care, fueled by their own individualism and support from like-minded influencers, bathed in an anti-science and anti-expert mindset, targeted with messages and content that are hyper-personalized through social media and other technologies, falling deeper and deeper into the grips of an immersive tribe with millions who share the same views on everything from politics to economics to health. It's not hard to imagine because all of these factors are happening *right now*, and have been growing for a number of years. What's new is how these factors could combine to shape one or more health sects, leading to a scenario not unlike that laid out in the opening of the chapter. Individual healthcare clinicians, clinics, hospitals, research facilities, universities, health systems – all developed or spun to cater to a specific health sect. Dr. Ryu, CEO at Geisinger, sees the potential for this future, and the underlying dynamics, and it's not a positive view.

> *I don't want to be all doom and gloom, but misinformation is so easy to propagate with social media and technology. It's really hard to discern trustworthy sources from untrustworthy sources. There will always be misinformation, but the level of it during Covid was shocking. We see it everywhere, regardless of which side of the political spectrum one looks at. It's news meets entertainment meets sensationalism, and it further polarizes the country because everything has now been politicized.*

Examples of the early stage formation of alternative health sects are not hard to find.

○   ○   ○

In the summer of 2021, the Minnesota Board of Medical Practice suspended pediatrician Dr. Robert Zajac for telling parents of his patients that vaccines weren't safe. A story on the ruling outlines how Dr. Zajac took the matter to federal court, "claiming that his free speech and due process rights were being violated." Additionally, "Zajac told board investigators that he did recommend the CDC's vaccine schedule, but the clinic's website said it was a 'non-judgment clinic' about alternative schedules." [177] While we might understandably expect the courts or state medical boards to stop these kind of "contrarian" medical practices dead in their tracks, the ruling of judges is often determined by their political backgrounds. State medical boards are bound by law and the U.S. Constitution to regulate the practice of medicine, and should theoretically act above political persuasion. But as we've seen in many other aspects of government over the past decade, from the U.S. Justice department to state election boards and officials, nothing seems to be out of the reach of those who would want to instill a political persuasion to government activities. As with many states, for example, members of the Minnesota Board of Medical Practice are appointed by the state's governor. In September 2021, the Republican county commissioners for Idaho's most populous county, which contains the capitol of Boise, replaced a 15-year member of its regional health board and a former president of the American Academy of Family Physicians – who had been dismissed for his support of pandemic restrictions – with a physician, Dr. Ryan Cole, who was outspoken on Covid-19, calling coronavirus vaccines "fake." According to an article in *The Washington Post*, the appointment, supported by hundreds of letters submitted by residents, was seen by critics as a politically motivated maneuver, "Cole's elevation to a public health-care role is an extreme example of GOP-driven resistance to not only mandates but basic medical guidance." [178]

○   ○   ○

Right as this book went to the publisher in August 2021, the use of ivermectin galloped into the national spotlight. The drug (ironically created by Pfizer) to help the deworming of domestic animals such as horse and sheep became the stuff of social media legend as those opposed to Covid-19 vaccines began taking the drug to treat the virus. After being touted by right-leaning media personalities such as Laura Ingraham and Tucker Carlson, as well as Republican politicians such as Senators Ron Johnson from Wisconsin and Rand Paul from Kentucky, ivermectin seemed to reach critical mass when popular podcaster Joe Rogan, mentioned previously, caught Covid-19 and claimed to have taken ivermectin (along with a slew of other treatments). In Arkansas, the state's medical board began investigating a doctor who claimed to have prescribed the drug "thousands" of times to patients, including inmates at an Arkansas jail. In an article on the case in CNN, the doctor defended his practices, stating:

> *Do you want to try and fight like we're at the beaches of Normandy? Or do you want me to tell what a lot of people do and say – oh, go home and ride it out and go to the ER when your lips turn blue?*[179]

Later reporting showed many of the inmates claimed they were not told that what they were given for Covid-19 was an anti-parasitic drug, and also disputed claims by both Dr. Karas, quoted above, and the county sheriff, that the use of the drug was voluntary.[180] All of this while public health officials stated there was no scientific evidence that ivermectin had any positive effect on Covid-19, and that further, misuse of the drug – especially in the form found at feed and livestock stores – could have severe medical side effects. The FDA has warned that taking ivermectin is "dangerous and can cause serious harm."[181] On September 2, the American Medical Association, American Pharmacists Association, and American Society of Health-System Pharmacists issued a joint release warning against the use of the drug, which had no FDA approval for Covid-19 treatment, citing a five-fold rise in calls to poison control centers due to ingestion of ivermectin.[182]

And yet, despite no research-backed scientific evidence of the efficacy of the horse-dewormer to treat Covid-19, a judge in Butler County, Ohio, just outside of Cincinnati, ordered a local hospital to administer ivermectin to one of its patients based on pleas of the patient's wife. (Two weeks later, another Ohio judge reversed this decision, stating, "Judges are not doctors or nurses.")

o   o   o

Many followers of former President Donald Trump launched a medically focused national tour called ReAwaken America, which sought to tout messages of "health and freedom." Events across the country featured speakers such as Simone Gold, a leader in the group America's Frontline Doctors, who participated in both the event at the Supreme Court in 2020 touting hydroxychloroquine as well as the January 6, 2021, attack on the U.S. Capitol; Scott Jensen, a physician and candidate for governor of Minnesota, who claimed in 2020 that doctors were over-diagnosing Covid-19 for financial gain; and of course, Stella Immanuel herself. Other famous (infamous?) participants included Michael Flynn, Trump's former National Security Advisor who was pardoned by the president after he pled guilty to lying to the FBI about his contacts with Russia; Roger Stone, another former advisor pardoned by Trump after his conviction for lying to Congress; and Mike Lindell, CEO of MyPillow and prolific conspiracy theorist.[183] The events have been used to spread misinformation on everything from the 2020 presidential election to Covid-19 issues such as masking, vaccines, and ivermectin. Irwin Redlener, who leads Columbia University's Pandemic Resource and Recovery Initiation, told *The Guardian* in a story about the tour, "I'm actually embarrassed by the fact that there are doctors fully into this craziness."

o   o   o

So how do hospitals, health systems, and other providers prepare for health sects? In considering a future with clearly identified health sects such as Mainstreamers, Progressives, and Contrarians, providers are placed between the proverbial rock and a hard place.

CHRIS BEVOLO

The Rock – Corporate social responsibility

On one hand, there's likely no way to avoid the politicization of
healthcare, as many of those we spoke to pointed out. While healthcare
providers used to be above the political fray, avoiding for the most part
the controversies of the day, both the Covid-19 pandemic and social
justice movement may have ended that enviable position forever. Paul
Matsen, Chief Marketing and Communications Officer at Cleveland
Clinic, believes both the events of 2020 and changes in communications
channels have forced a new approach on hospitals and health systems.

> *You have to go beyond corporate responsibility, and you
> need to be very clear about values, which is an increasing
> component of brand perception and value. Today, it's
> expected and observed at a much greater level. There's
> also an incredible immediacy of information – everyone
> saw what happened at the Capitol, or in Atlanta, or
> Boulder, immediately. That demands a different mindset.
> We are expected to engage in these issues. For example,
> The Cleveland Clinic issued a statement about the
> shooting involving the Asian spa in Atlanta. This is a
> palpable change – ten years ago, organizations like ours
> just didn't respond at all.*

Research has shown over and over that consumers are increasingly
taking into account social responsibility related to brands they prefer,
particularly for younger generations. As just one example, a 2019 study
showed that two-thirds of consumers around the world said they would
buy from a brand or boycott it solely because of its position on social or
political issues.[184]

Sandra Mackey, Chief Marketing Officer at Bon Secours Mercy
Health, also believes 2020 was a turning point.

> *There is a social justice movement that is here to stay,
> it will continue. From what we have seen over the
> course of last year, the political divide is becoming*

more transparent, and it's taking on a life of its own. We have witnessed the need for social justice at a level we haven't seen for decades, in terms of the public's engagement in these issues. There's no turning back, no turning away. We are raising a generation of purpose-driven youth who will dominate the conversation over the next decade. There will be greater consumer expectations based on social issues for years to come. Because of that, there will be far more awareness and purpose for brands to demonstrate corporate social responsibility.

As with other organizations, hospitals and health systems are driven today to speak out on social issues not just because they believe in them at a leadership level, but because their employees demand it. Wright Lassiter, President and CEO of Henry Ford Health System:

This country, for lots of reasons, is going through an awakening, and there's a notion for advocating for things that are important. There is an expectation that organizations like ours need to take a stand on issues. If not for anything else, our employees will demand that we step up and lean in on these issues. There is no doubt our organization will play an advocate role.

Sometimes, hospitals and health systems will have to deal with their very own clinicians who are making the wrong kind of political news – or when there is a perception the organization is involved. Remember the start of the chapter, with the 2020 press conference featuring Dr. Stella Immanuel and her controversial claims about Covid-19. One of the clinicians also appearing on the steps of the Supreme Court that day was Dr. Simone Gold, the emergency and general practice physician mentioned early as a speaker on the ReAwaken America tour, who is featured in another video talking about Covid-19 while standing in front of Cedars-Sinai Medical Center in Los Angeles. This forced Cedars-Sinai itself to have to address the controversy publicly, issuing a statement saying, "there is no one by that name on the staff at Cedars-Sinai or affiliated with Cedars-Sinai."[185]

There is also a danger in not being authentic in speaking out on political issues. Many hospitals and health systems hesitated to jump too soon or too aggressively on the racial justice movement stemming from George Floyd's murder due to their own struggle with racial equity, such as having leadership groups or boards made up mostly or entirely of white executives (and also mostly or entirely male). There can be a concern that political statements can come off as opportunistic or hollow if not handled right. Further, some brands can take things too far. In his critically acclaimed special "Inside" that poked fun at many of the social trends of the day, comedian Bo Burnham excoriated brands who mishandled social responsibility with a satirical bit where he posed as a consultant, asking the existential question, "Who are you, Bagel Bites?"

While Bagel Bites or Budweiser or Minute Maid may be able to minimize the degree to which they position their brands on social justice issues, hospitals, health systems, and other providers have no such out. Healthcare providers play a crucial role in society, and their beliefs and actions in the areas of social responsibility have a direct impact on core challenges in the U.S. such as health disparities and health inequities. Simply put, healthcare providers can no longer sit on the fence – they must take a stand. Which, of course, puts them right up against the potential "hard place" of those health sects with different political views.

The hard place – appealing to health sects with different political views

It might be impossible for an organization like Henry Ford Health System, based in a community such as Detroit with its history of racial strife and injustice, with a Black leader in Wright Lassiter who is passionate about social and racial justice and equity, and as an organization with a highly-diverse workforce that has been recognized a national leader in diversity and inclusion, to NOT publicly support racial justice issues. At the same time, how does such an organization or others like it serve those who don't hold the same level of attention to or passion for racial justice issues, or going further, have opposing views? If two thirds of Americans want brands that speak out on social issues, it begs the question: what do those two thirds want to hear? If you're Major League Baseball and you move the All-Star Game to support what you deem are voting rights, what do you say to the large percentage of the population that see the issue through the lens of election security, not voting rights? No major healthcare organization (or, likely, minor) is designed to cater to only certain segments of the political population. Most, in fact, seek to actively seek out and support *anyone* who needs clinical care, regardless of race, creed, religion, gender orientation, income level, or other demographic attribute. Says Laura Schoen, Chief Healthcare Officer for DXTRA Health Integrated Solutions and Global Healthcare President at Weber Shandwick:

> *Hospitals and health systems will have to have a point of view on this dynamic – they will have to be prepared to deal with these issues. And not just at an organizational level, but down to an individual clinician level. How will you deal with emboldened tribes? How will we deal with these challenges?*

While brands, including hospitals and health systems, are increasingly expected to speak out on political issues, they will also simultaneously have to learn how to appeal to, or at least manage, consumer segments with differing and powerfully embedded political views. Chris Perry, Chief Innovation Officer at Weber Shandwick, and one of the authors of the provocative report "What Comes After the Coherence Crash" mentioned earlier, poses these fundamental questions for brands:

> *If we're banding together in forums tailored to particular interests… can organizations enhance our communities with relevant participation and perspective? If individuals are increasingly moving from the public into private networks…how can businesses and marketers use these*

*same networks to connect and empower people to make
their mark on the world? If facts are socially-constructed
versus authoritatively told…do we understand the means
for how this happens, along with the dis- or misinformation
risks that coincide with reality-building?*[186]

Today, healthcare providers face challenges related to the
politicization of healthcare such as:

- How does a doctor convince someone with anti-vaccination beliefs to take a life-saving vaccine?
- How do public health officials achieve adherence to critical strategies such as mask mandates or social distancing?
- How does a surgeon convince parents who follow Christian Scientists orthodoxy of rejecting modern medicine to pursue a life-saving surgery for their child?

Tomorrow, with the rise of health sects, providers will face a different
level of challenges:

- How does a hospital convince an emergency room patient to seek follow up care when that patient vehemently disagrees with the hospital's public stance on racial issues?
- How does a physician deal with a patient who claims their research, based on an organization or academic institution pushing intentionally politicized studies, is superior to medically accepted research on their clinical issue?
- How does a clinical administrator deal with a patient who is combative because that patient isn't allowed to choose a white nurse?
- How does a health system deal with a boycott organized by one if its own clinicians based on that system's stance on a public health tactic such as treating drug addicts with a needle-exchange program, or going door to door to educate lower-income neighborhoods on the importance of taking the Covid-19 vaccine?

How will healthcare providers serve their communities with divided health sects? Can they learn to target these different segments effectively? What will happen if politically oriented healthcare organizations emerge? How will legacy hospitals and health systems compete? How would politically oriented provider organizations, research institutions, and healthcare influencers alter the ability of the country to address ongoing and future public health crises? The challenges healthcare providers have always faced will be expanded by an entirely new set of issues brought on by the rise of health sects. Here's Russ Meyer, Senior Director of Brand Strategy at CVS Health:

> *Sorting of brand by political orientation, this is growing below the radar and will surprise a lot of people. When you look at legacy health systems, religion is already wrapped up in this space. Now, given everything we've seen and the need to speak out on political issues, and the immediacy of communications, consumers will be unable to avoid the religious or political bent of a health care organization. This could definitely factor into a consumer's choice, and in fact be a key driver of brand choice. It's all just part of our reptile brain.*

Chapter 8

PREDICTION

Disparity Dystopia

In the 21st Century earth was diseased, polluted and vastly overpopulated. Earth's wealthiest fled the planet to preserve their way of life.

That's the superimposition at the beginning of the 2013 science fiction movie *Elysium*, starring Matt Damon. Damon plays a character named Max Da Costa, a factory worker who lives in a future Los Angeles, shown as an overpopulated, crimes-ridden, garbage strewn hellscape with children begging in the streets and skyscrapers turned into giant tenements. Early in the movie, Max has his arm broken by the authoritarian robot cops patrolling his neighborhood, and when he visits the hospital, it's a chaotic scene: the waiting room is overrun with patients, as are all the halls. The hospital is clearly dilapidated, dirty, and disorganized. There is a mob scene at the front desk as patients and their family members fight to be seen, and Max's physician friend has little time to spare as she rushes off to the next emergency.

Contrast these images of a blighted LA with Elysium, the utopian space station orbiting the earth's atmosphere. A spinning marvel of modern technology, Elysium is gorgeous with its green trees, modern, clean buildings, and singing birds. To protect their perfect world, citizens of Elysium prevent citizens of Earth from travelling there without authorization. As an example, dozens of Earth's citizens steal transports early in the movie to make a desperate attempt to reach Elysium. That's because, on Elysium, the world's wealthiest have access to technology called a Med-Bay, which can cure an individual of any disease or injury. Two of the transports are shot to smithereens, while the one that breaks through includes a mom who rushes her injured child to the nearest Med-Bay for treatment. They are promptly arrested and sent back to earth. The plot of the movie revolves around Max's attempt to reach the space station Elysium after he receives a fatal dose of radiation in a workplace accident. He's given five days to live, but if he can reach the flying Eden and use a Med-Bay, he can save himself.

I won't spoil the ending, but given Matt Damon is our hero, you can probably imagine the outcome. A decent science fiction film, (though it will make you wonder what happened to Jody Foster's career), Elysium is clearly an exaggeration. The movie paints a worse-case, ultimate outcome of the inequities and disparities faced by those in the U.S. and across the world. It's a work of fantasy, with an end-game where the haves – both in terms of wealth and health – are literally separated from the rest of humanity, the have-nots, by hundreds of miles in space. Of course, in real life, we'd never experience such a gross display of inhumanity – our institutions, our government, our leaders, and us, the people, would never allow it.

As I sit here writing the first draft of this fifth and final prediction, Disparity Dystopia, the richest man on earth, Jeff Bezos, is eight minutes from launching into space on the New Shepard rocket, built by his company Blue Origin. The plan is to launch more than 62 miles into the atmosphere, besting the 50-mile distance achieved by another billionaire, Richard Branson, when he rode a rocket built by his company, Virgin Atlantic, one week ago. Perhaps the company furthest along in advancing private space travel is SpaceX, run by rebel billionaire and entrepreneur Elon Musk (Musk's first ride into space will actually be on Virgin Galactic). This billionaire space race/ego rivalry has become a focal point for conversation, debate, and outrage related to the growth in wealth for the wealthiest coming out of 2020 and the

Covid-19 pandemic. Bezos, for example, whose wealth is estimated at more than $200 billion, saw his wealth increase more than $70 billion during the pandemic as his company, Amazon, became for many the sole source of acquiring food, supplies, and more.

The contrast of the richest getting so much richer coming out of a global health crisis understandably is gaining attention. In his speech before Congress in April 2021, President Joe Biden said, "Twenty million Americans lost their job in the pandemic. At the same time, roughly 650 billionaires in America saw their net worth increase by more than $1 trillion, and now they're worth more than $4 trillion."[187]

Turns out that was even a somewhat conservative estimation by the president. An update on July 14, 2021, claimed that in the 16 months since the start of the pandemic in the U.S., "the combined wealth of 713 U.S. billionaires has surged by $1.8 trillion, a gain of almost 60 percent. The total combined wealth of U.S. billionaires increased from $2.9 trillion on March 18, 2020, to $4.7 trillion on July 9, 2021."[188] Another report claimed that globally, nearly 2,400 billionaires saw their wealth increase 54%, or a combined $4 trillion, in the year following the start of the global pandemic.

In an Instagram post, Dan Price, an outspoken entrepreneur who gained fame by guaranteeing all of the employees at his company a minimum salary of $70,000 in 2015, posted the following in July 2021: "In the pandemic, the world added a record 118 million people who are chronically hungry and global billionaires added a record $4 trillion to their wealth. The cost to end world hunger ($330 billion) is what billionaires made in one month and instead they're going to space."

The idea of the nation's wealthiest citizens enriching themselves while millions suffer and more than 600,00 Americans have died (to date) during the Covid-19 pandemic is the perfect backdrop for our fifth prediction. Debates about wealth and income inequities have raged for decades, but they are parallel, and not unrelated to, debates about the level of health and healthcare inequities and disparities in the U.S. Like wealth inequity, health inequity was an issue long before Covid-19 first struck. But like wealth disparity, health disparity came to the forefront of the national conversation *because* of Covid-19. In both cases, whether we're looking at the concept of disparity or inequity, we're talking about a gap, and to really put a fine point on it, a gap between the *haves* and the *have nots*. Unfortunately, Prediction Five, doesn't not bode well for this gap...

> *The Covid-19 pandemic shone an ugly light on the disparities that have plagued the U.S. healthcare system for decades. Unfortunately, that health gap is more likely than not to expand, as the "haves" gain access to increasingly more expensive medical treatments, health services, and personalized care, while the "have nots" face growing shortages of basic health resources, from clean water and air to physicians and clinicians, rural healthcare, and more. This shift will be compounded by the mental health crisis, which disproportionately affects systemically disadvantaged populations and groups outside traditional healthcare access channels (teens, for example). All while those entities that might address these disparities increasingly struggle financially – health systems, health plans, state and federal governments – and others lack the incentives to focus on the growing issue.*

So Elysium, sure, that's a stretch. But as I write this, and as everyone who is reading this is well aware, the inaugural Bezos space flight has successfully returned to earth.

The expansion of the health gap

Many books have been written about the global health gap. As we noted in Chapter 3, there are distinct differences between health disparities and health inequities, as well as healthcare disparities. For the purposes of this discussion, rather than parse between the three different areas, we'll consider these critical issues holistically and refer to them collectively as the "health gap." (Of course, discussions beyond this one and practical solutions must address these different components distinctly as appropriate.) Our intent here is not to rewrite those books, but instead try to paint the very discouraging picture of what will happen in the coming decade if dramatic action is not taken to address the growing health gap between the *haves* and the *have-nots*. By *haves*, we're referring primarily to those on the higher side of the wealth and income gap, those in the majority racially (white) and gender (male, cisgender), and those with higher education profiles (college or higher). The *have-nots*? Communities of color, the poor, LGBTQ+, the undereducated. While the health gap hits these populations in sometimes vastly different ways, they are all on the wrong side of that broadening chasm.

Our prediction focuses on the U.S. because that's the situation we understand best. But there's no denying that a health gap exists globally, and in many cases, is worse than what we experience in the U.S. Going further, it's likely foolish to try and consider the health gap in the U.S. separately from the global scene, because the latter will most definitely affect the former in substantial ways, from the spread of infectious diseases like Covid-19 to the migration of populations due to climate catastrophe to the advance of medical science and innovation. Nevertheless, if only to keep the conversation manageable, we'll focus on the health gap here in the U.S. over the next decade.

What makes this prediction discouraging from our perspective is that in considering the widening health gap, we're not just talking about the "rich getting richer" in terms of health and healthcare, or the "poor getting poorer." We're talking about *both*. If the health gap can be represented by a chasm, the ledges on both sides are crumbling into the abyss, enlarging the breach in both directions. And, again, while this pull in opposite directions has been happening for decades, the Covid-19 pandemic is a watershed event in terms of the health gap, both in further highlighting existing disparities, while at the same time contributing to greater disparity. To understand where the next decade may go, we have to quickly review where the U.S. was with our health gap, and what has changed as a result of the Covid-19 pandemic.

A long history of disparity

For our discussion, we are taking for a given that the health gap exists, and that it plays a significant role in the lives of the *have-nots*. We will not devote much space to building this case, and those needing that case should probably stop reading here – if you're not convinced a health gap exists and is a fundamental, life-or-death issue for tens of millions of Americans, you probably won't get much out of the rest of this chapter. But just to refresh ourselves on the health gap, here are some stark reminders from a 2019 report from the U.S. Department of Health & Human Services:

- For about 40% of quality measures, Black people (82 of 202) and American Indian people and Alaska Native people (47 of 116) received worse care than White people. For more than one-third of quality measures, Hispanic people (61 of 177) received worse care than White people.[189]
- For nearly a quarter (24 of 102) of quality measures, residents of large central metropolitan areas received worse care than residents of large fringe metropolitan areas.[190]
- In 2018, White people were 60% of the U.S. population and approximately 57% of physicians (Figure 7). Asian people were about 6% of the U.S. population and approximately 17% of physicians. Black people were 12% of the U.S. population but only 5% of physicians.[191]
- In 2019, 33.2 million people of all ages (10.3%) were uninsured at the time of interview.[192]
- In 2018, high-income Hispanic and Black people were less likely to have any private insurance compared with high-income White people.[193]
- In 2019, among adults ages 18-64, the percentage who were uninsured at the time of interview was higher among those who were poor (25.8%) and near poor (26.8%) compared with those who were not poor (9.0%)[194]
- In 2019, Hispanic adults were the most likely to lack health insurance coverage, while non-Hispanic White and non-Hispanic Asian adults were the least likely to be uninsured. Non-Hispanic Black adults were more likely than non-Hispanic White and non-Hispanic Asian adults to be uninsured.[195]

- Black people had worse access to care than White people for 48% of access measures. Asian people had worse access to care than White people for 32% of access measures. Native Hawaiian/ Pacific Island people (NHPIs) had worse access to care than White people for 25% of access measures. American Indian people and Alaska Native people (AI/ANs) had worse access to care than White people for 55% of access measures. [196]
- According to CDC research, in 2017, Black people accounted for 13% of the nation's population but represented 43% of all new HIV cases.[197]
- In 2017, Black people had 6.6 HIV infection deaths per 100,000 population compared with 0.9 per 100,000 cases for White people.[198]
- From 2000 to 2018, only 5% of the metrics for disparities in quality of care experienced by Black people were narrowing.[199]
- Of the 53 quality measures with a disparity at baseline, disparities between Hispanic people and non-Hispanic White people did not change for 48 (91%) from 2000 through 2018.[200]
- In 2017, 83.3% of American Indian/Alaskan Native hospital patients received influenza vaccinations compared with 93.8% of White people. [201]
- High-income groups performed better than other income groups on 55% of all quality measures.[202]
- In 2017, the percentage of people without a usual source of care who indicated a financial or insurance reason for not having a source of care was higher for poor, low-income, and middle-income people compared with high-income people (20.3%, 18.3%, and 12.7%, respectively, vs. 6.5%).[203]
- In 2017, the rate of hospital admissions for short-term complications of diabetes was three times as high for adults in the lowest income group (101.0 per 100,000 population) compared with adults in the highest income group (32.9 per 100,000 population).[204]
- Uninsured people had worse care for 62% of quality measures, and people with public insurance had worse care for 47% of quality measures.[205]

The list, unfortunately, could go on and on (The 2019 HHS report was 274 pages long). And it doesn't necessarily provide the bigger picture context needed to truly absorb the depth of this issue. For example, as of 2018, life expectancy among Black people was four years lower than White people, with the lowest expectancy among Black men.[206] Across America, Black men under 50 are twice as likely as white men to die of heart disease.[207] In fact, studies have shown disparities drive higher incidents of many health issues in communities of color, including depression and mental health issues, neonatal mortality, low birth rate, cancer, and the prevalence of chronic disease. A 2011 study estimated that the economic costs of health disparities due to race for Black, Asian American, and Hispanic people from 2003 thru 2006 was a little over $229 billion.[208]

The *have-nots* also experience the U.S. healthcare system in worse ways. A 2020 study released by the Kaiser Family Foundation found that among Black women who have a child under the age of 18, 37% say they have been treated unfairly based on their race while getting health care for themselves or a family member in the past year, and 41% had an experience where a healthcare provider talked down to them or didn't treat them with respect. Roughly 22% of Black people surveyed said they had encountered a physician who didn't believe they were telling the truth, compared with 17% of White people. Not surprisingly then, the study also showed that compared to White adults, Black adults are 19% less likely to trust doctors (59% vs. 78%), 14% less likely to trust local hospitals (56% vs. 70%), and 11% less likely to trust "the health care system" (44% vs. 55%) to do what is right for them and their communities.[209]

Further, these statistics only capture health and healthcare disparities. The list of examples of health inequities would be equally long. For example, in 2019, the median Black household earned 61 cents for every dollar of income the median white household earned, while the median Hispanic household earned 74 cents.[210] Or a 2019 report that shows America's wealthiest spend a lower percentage of their incomes on their housing than they did a decade ago, despite their incomes rising, while poorer Americans are having to spend a higher percentage of their income on housing.[211] Or a 2019 study that shows those in the

LGBT community collectively have a poverty rate of 21.6%, which is much higher than the rate for cisgender straight people of 15.7%, and that among the LGBT, transgender people have especially high rates of poverty—29.4%.[212]

What is one thing all of those statistics *do* have in common? They reflect the state of the health gap *before* Covid-19 hit. And if things were bad before, well...

The consequences of Covid-19

We've heard over and over that the Covid-19 pandemic shed a brighter light on the existing health and healthcare inequities and disparities in the U.S. For example, confusion at the outset of the pandemic on the cost of testing and what would be covered by insurance or the federal government highlights how millions can't just pursue the care they need without serious financial consideration. How community and rural hospitals suffered disproportionately in terms of financial loss and federal support. How one of the greatest obstacles to vaccine adherence in black communities is the deep distrust of the U.S. government, given the health atrocities such as the Tuskegee Study in the 1930s (where 600 Black men were used for human experimentation in the study of untreated syphilis). Or how Covid-19, like many diseases before it, hit Black and Hispanic populations harder than White populations. But in considering what the next decade holds, and our point of view that things are likely to get worse in terms of the health gap, it's important that we consider how the pandemic itself made things worse. An article from Kaiser Health Network paints a horrible scene:[213]

- The average life expectancy for Black Americans dropped more than *three years* in 2020 compared with 2018. Hispanic Americans dropped nearly *four years*. Compare those numbers to the drop in average life expectancy for White Americans of 14 months. (According to CDC reports, the 2020 drop in life expectancy for Black people was the largest one-year drop since the Great Depression.)[214] Dr. Steven Wolf, a professor at Virginia

Commonwealth University and head of the study, called the change "pretty catastrophic," noting that most year-to-year changes are rarely over a month or two either way. During the time of the study, the change in life expectancy was nine times greater in the U.S. than that of 16 other developed countries.

- The mortality rate in the U.S. jumped 23% in 2020, mostly because of Covid-19, but also because of a spike in severe health incidents such as strokes or heart attacks that went untreated.
- Research shows that people with low incomes live an average of seven to eight years less than those who are financially secure. The richest 1% of Americans live nearly 15 years longer than the poorest 1%. According to a February 2021 report by McKinsey & Company, Black and Hispanic people in the U.S. won't recover their pre-pandemic income levels until 2024.
- Poverty levels jumped from 10.7% of Americans in January 2020 to 11.3% one year later. More than 20 million American struggle to feed themselves. According to Dr. Otis Brawley from John Hopkins Medicine, there is a clear and direct link between poverty and health issues. "Poverty causes a lot of cancer and chronic disease, and this pandemic has caused a lot more poverty."
- Women have also suffered from the pandemic, particularly given their primary role in raising children. According to research from the National Women's Law Center, women have lost a generation of labor force participation gains by having to stay home and/or quit their jobs to care for their children.[215]

Of course, many believe the impact of Covid-19 could have been dramatically reduced had the country made difference decisions along the way.

Laura Schoen, Chief Healthcare Officer for DXTRA Health Integrated Solutions and Global Healthcare President at Weber Shandwick, was one of many experts we talked to who were dismayed at how poorly the U.S. responded to and managed the pandemic.

I'm surprised that what broke the camel's back was a pandemic. We thought we had a certain level of control

on transmittable diseases, and we have invested so much
on understanding infectious disease. This is something
that happened 100 years ago, and now it has happened
again, almost blow by blow. And yet how could we be
so unprepared for Covid? In some ways we are over-
confident in our ability to manage disease and medical
issues. We've had some sparks of concern before – Ebola,
SARS, etc. But when Covid-19 hit, we didn't have even
the most basic supplies, such as PPE, prepared. Being
based in New York City, I saw first-hand the challenges
they faced.

Schoen goes on to point out that the effect of Covid-19 on health disparities won't stop when the virus is under control. There was a shortage of oxygen in India as Covid-19 rampaged across that country. And there has been an ongoing discussion about global vaccine distribution, with richer nations buying most of the supply – and even considering adding additional booster shots – while poorer nations go without the vaccine altogether. Says Schoen:

Covid has really revealed very big issues. Globally, how
do you equitably distribute what's needed? Vaccines,
oxygen, ventilators, tests. We'll see the same questions
and challenges as we continue to produce more high-tech
treatments. Who will be able to afford what? And who
will decide who has access?

And of course, the challenge isn't over. As I write this book, the Delta variant is flaring across the U.S., spreading rapidly among the unvaccinated and affecting a much younger group overall than the original virus did in 2020.

So let's recap. The health gap in the U.S. was a colossal issue before 2020. The Covid-19 pandemic not only allowed us to see that health gap in a new way, but it also contributed to the widening of that gap. With that as backdrop, what will we see with the health gap in the coming decade? Well as I've laid out, if it was already bad, and Covid-19 made it worse, we think that without earth-shattering intervention, that trend will simply continue.

Here's how Danah Boyd, principal researcher at Microsoft Research, put it when considering where the next 10 years may take us:

> We haven't hit peak awful yet. I have every confidence that social and civic innovation can be beneficial in the long run (with a caveat that I think that climate change dynamics might ruin all of that). But no matter what, I don't think we're going to see significant positive change by 2030. I think things are going to get much worse before they start to get better. I should also note that I don't think that many players have taken responsibility for what's unfolding. Yes, tech companies are starting to see that things might be a problem, but that's only on the surface. News media does not at all acknowledge its role in amplifying discord (or its financialized dynamics). The major financiers of this economy don't take any responsibility for what's unfolding.[216]

Let's take a look why we believe we're headed for a Disparity Dystopia in this country by considering how the health situation for the *haves* will actually get better, and more importantly, how the *have-nots* could face even greater challenges than they see today.

The have's – the healthy get healthier

Our first prediction, The Copernican Consumer, provided a rosy picture of the future in terms of personal health and wellness. Body monitors and Apple Watches. AI and digital therapeutics. Individualized care and customized wellness. Woebot and the Betterment of healthcare. Genome mapping and digital twinning. The future is bright and transformative and all about you, the healthcare consumer.

If you can afford that future, of course. If you can spare $400 or more for an Apple Watch, or membership in a wellness-oriented program, or pay for genomic testing or therapies. We heard from Schoen in Chapter Four about the advances in personalized medicine and genomics. Suzanne Sawyer, Chief Marketing and Communications Officer at Johns Hopkins Medicine, was another of the experts we spoke with who pointed out the promise – and financial challenge – posed by advances in therapeutics. She points out that some of the new therapies are extraordinarily expensive. Can the private payor model survive the growth in this area?

If you're a *have*, you're much more likely to have commercial insurance that may cover these costs. I'll use myself as a financial test case. I was diagnosed with Crohn's Disease in my thirties, and for the last two decades I've used biologics – medications that are derived from living organisms – to help keep the disease at bay. I have to undergo a 3-hour infusion every 8 weeks, and each treatment costs thousands of dollars. Without a job that provides strong health insurance, the vast majority of us would not be able to afford that treatment. A July 2021 article in *Modern Healthcare* notes that major insurers such as UnitedHealthcare, Aetna, and Cigna were clamping down more forcefully on coverage for biologics, making patients switch to cheaper alternatives, or in some ways restricting the use of the drugs altogether.[217] (I experienced this personally when UnitedHealthcare, my insurer, forced me at the beginning of 2021 to switch my Crohn's medication, Remicade, after years of successful use in staving off severe effects from the disease.)

If you're a *have* financially, then you've been in pretty good shape in recent years. For example, the wealthiest 1% of Americans holds 32% of the country's wealth, up from 23% in 1989. The top 10% holds 70% of the wealth, up from 61% in 1989. And the bottom 50% of the country, who have never owned more than 5% of the wealth, is down to just 2% as of 2021.[218] And we know if you are a Black or Hispanic person, you're even worse off. For example, the median household wealth of the typical Black family was $6,674 in 1968, compared with $70,786 for the typical White family. In 2016, adjusted for inflation, that number had increased to $13,024 in 2020 for the typical Black family, and to more than $149,700 for the typical White family.

Much of healthcare is oriented toward the *haves*. Hospitals and health systems, who have to compete for patients to ensure they have enough revenue to stay viable, often target those with higher incomes and commercial insurance coverage because there is higher reimbursement on clinical care from commercial insurance than from government-sponsored coverage such as Medicare and Medicaid. (Those commercially insured patients help cover the cost of publicly-insured patients and those who are underinsured or uninsured through the controversial practice of cost-shifting. On one hand, some argue that hospitals are gouging commercially insured patients, sometimes charging 2-3 times that of other patients. Others argue, as providers do, that without cost-shifting, they would go bankrupt as the reimbursement from Medicare, Medicaid and of course the uninsured does not cover the cost of care.) Some physicians have opted to not even accept Medicare given the lower reimbursement rate, though the total number may be lower than most would expect (a 2020 showed that roughly 1% of non-pediatric physicians formally opted out of Medicare in 2020).[219]

While most hospitals and health systems follow ethical standards and strive to treat any and all patients who need care, targeting and selective care for those of a better financial status is commonplace. Schoen relays a story about a friend seeing a top surgeon in Manhattan, and upon hearing about the potential procedure expressed concern about whether insurance would cover it. "Don't worry," said the physician. "You wouldn't be in here talking to me if your insurance didn't cover it. I have three people in my office who screen that ahead of time. I don't even talk to people without coverage."

Concierge medicine is another benefit of being a *have*. These membership-style practices provide a far higher level of attention and a far more superior experience than standard providers can afford to provide. The Concierge Medicine Research Collective reports that the average concierge doctor sees between 6-8 patients a day.[220] Compare that to research that says the average PCP sees 20 patients a day.[221] Consider "The Lanby," a Manhattan-based concierge practice with the slogan "Discover what it feels like when health meets hospitality." The website promises "The best of concierge and urgent care in one place. Next-day availability. Short waits. Long Visits. Seamless specialist referrals," and says the clinic is "A club inspired by your favorite New York restaurants & hotels." The Lanby doesn't take insurance, but instead charges a base rate of $2,400 annually for membership. Annual concierge membership fees can run to $5,000, $10,000, or even $50,000 a year.

In a country that celebrates individual and financial success, most don't argue with a "to the victor goes the spoils" society, even when it comes to healthcare. There is nothing inherently wrong with concierge medicine, or those who can hold down the right job enjoying the benefits of commercial insurance. The conversation starts when the disparity between the *haves* and the *have nots* becomes gratuitous, and when that disparity continues to grow and grow. I've provided just a glimpse into the ways the health gap is growing on one end – access to and the ability to afford better products and services related to health and healthcare for the *haves*. But it's more illustrative to consider how the gap is widening from the other direction, how the *have nots* are experiencing less and less, and how, as we predict, this is only likely to become worse over the next 10 years. And any discussion of the widening health gap has to start with its most obvious indicator – healthcare costs.

The have nots – there's nowhere to go but up from here…except for down

Perhaps more than any other issue, those we interviewed for this book shared one common view: surprise at how little we've done over the past decade to solve for the affordability issue in healthcare, and, as a result, how something will have to give. Here's Adam Brase, Executive Director – Strategic Intelligence at Mayo Clinic:

> *We're still dealing with some of the same issues we've dealt with since the 80s, and we can't figure them out. Affordability, health disparities. In the last 10 years, these have only grown as issues, which is increasingly worrisome. They aren't new issues. We can't become more and more expensive. But yet, solutions are pretty elusive. The pressure is on healthcare, and rightly so, to solve for the affordability crisis, and focus on health inequities. This simply can't continue – how can we be complacent in*

the face of that? Health disparities are a huge challenge, that extend well beyond the medical realm. Yet, there is so much more we can do.

Dr. Ryu, CEO of Geisinger:

Affordability – we have not solved for this. The trend is heading to an unsustainable place for us. The Medicare Part A trust fund for hospitals is now projected to go negative in 2023 or 2024. There will be patches to try to stem this, but it represents a very serious problem. Healthcare costs will continue to climb in a way that all players will struggle to keep up with – government, employers, and consumers.

Wendell Potter, healthcare expert, consultant, and author:

The idea of costs – it's unsustainable. Keep an eye on the employer community. They are waking up to realize they've been sold a bill of goods in terms of cost management from insurers and third-party administrators. These companies aren't really controlling costs at all, and employers are growing tired of continuing to shift cost to employees. Even the giant insurance companies, at their current size, are not meaningfully bending the cost curve. There is just a limit to how much you can squeeze the stone. What is the real value proposition of these insurers anymore? The value of their primary purpose – cost control – is not working anymore. In a recent survey from the Kaiser Family Foundation, 87% of large company CEOs said the government needs to play a larger role in healthcare in the U.S. The free market is not working, and costs keep going up. Corporations have been fierce defenders of the free market, but that's changing.

David Goldhill, healthcare policy expert, board member at the Leapfrog Group, and currently CEO and co-founder of Sesame:

The amount of care paid directly by patients has soared over the past decade, since the ACA, and not just in commercial insurance, but also in Medicare and through the individual ACA exchanges. The average family deductible is four to five thousand dollars. When you strip out those with higher income, and strip out the single percentage of chronic patients who bust through their deductible every year, most consumers essentially pay for 100% of their healthcare out of pocket every year. They simply never meet their deductible.

Additionally, a sea change in terms of employer-sponsored health insurance may be around the bend, and it doesn't necessarily bode well for consumers. While it hasn't made big headlines yet, a policy change under the Trump administration would allow employers to fund insurance premiums through a vehicle called the Individual Coverage HRA, or ICHRA, using pretax dollars. This could have huge ramifications, because prior to this change, companies could only claim tax benefits from their health insurance provided through their own organization. Now, organizations could provide employees with tax-protected funding through ICHRAs and force them go out and purchase insurance on their own on the individual market. That would allow companies to get out of the business of managing health insurance altogether, leaving it up to workers to fend for themselves with their allotted funding. Says Kyle Rolfing, serial entrepreneur in the healthcare consumerism space:

This is the 401k of healthcare. It takes the administrative cost and risk off of the employer and puts it on the employee. Here's your money – now go out and find your own plan.

We touched on this briefly in Chapter Five, and the outcome of such a shift for consumers would likely not be positive. Wendell Potter, healthcare expert and author, for one, sees the writing on the wall.

One of the most outspoken advocates for a federally sponsored public health insurance option is Jacob Hacker, who wrote the amazing book, The Great Risk Shift. *In it, he explains how the U.S. has continued to shift risk from companies to individuals, and points the dramatic move from defined benefit pension plans to defined contribution plans like the 401k. How did that work out for everyone? Before, most middle-class workers could count on a solid pension to carry them through retirement. Now, the number of people who are financially prepared for retirement is alarmingly low, and maybe the biggest reason for that was the shift of responsibility for saving for retirement from companies to individuals through the 401k. This (the ICHRA) is more of the same thing. This is going to happen in healthcare, and you will see more and more employers taking this path. It may or may not be good for employees – it definitely wasn't good for them in retirement. It will be sold as providing "freedom" and "choice" to employees, just as Haker said shifting risk to individuals has been framed by what he calls the "personal responsibility crusade" in this country. But just like individuals were not ready to take responsibility for their own retirement, they won't be ready to take responsibility for their own health coverage.*

A study released by the Rand Corporation in 2019 showed that those U.S. households in the middle of the income spectrum spent between 19.8% and 23.3% of their income on healthcare. For the bottom fifth of households by income, they spent on average 33.9% of their income on healthcare.[222] For many families, their health insurance premiums alone have now become their single biggest monthly expense, surpassing their rent or mortgage payment. I'll never forget watching a keynote presentation by the great Uwe Reinhart about a decade ago, where he said that, based on the then rate of inflation for healthcare costs, families would, within our lifetimes, spend every last cent of income on healthcare, leaving nothing for food, housing, clothing, transportation, or anything else, without a dramatic change to our system.

In July 2021, *The New York Times* reported on a study released by JAMA that found Americans owed more than $140 billion in unpaid medical bills held by collections agencies, up from $81 billion in 2016.[223] As the story points out, this only accounts for debt that has been sold by providers to collection agencies, not all outstanding medical debt. On one hand, this is a fair measure to use, because it's a metric that in one way reflects the level of debt that was unmanageable by borrowers (the assumption being that it was not paid in time to the issuer, thus sold to a collection agency for more aggressive pursuit). Nevertheless, there would be far more debt counted if researchers were able to account for money still owed to providers but not yet sold to collection agencies, or perhaps even worse, medical debt that was covered by other forms of consumer lending, such as credit cards or home equity loans. As Potter points out, the story is ugly in even more ways given that much of this debt is held by those *who have insurance*:

> *Not counted in that total are the medical bills patients are putting on their credit cards and trying to pay off. Undoubtedly, many of those patients will never pay them off. Another crucially important fact the Times story does not mention is that much of Americans' medical debt –maybe more than half of it – is owed not by the uninsured but by people who have health insurance. The Commonwealth Fund's most recent research found that more than 40% of people with individual plans and more than a quarter of people with employer-sponsored coverage are now underinsured and consequently unprepared for a serious diagnosis or accident. An alarming 43.4% of adults between the ages of 19-64 are now inadequately insured.*[224]

No matter how you slice it, healthcare affordability is a growing issue. Medical costs continue to be the number one reason cited by those filing for bankruptcy, with a 2019 study showing two-thirds of all bankruptcies were tied to medical issues.[225] Average worker wages, accounting for inflation, have remained stagnant for nearly four decades (though inflation driven by Covid-19 in 2021 is changing that, though for how long or to what degree is unknown). By definition, healthcare *haves* are those with higher incomes and more wealth, insulating them from the ever-rising tide of healthcare costs. The *have-nots* will continue to experience flat or lower incomes combined with rising medical costs, maybe the number one reason the health gap will continue to widen in the coming decade.

The aging of America

While health disparities are often thought of in terms of race or gender or income, there are also healthcare inequities related to age. And as we all watch the Baby Boomers flow through the healthcare field, this will lend to the growing Disparity Dystopia over the coming decade. In a report released in July 2021, The Advisory Board reiterated how Boomers will jolt healthcare providers. The highlights include:[226]

- By 2030, all Boomers will be eligible for Medicare.
- By 2060, the share of the U.S. population that is eligible for Medicare will increase from 17% to 23%. Over half of this increase will occur by 2030, with over 17 million Baby Boomers added to Medicare in the decade ahead.
- By 2030, eldest baby boomers will start to age into the "old-old" (85 and older) cohort, and more than half of the generation will have passed the "young-old" years (65 to 74 years old). This is a problem because this cohort will be passing out of the ages where surgical solutions make sense, further sapping providers of much needed revenue and margins.

As the report rightly points out, all of this will put the financial squeeze on providers, forcing many to reduce or retract services and access, further widening the health gap for those struggling with costs and access.

Of course, everyone in the industry has been bracing for the Boomers, but in terms of a growing health gap, the issue is even broader. Beyond just the Boomers, the U.S. overall is an aging society, which will have ramifications beyond overflowing ICUs and overwhelmed PCPs. Take for example the fun but oddly scary fact that by 2030, there will be more grandparents than grandchildren in the U.S. Many of our society's core safety net programs, such as Social Security and Medicare, are funded by the wages of younger working generations. When there are more non-working elderly taking from these funds than there are workers contributing, we have a problem. That's a driving factor for why the Congressional Budget Office predicted in 2020 that the Medicare trust fund will run dry in 2024 without an increase in funding, a decrease in benefits, or both.[227] Currently, the Social Security trust fund will run out by 2035.[228] Barring some unforeseen miracle, those depending on Social Security will see a reduction in payouts and possible higher age eligibility, and those needing Medicare will see higher premiums and lower coverage. In both cases, that means those who depend on these government programs the most – the *have nots* – will see lower income combined with higher medical expenses. Combine that with lower than needed retirement savings, and many seniors will be forced to work far past the traditional age of retirement, which in some cases can actually boost their personal health, but in others add stress and increase health risk.

And like at any age and seemingly with everything else, health disparities are worse for older people of color. Older Black people are more likely to get dementia than their white peers.[229] Recent data show higher COVID-19 hospitalizations for Black, Hispanic, and American Indian/Alaska Native Medicare beneficiaries, with rates even higher for people of color who are dually enrolled in Medicare and Medicaid.[230] Long-term care facilities with predominantly Black and Hispanic residents have significantly higher numbers of infections and mortalities compared to facilities with predominantly white residents.[231]

Falling behind with technology

Another factor in the widening health gap is how the *have-nots* struggle to keep up with advancing technology. Covid-19 saw a revolution in the use of virtual care, the ultimate example of how necessity is the mother of invention. But the ability to use virtual care requires the technology – personal computer or smart phone – and the understanding of how to use it. The digital divide is real, and while there are improvements in some areas, many Americans – in particular the poor, rural, communities of color, and the elderly – struggle with the technology most of us take for granted,

According to results from a national Pew Research Center survey released in June 2021, only 24% of adults with incomes of less than $30,000 own a smart phone. Only 41% said they owned a laptop or computer, and 43% said they have home broadband internet service, another requirement of virtual care. Compare that with those earning more than $100,000, 63% of whom said they own a personal computer, a smartphone, a tablet *and* have home broadband.[232] Dr. Erica Taylor, Associate Chief Medical Officer of Diversity, Equity, and Inclusion for the Duke Health physician organization, was an early adopter of virtual care, and sees the benefit of using the platform to reach systemically disadvantaged communities. But she also sees the challenge:

> *Well before Covid, when telehealth was still an emerging innovation, I was one of the first providers to implement virtual visits. I often conducted post-op visits using video. It helps us serve those where physical access is a challenge. We're using telehealth for patient education, not just clinical support. It's a huge asset that was accelerated by Covid-19, but is really driven by technology innovation development. With that, we cannot miss those who aren't tech comfortable, or who don't have access to digital or internet capabilities. The digital divide is real! There are some patients who have to go to the library just to get internet access.*

The concern, of course, is that the increased use of virtual care and other technologies doesn't result in broadening the health cap rather than improving it. As someone who has been immersed in caring for aging and sick parents, I can attest that even when many elderly do have computers or smart phones, that doesn't mean they are proficient in them. (Before my mom passed in the Spring of 2021, my kids would get a kick out of her signing every text message she sent. She also never learned how to reply to an email, always starting a new one to further a conversation.) The continued aging of America and the rapid advancement of technology are two titanic forces pulling in opposite directions.

In Chapter 4, we touched on the biases that are often built into Artificial Intelligence technologies. While AI is a computer-driven platform that leverages data to learn, AI algorithms are programmed by humans, meaning any bias existing in those humans – or in the data used in the platform – may show up in how the AI learns and the insights it produces. For example, a report from Reuters claimed that an AI-driven recruiting tool developed and used by Amazon effectively "taught itself that men were preferable candidates."[233] Media outlet *ProPublica* exposed a substantial racial bias baked into the Correctional Offender Management Profiling for Alternative Sanctions, or COMPAS, platform, which is used by state court systems across the United States to provide guidance on sentencing by estimating the likelihood of recidivism in a convicted criminal. ProPublica found that:

> ...the statistical results the algorithm generates predict that Black defendants pose a higher risk of reoffending than a true representation, while suggesting that white defendants are less likely to reoffend. Black defendants were almost twice as likely to be misclassified with a higher risk of reoffending (45%) in comparison to their white counterparts (23%).[234]

One of the most famous stories of AI bias involves hospitals themselves. A software algorithm developed and sold by Optum and used by hospitals with more than 200 million patients annually was found to systemically discriminate against Black people. In 2019, a study conducted in *Science* magazine showed that Black people were assigned lower risk scores than equally sick White people, and that only 17.7% of patients who were assigned to receive extra care were Black, when researchers determined that an unbiased assessment of the data would have seen that number at 46.5%. One of the outcomes of these biases was that the data showed the care provided to the average Black patient cost an average of $1,800 less per year than the care given to a white person with the same number of chronic health problems.[235]

Smart phones, AI, laptops, virtual care, social media platforms, the Internet of things – all of these make life better and more enjoyable for the majority of Americans. But for those falling on the *have-not* side of the growing health gap, they hold both the promise of better healthcare access and outcomes, but also the potential to fall farther and farther behind.

The biggest health crisis of all – climate change

Adam Brase of Mayo Clinic has one of the coolest jobs around. He's paid to just think about the future and make predictions, predictions that help shape the strategic vision and actions of one of the top health systems in the world. When we talked about what he saw coming over the next decade that would change how consumers engage in healthcare, climate change was near the top of the list.

One of the issues we don't hear about as much related to health and healthcare, but is real, is climate change. It's not really on the radar for most healthcare providers, but we need to care about this, if only for crisis management. For starters, hospitals and health systems are huge generators of carbon emissions. Younger consumers are watching organizations for environmental and political stances, so we need to really pay attention to this. But that's nothing compared to how climate change will have an explicit impact on hospitals and health systems. Consider the local health care crises caused by things like hurricanes, wildfires, or the winter storm in Texas that knocked out power for millions and caused more than 200 reported deaths. What planners aren't accounting for is the increased nature of these weather-related

219

emergencies and the greater repercussions of each, including the introduction of new vector diseases caused by climate change. Five-hundred-year floods now happen every decade.

Just consider this summer, which is only half over as of this writing. June of 2021 was the hottest June on record. Before 2021, Seattle had experienced a grand total of three days with temperatures exceeding 100 degrees, none of them consecutive. In June, the city experienced three *in a row*, including one day that reached 108 degrees. On June 28th, Portland, Oregon saw a high of 116 degrees. Portland Oregon! According to the U.S. Drought Monitor, more than 58 million Americans are currently living in an area affected by drought.[236] An estimated 25 million people rely on water from Lake Mead, which is currently at its lowest level since the reservoir was created in the 1930s, with the threat of the water source becoming a "dead pool" (where water levels are so low they no longer will leave the lake), within two years.[237]

There's no question climate change, whether it's more extreme weather events, drought leading to water shortages in the American West, or rising ocean levels threatening coastal cities, will have ramifications for the healthcare system in the U.S. A 2020 article in *Health Affairs* cites the fact that of 158 hospital evacuations between 2000 and 2017, nearly three-quarters were for climate-sensitive events, and that almost 250 hospitals simultaneously lost power in intentional power outages in California because of wildfire prevention measures. It cited a study that claimed that 10 climate sensitive events in 2012 cost more than $1.5 billion in increased hospital admissions, outpatient and home health care visits, and medication use.[238]

The same article goes on to show, you guessed it, how climate change will have an outsized effect on the *have-nots* of healthcare, stating that the poor and people of color experience the most risk for health issues stemming from the adverse effects of climate change. In just one example, it says, "Black (people) in the U.S. are 52 percent more likely to reside in areas that are prone to heat-related risks, as are non-Hispanic Asian people (32 percent) and Hispanic people (21 percent), compared with non-Hispanic White people."[239]

One of the authors of that 2012 study, Vijay Limaye, a climate and health scientist at the Science Center at the Natural Resources Defense Council, wrote an opinion piece in August 2021 in the *Washington Post* calling for increased consideration of climate change on public health, and claiming even the staggering costs found in the 2012 review didn't adequately capture the impact, and he too calls out the inflated impact of climate change on the have-nots:

> *Many research studies show that climate change is hitting the most vulnerable communities the hardest. Medicaid and Medicare patients shoulder a hugely disproportionate share of climate-sensitive illness costs, according to our research. Nearly 1 in 3 American adults reported difficulty in paying for necessary medical care in a recent survey, and when people delay or avoid medical treatment for existing ailments, they can be even more susceptible to further harm from a rapidly destabilizing climate.*[240]

Another article in the *Washington Post* in June 2020 paints a similar picture. In it, Penn State University meteorologist Gregory Jenkins said climate change was directly connected to racism, because "it dictates who benefits from activities that produce planet-warming gases and who suffers most from the consequences." For example, one study showed that Black people and Hispanic people are exposed to far more air pollution than they produce through actions like driving and using electricity. Compare that to White Americans, who benefit from better air quality than the national average, even though their activities are the source of most pollutants. And finally, another study showed how the most economic harm from climate change over the coming years will disproportionally hit the poorest counties in the U.S., which typically have a far higher population of Black people, Hispanic people, and other communities of color.[241]

Going back to the historically hot summer of 2021 in the western U.S., this description from another *Washington Post* story seems to sum up the intersection of climate change and the *have-nots* of healthcare.

> *Yet as officials assess the staggering toll of recent heat waves — at least 115 deaths in Oregon — they are realizing their social infrastructure is equally in need of repair. Long-standing inequities in housing and health care put the region's poorest residents at greatest risk. Official warnings and government services didn't reach those who most needed the help. Almost every victim of the heat wave died alone. 'The deepest challenge is the intersection of the ecological crisis and the social justice crisis,' said sociologist Eric Klinenberg, an expert on climate disasters. 'If we're not responsible for one another, that's a recipe for mass fatalities.'*[242]

Right before going to press for this book, the Department of Health and Human Services announced that it was opening an office to consider climate change as a public-health issue. An article on the announcement in the *Wall Street Journal* stated that the goal of the office was to "address what the White House says are health risks, including those that disproportionately affect poor and minority communities," and, in a quote from Health and Humans Services Secretary Xavier Becerra:

> *Its mission is to protect the health of people experiencing a disproportionate share of climate impacts and health inequities from wildfires to drought, to hurricanes and floods.*[243]

The decade ahead – a dark picture

Increasing healthcare costs and the affordability crisis. The aging of America. The digital divide. Climate change. These are four of the primary reasons why those who suffer the most in the U.S health system from disparities and inequities will likely see their situations worsen over the coming decade. There are of course plenty of other reasons, such as the fact that major health issues gripping the U.S. – obesity, mental health, the opioid crisis, etc. – all disproportionally affect people of color, the poor, and the elderly. Or that while millions have marched for social justice in the year following the murder of George Floyd and other horrific racial incidents, real progress in the areas of police reform, or educational reform, or state and national policy, have been incremental at best.

As always seems to happen, whenever there is some advancement made in racial issues, there is a subsequent backlash and reversion among many, which will make true progress difficult in the coming decade. Right now, roughly 70% of Black Americans say that the U.S. health care system treats people unfairly based on their race or ethnic background very often or somewhat often, compared to 41% of White adults and 43% of Hispanic adults.[244] A survey released in the fall of 2020 showed that less than half of those surveyed, 45%, felt social justice protests would lead to meaningful change, while 48% believed they would not.

Or consider the growing crisis in rural healthcare. Or the fact that the U.S. is twentieth out of the top 20 industrialized nations in child mortality. It's worth repeating: the health gap has been bad for decades, it was made worse by Covid-19, and it looks to only grow in the coming decade. Are there any signs of hope?

There are many organizations that prioritize studying and trying to repair the health gap in the U.S. For the federal government, that includes everything from the Health Resources and Services Administration, the Centers for Medicare & Medicaid Services, and The Agency for Healthcare Research and Quality, to the National Institutes of Health, VHA, and CDC. Most states have at least one department and/or initiative focused on health disparities, as do many counties and cities. Most of the national healthcare associations call improving health disparities a top priority, including the American Hospital Association (AHA), the American Medical Association (AMA), the American Nurses Association (ANA), the Association for Health Insurance Plans (AHIP), and many others. There are hundreds of non-profits, charities, foundations, and non-government organizations dedicated fully or in part to addressing the health gap. And the vast majority of hospitals, health systems, and other providers claim to make solving health disparities a priority.

So there's no lack of effort on the part of governmental, corporate, and private organizations to address the seemingly endless array of issues tied to the health gap. But that has been the case for at least the last two decades, and in some instances, for far longer than that. Yet again, not only has progress been incremental at best, Covid-19 has made things worse. Consider the reluctance of hospitals to really take responsibility for health issues beyond their walls, as called out by Dr. Ryu in Chapter Seven.

Of course *some* health systems *are* taking dramatic steps in this area, such as investing in public housing, community health programs, or other areas where social determinants of health are a factor. One interesting example is how more and more health systems are trying to tackle gun violence in their communities. The strategy is similar to that leveraged by healthcare organizations during Covid-19. Many invested heavily in public health communications around hand-washing, social distancing, mask wearing, and vaccine adherence, even though theoretically that's the job of public health institutions. But leaders realized if they wanted to slow the flood of Covid-19 patients ending up on vents in their ICUs, they could play a role upstream in helping prevent the spread of the virus. The same logic applies to gun violence. Dr. Ryu believes that, as with other aspects of the health gap, hospitals and health systems can play a greater role.

> *Reasonable people will disagree on this topic, but gun violence needs to be addressed as a public health issue. For emergency room doctors, gun violence and trauma are public health issues. It's not a stand-alone event, and data shows that it's just like a chronic disease. Sometimes it is a one-time senseless event, but many other times it's a dynamic in the community. Hospitals and health systems have a role to play in this. It's a prevention issue, just like Covid or diabetes or food insecurity. And playing a role in public health issues isn't new for us. Healthcare professionals were part of the early mobilizers behind seat belts and car seats. The top advocates were pediatricians – they see the outcome in the hospital if we don't prevent*

*these issues. Gun violence, smoking, car accidents — it's
basic health 101, and we should be involved.*

Dr. Erica Taylor, Associate Chief Medical Officer of Diversity,
Equity, and Inclusion for the Duke Health physician organization, and
the first Black female orthopedic surgeon at Duke Health:

> *Health disparities, social justice, microaggressions,
> unconscious bias. For the next 5-10 years – how do you
> analyze information and act on it? Currently there is
> a lack of education in the healthcare community on
> how to make sense of the demographic data we have on
> patient outcomes and experiences, and then utilize it
> appropriately to make thoughtful change. The hope is
> that we see diversity through the lens of their experiences.
> It's our number one social responsibility. We've too often
> just stayed in our own sectors as caregivers – 'If it's
> not healthcare then it doesn't have to do with me.' Not
> anymore. We will see a greater call for accountability
> and change from consumers and other organizations.
> Hopefully, DEI will stop being a separate initiative,
> but instead become integrated in everything we do. All
> initiatives, all departments, all processes.*

What about moving to a new model, such as Medicare-for-all,
or a government-run health system like the National Health Service
in England? Jarrett Lewis, partner at Public Opinion Strategies, and
a researcher and pollster focused primarily on healthcare, says that
the majority of Americans believe that the federal government should
serve as a backstop for healthcare coverage. Yet the majority also
believes insurance should be provided by private payors rather than
the government. That means the political leverage for something like
Medicare-for-all is likely still a ways off.

But even a single-payor solution, or a fully government-run system,
is not a guarantee of a full solution for health disparities. Nate Kaufman,
managing director at his healthcare consultancy Kaufman Strategic

Advisors, a long-time healthcare executive, and outspoken critic of our current health system, points to the fact that in their current state, Medicare and Medicaid do not provide enough reimbursement to cover the costs of providing care. This has been the number one factor driving independent physicians to shutter their private practices and join larger systems, he says.

> *Right now, roughly 65-70% of revenue for health providers comes from government-sponsored programs like Medicare and Medicaid. Because current reimbursement levels from that payor don't cover current costs, access and quality will continue to be hampered. Something has to give. We can't expect an expansion of Medicare to drive the necessary change – so many more physicians will resist or drop out.*

Kyle Rolfing calls out how attempts to solve for disparities through extensive social programs have often had the oppositive effect.

> *It's so interesting, the more we try to make things the same and equitable across the board for people, the more we actually bifurcate delivery of what we're dealing with. Take a look at nationalized medicine in Canada or European countries – there's a whole different market for those who can afford more. Look at private education as another example. It creates a greater divide. Equity can often lend to forced bifurcation based on what you can afford, so it can be a good and a bad thing. Bifurcation goes against equity, which was the intended goal in the first place.*

The truth is, we're a long way from any kind of Medicare-for-all solution in the U.S. It's definitely possible we could see legislation that moves us closer to this, or at least to a public-option, by 2030. But again, even if we did, that would probably not solve for the health gap on its own. In the end, it may take more than programs and initiatives, more than hospitals and health systems focusing on the issue, more than changes in the U.S. health system itself, to truly alter the health gap. Here's Scott Weber, Chief Marketing and Design Officer at M Health Fairview:

> *Polarization between the haves and have nots will get worse. This country is at a real reckoning point around values. What we have a right to versus privilege and entitlement. I have no idea how this will be resolved, but the next five years could have a material influence on the future in this regard.*

The point is that the ultimate solution to the devastating health gap in this country likely lies less with the programs and actions we take, and more with the mindset and values of the country as a whole. Given where this country has been, and where it is today, there's every reason to question whether we as a nation can make the fundamental changes necessary to change our mindset about our collective health and the gaps that exist. I'll leave the final words to Marco Bevolo, a long-lost relative (maybe sixth cousin first removed?) who is a futurist, designer, lecturer, and researcher, with a degree in humanities, and a PhD in social and behavioral sciences. Among other positions, Marco was one of the strategic design leaders at Philips for a decade, and is currently Principal at his own consultancy, Marco Bevolo Consulting. He's a globally respected author and speaker currently living in Eindhoven, Netherlands, and has studied (and experienced) the health system of a number of European countries, including Italy and the Netherlands, as well as the health system in Japan thanks to his wife, who is from there. He said he admires what the ACA set out to do, and he enjoys the level of care he receives in the Netherlands through a unique mix of "universal healthcare rights" for all citizens, enabled by the private insurance sector. That said, from his experience, the solution to the health gap in a country like the U.S. will depend primarily on who we want to be as a country.

Healthcare is to a large extent a cultural notion. For example, most experts would say we have learned from the Covid-19 pandemic that the marketplace does not work if there is only the market to take care of vaccinations, or regulations, or solving for care. It's a huge learning of the pandemic. The Trump administration tried as much as possible to ignore the pandemic, to keep the economy going. But at a certain point, the pandemic doesn't conform to that. I understand there are many in the U.S. who don't want the government to interfere in their private lives, but we can see how Covid-19 was more difficult to manage without universal care.

Chapter 9

Conclusion

When we first set out to explore how the next decade might unfold in healthcare, we tried to wipe our mental slate clean and let the data, insights, and opinions lead us wherever they needed to go. Oh, we had preconceived ideas about what our world might look like in 2030, and those absolutely influenced our thinking as we went through the process of developing and assessing concepts and themes. After all, collectively, we knew a little something about this industry, which trends were most important today, and what new trends might emerge. But we explicitly designed our process to not jump to any conclusions, or establish any predictions at the outset that we would then backfill and rationalize to substantiate.

A great example of this is the second prediction – Constricted Consumerism. I've spent most of my career consulting healthcare organizations that they had better get with consumerism or expect to be left behind. And certainly, there are aspects of that advocation that still hold true. But now, I'm a little more skeptical. Now, I see a bigger, broader picture of all the ways healthcare consumers are twisted and turned, halted and delayed, funneled and ushered – often to their own detriment. Had I have followed my instincts prior to doing this deep dive, I might have doubled-down on the import and influence of consumerism. Now, the "promise" of consumerism is stained and constrained for me, and I will be ever more wary on both a personal and professional level.

While it was completely unintended, it's worth noting the way the predictions become darker as we move through them. While I wield pessimism like a shield at a micro-level to help get me through the day, I am at heart an optimist, thinking in general that everything will eventually work out. While I've spent my career in healthcare shouting and cajoling and pontificating about the dramatic need to, finally, dammit, change already, I've always levelled that demand through the lens of opportunity. If I had a personal mantra, it was Critical Cheerleading. We're so far behind! Wake up! We must change! Because the promise is so, so great. And we can do it!

Looking back now on these five predictions, there is definitely a thread of doomsaying as we move forward through them. We start with the wonder of the Apple Watch and consumer empowerment and end with a deeper political divisiveness and continued societal struggles helping those who most need it. Is this just a coincidence? Or is there something deeper going on? Maybe an overall darkening of outlook brought on by a devasting 18 months as a country, coupled with my own personal loss of a parent just two months ago as I write this. In consideration, I actually think (and hope) it's neither, but rather a clear-eyed take on the world around us. And if that perspective is increasingly negative, well then, that's a fair evaluation of the facts as they are presented. It's certainly possible, then, that were one to read just the five predictions themselves, one might also walk away feeling despondence and despair. But recall our purpose for taking this project on in the first place, from Chapter One:

> Our goal in publishing the five predictions you'll find here is not to be right as much as it is to spark conversation. Because the truth is, in all five cases, the trends we're predicting are already under way. In some cases that may be a good thing, in others, clearly not a good thing. But by sparking conversation now, maybe there are those who read these predictions who will set out to either ensure they do happen as articulated, or who will fight like mad

to prevent them. Either way, having the conversation now about how consumers and healthcare will change in 10 years will, at a minimum, better prepare all of us in the healthcare industry for what may come. And given some of the predictions, that is a very important goal indeed.

In other words, the first step in solving a problem is admitting you have one. Regardless of the level of angst or helplessness these predictions may invoke, the issues are the issues. Affordability, disparities, political division, shrinking consumerism, climate change – it does no good to ignore these or minimize them in some way. If we want to improve our health system, improve the health of Americans, and build a better world, it starts with putting all cards on the table.

It's with that spirit that we encourage you to take this book and employ it in improving your life, improving your organization, improving the industry, or improving the world. These are our predictions, and no matter how much research we did or how many experts we consulted with, they may be right, or they may be wrong. In all likelihood, they will fall somewhere in between, on a spectrum from "pure garbage" to "nailed it." But no matter where they fall, they should spark thought, conversation, and maybe, action.

Start a book club with the peers in your department or organization and discuss your takeaways. Which predictions hit home? Which missed the mark? Why, and why are your opinions different from those of your co-worker or colleague? How far afield are the predictions from that of your own organization's outlook? How might the contents of the book change that outlook?

Start your own prediction market. Place odds on the predictions and take bets. The odds that we'll see half the AMC's shrink in size and end up as smaller, less powerful downstream vendors of high acuity care? Let's call it 15:1. Or maybe you think it's pure bullshit and give odds of 50:1. Set a deadline (December 31, 2030, seems like a good one) and track the odds. Does that 50:1 drop to 25:1 when the first AMC goes bankrupt? Or maybe it jumps to 100:1 when Amazon announces it's giving up on healthcare altogether. Crowdsource the odds, letting those with deeper and varied expertise shape the market. I can tell you one thing, if your health system CFO puts all his money on the 50:1 odds that a certain former president will start his own chain of clinics, she may know something you don't.

Argue. Agree. Debate. Dispel. Disprove. Pile on. Expand. As soon as this book is published and out of our hands, these ideas are yours to do whatever you want to with. For us, there's no going back. Sure, we may come to change our minds on these predictions, and someday laugh about how far off we were. But if the end result is a reader saying "hmph," and placing the book on her shelf, then we have failed. Our hope is that by calling attention to the potential outcomes predicted in this book, those who hope to impact them can leverage our thinking to their benefit.

It's extraordinarily humbling to put your opinions on the table for all the world to see and critique. What if we missed something obvious? What if we misinterpreted a key piece of data? What if we're just wildly off in our thinking? But we are willing to take that risk, because the issues at hand are too big to ignore. We've done our best to understand the potential future in serious and provocative ways, and we're comfortable with whatever may come from our thoughts. The question is now, what risks are you willing to take?

APPENDIX

Interviewee Biographies

Marco Bevolo
Researcher and Lecturer
Breda University

Dr. Marco Bevolo, PhD, is currently Adjunct Professor of "Design Futures" at World University of Design, India, and a Researcher and Lecturer at Breda University of Applied Sciences, The Netherlands, in international leisure management and sciences. He earned his PhD on the role of design in generating urban futures at the Graduate School, Faculty of Behavioral and Social Sciences, Tilburg University. In 1999-2009, he was a Director at Philips Design headquarters in the Netherlands. He led programs in cultural trends, in brand design, and in advanced business development. He directed foresight and strategic design projects for Philips Medical Systems, Philips Semiconductors (now NXP and Nexperia), and joint ventures with SHL Telemedicine, AEG Licht, and more. He is the founder of Marco Bevolo Consulting, working in foresight, futures research, and strategic design for selected customers in Europe and Asia, including FIAT Chrysler Automobiles (now Stellantis); Chamber of Commerce of Turin, Italy; Municipality of Eindhoven, The Netherlands; Lighting Design Collective, Helsinki / Madrid; 515/BBB, Turin / Berlin, and more. In this extracurricular capacity, in the lustrum 2010-2016 he has been the Principal Researcher on Urban Futures for Philips Lighting, now Signify, in EMEA and Poland. He has contributed to seminars and events with the School of Design, Politecnico di Milano, Italy; Emerson College, Boston; the UNAM Post-graduate School of Architecture, Mexico City; Domus Academy, Milan; IED, Milan; and more. He has been 2019 Visiting Scholar at Vancouver Island University, Canada. He had his research published on: Journal of Consumer Marketing; Research in Hospitality Management; Journal of Tourism Futures; World Futures Review; Place Branding and Public Diplomacy, and more. He printed books with Palgrave; Gower, then Taylor & Francis; EMAP Books; and more. He is the recipient of an Emerald Literati Award and of two ESOMAR Best Conference Paper. He lives and works in The Netherlands, in Japan, and in Turin, Italy.

Adam Brase
Executive Director, Strategic Intelligence
Strategy Department
Mayo Clinic

Adam Brase is the Executive Director of Strategic Intelligence at Mayo Clinic. He leads a team of analysts and researchers who assess the external environment, market conditions and consumer attitudes and behaviors to identify trends, threats, and opportunities that impact Mayo Clinic strategies. He's extensively involved in Mayo Clinic's strategic planning efforts and was one of the key authors of Mayo Clinic's 2030 strategy. Prior to his current role, he served as the senior marketing executive for Mayo Clinic and held various other senior leadership roles in Public Affairs during his 20-year Mayo Clinic career. In addition to strategic intelligence and strategy development, Adam has extensive experience in marketing and advertising, internal and media communications, community engagement, voice of the consumer and brand management. He's been awarded Mayo Clinic's excellence in leadership and excellence in teamwork awards. Before coming to Mayo Clinic, Adam was the Director of Communications at Rochester Public Schools, Minnesota's 4th largest school district. As a meteorologist at KTTC-TV in Rochester, Minnesota, he developed and delivered daily weather forecasts. His career experiences also include work at the Federal Emergency Management Agency and the University of North Dakota. Lessons from each of these experiences have helped him to become a trusted advisor and leader. Adam holds a Master's in Business Administration and additional degrees in Communications and Meteorology. He serves as an elder at Christ Community Church in addition to serving on other community boards. His family also serves as licensed foster parents for infants awaiting adoption.

Yumin Choi
Healthcare Team Lead
Bain Capital Ventures

Yumin joined Bain Capital Ventures in 2017 and leads our healthcare team. He is based in Boston and invests across venture and growth stages. Yumin was previously General Partner at HLM Venture Partners, a healthcare-focused venture fund. Yumin spent 10 years at HLM, where he led a variety of investments across healthcare IT and services sectors. He served as board director for AbleTo, mPulse Mobile, Oceans Healthcare, Payspan (acquired by Primus Capital), Spinal Kinetics, and Vets First Choice. He was also board observer for Imagine Health, Nordic Consulting (acquired by Silversmith Capital Partners), Persivia, and TYRX (acquired by Medtronic). Yumin serves on the Board of Trustees for Newton-Wellesley Hospital and Mass. Eye and Ear. He is on the New England Venture Capital Association's Board of Directors and was previously chair of New England Venture Network. He is also on the Board of Advisors for the Boston Symphony Orchestra. Yumin served as a lecturer in the Gordon Institute at Tufts University where he taught entrepreneurial finance. Yumin was born in Seoul, South Korea and moved to Hawaii at the age of 10, where he attended Punahou School. Outside of work he enjoys golfing, fly fishing, and bird hunting, and can be found listening to his vinyl record collection. Yumin received his BS in Entrepreneurship and Finance at Babson College.

Danny Fell
Marketing Consultant and Senior Strategist
Optum

Danny Fell has over thirty years of healthcare marketing and advertising experience working with some of the largest healthcare brands in the country. Nationally recognized for his writing and speaking on topics ranging from healthcare ratings and rankings to digital healthcare strategies, Danny has written articles appearing in *HealthLeaders, Modern Healthcare, Strategic Health Care Marketing* and *The Journal of Healthcare Management* among others. He is the co-author of *A Marketer's Guide to Market Research* and a member of the editorial advisory board of eHealthcare Strategy and Trends. In addition, Danny has served on the board of the American Hospital Association's Society for Healthcare Strategy and Market Development, and as president of the Tennessee Society for Healthcare Marketing and Public Relations, and is an active member of the American Marketing Association and the American College of Healthcare Executives. In 2012, Danny was honored as the very first recipient of the John A. Eudes Vision & Excellence Award for his contributions to digital innovation and thought-leadership within the healthcare industry. Danny currently works with health systems across the country as a senior strategist with Optum where he focuses on consumer engagement, predictive modeling, and digital transformation.

David Goldhill
Co-founder, CEO
Sesame

Through his writing and advocacy, David is a leading national voice for market-based health care reform. Prior to founding Sesame, David served as

President and CEO of the Game Show Network, President of TV at Universal Studios, Founder and CEO of INTH, and CFO of Act III Communications. He is the author of the *Atlantic* cover story "How American Healthcare Killed My Father" and the follow-up book, *Catastrophic Care: Why Everything We Think We Know about Health Care Is Wrong*. David is chair of The Leapfrog Group, the nation's leading advocate for health care transparency.

Matt Gove
Chief Marketing Officer
Summit Health

Matt Gove is Chief Marketing Officer for Summit Health, a first-of-its-kind merger bringing together New York's largest urgent care provider (CityMD) with one of the largest independent physician practices in the country (Summit Medical Group). In this role, Matt oversees brand, marketing, and communications for the combined organization, driving revenue through customer acquisition and retention, physician-centric marketing, and helping the organization design and implement a modern digital patient experience. Matt joined Summit Health in September 2019 and is based in New York. Prior to joining Summit Health, Matt served as Chief Consumer Officer for Atlanta-based Piedmont Healthcare, where he was responsible for marketing, patient/consumer experience, communications, community benefit and government relations for Georgia's largest health system. Under Matt's leadership, the Piedmont team established a reputation as a national leader in consumer-centric marketing and digital experience design, winning more than 100 local and national marketing awards, and he was individually recognized as AMA/Atlanta Corporate Marketer of the Year and American Business Awards Marketing Executive of the Year. Earlier, Matt was a core member of the executive team that engineered an $80 million operational turnaround and raised more than $300 million for capital improvements at Grady Health System, helping revive the critical safety net institution. As Grady's Senior Vice President of Marketing and External Affairs, he helped reposition the Atlanta institution, establishing a new look and feel and reconnecting Grady to business, media, and community stakeholders. A commercial real estate refugee, Matt also served as Senior Vice President of Marketing and Communications with Atlanta's Cousins Properties, a national publicly-traded real estate developer. Earlier in his career, he launched a monthly commercial real estate magazine, covered the real estate industry for the *Atlanta Business Chronicle* and covered health care for the *Virgin Islands Daily News*. Matt holds a bachelor's degree in Psychology from Georgia State University and served on the university's Marketing Roundtable.

Bryan Hamilton
AVP – Marketing & Communications
Cincinnati Children's Hospital Medical Center

Bryan Hamilton transitioned from an 18-year career as a Global Brand Director at The Procter & Gamble Company to Assistant Vice President Marketing and Communications at Cincinnati Children's Hospital Medical Center in October 2017. At Cincinnati Children's, Bryan leads the strategic-thinking, integrated planning, communications, and creative execution across Service Lines, Creative Services, and Digital to enable the delivery of CCHMC's Strategic Plan and Growth Opportunities. Bryan's experience as a brand builder across diverse consumer targets provides great frameworks and insights in the development and implementation of innovative strategies and execution. Bryan has served on a number of non-profit boards, including Every Child Succeeds (First Vice-Chair); Co-Founder and Vice President of the Kilgour Foundation (Cincinnati Public School); P&G United Way Campaign Director; Advisory Board Member at Cincinnati State; and Deacon and New Ministries Leader at Knox Presbyterian Church.

Nate Kaufman
Managing Director
Kaufman Strategic Advisors, LLC.

Nathan Kaufman is Managing Director of Kaufman Strategic Advisors. With more than 40 years of experience as a strategist, executive and negotiator, he is considered one of the nation's healthcare industry experts. He is a strategic advisor to healthcare executives, boards, physician groups, and other healthcare companies. He is known for his practical advice focusing on succeeding in the new post-COVID, value-based risk environment. In addition, he is a seasoned negotiator and has successfully completed hundreds of transactions involving payor contracts, physician compensation, service line development, acquisition/ sale of surgicenters and imaging centers, restructuring employed physician groups, and developing clinically integrated networks. This provides Nate with a unique viewpoint since he not only studies industry trends but operates in the 'trenches,' which gives him a deep understanding of healthcare delivery. Nate is frequently a keynote speaker and facilitates board and management retreats. Given his vast experience with health systems, he will challenge the industry's conventional wisdom when he believes that it is not supported by evidence and/or it will not provide desired results. While his clients may not always agree with his perspective, they appreciate that Nate challenges them so that they will consider different points of view. Nate knows that health systems require realistic strategies (both short term and long term) that are financially feasible and will be supported by the majority of their practicing physicians. Nate is a noted author contributing more than 76 articles to healthcare literature. His education credentials include an MS in Health Systems from the Georgia Institute of Technology and a BS in Psychology from Emory University. Listed in Modern Healthcare's Class of 1987 Up & Comers of Rising Young Healthcare Management Talent.

Wright Lassiter III
President and CEO
Henry Ford Health System

Wright L. Lassiter III is the President and CEO of Henry Ford Health System, overseeing the $6.6 billion integrated health system comprised of five acute care hospitals, two destination centers for cancer care, orthopedics, and sports medicine, three behavioral health facilities, a regional health plan, and a wide range of ambulatory, retail, and other health services consisting of more than 250 locations across Michigan and more than 33,000 employees. Lassiter joined Henry Ford in December 2014 as President and assumed the role of President & CEO in 2016. Since his arrival, he led the Board and senior management through a comprehensive strategic planning effort to position Henry Ford for the future. Under his leadership, Henry Ford has completed two successful mergers, expanding its geographic footprint, and generating an additional $1 billion in revenue. Additionally, the Henry Ford brand has expanded globally under his leadership with the 2020 opening of partner hospitals in Saudi Arabia and India. The System has significantly increased its quality and financial performance, earning top honors in several publicly reported quality programs, and receiving both outlook and ratings upgrades from Moody's and S&P services. With a major focus on collaboration, the System has inked major partnerships with a host of organizations, including the Detroit Pistons, Michigan State University, General Motors, Syapse, Acadia Healthcare, Presbyterian Villages of Michigan, and Beckman Coulter. A seasoned health care executive, Lassiter has 30 years of experience working in large, complex health systems, including Dallas Methodist Health System and JPS Health Network in Fort Worth, Texas. Prior to joining Henry Ford, Lassiter was CEO of Alameda Health System in Oakland, California, where he was credited with leading the expansion and turnaround of the $865 million public health system. In 2021, Lassiter received the *Crain's* Detroit Business Health Care Heroes – Corporate Achievement Award. Cited for his commitment to finding solution, he was named "Michiganian of the Year" in 2020 by *The Detroit News*, as well as appearing in the 2020 "Top 10 Newsmakers" list by *Crain's Detroit Business* for the second time in three years. His other accolades include multiple year recognitions as "100 Most Influential People in Healthcare" by Modern Healthcare; "Top 25 Minority Healthcare Executives in U.S. Healthcare" by Modern Healthcare; "Top Blacks in U.S. Healthcare" by the Johns Hopkins Center for Health Disparities Solutions; and "20 People Who Make Healthcare Better in the U.S" by *HealthLeaders Magazine*. In 2011, *Fast Company* prominently featured Lassiter's work to rebuild Alameda Health. In addition to health industry recognition, Lassiter has received the Industry Award (2019) from Results Mentoring, the Corporate Leadership Award (2018) from National Medical Fellowships, and The Legacy Award (2014) from the Jobs and Housing Coalition. An avid community leader and advocate, Lassiter is the 2021 chair-elect for the American Hospital Association (AHA) Board of Trustees and will assume the AHA chair role in 2022, becoming the top-elected official of the national organization representing America's hospitals and health systems. Other non-profit board service includes Detroit Regional Chamber (Board Chair), Detroit Children's Fund, LeMoyne College, Invest Detroit, Motown Museum and Downtown Detroit Partnership. Additionally, Lassiter's board expertise is shared with several corporate interests, including serving on the Board of Directors of the Federal Reserve Bank of Chicago, Quest Diagnostics (NYSE: DGX) and DT Midstream, Inc. He serves as an advisor to Arsenal Capital Partners. Lassiter received his master's degree in Healthcare Administration from Indiana University where he graduated number one in his class and completed his bachelor's degree with honors in Chemistry from LeMoyne College.

Jarrett Lewis
Partner
Public Opinion Strategies

Jarrett Lewis is a Partner at Public Opinion Strategies, a national political and public affairs research firm, whose clients include leading political figures, *Fortune* 500 companies, and major associations. The firm is also part of the bi-partisan research team that conducts the *NBC News/Wall Street Journal* poll. Jarrett's work is heavily rooted in the healthcare industry and he has extensive experience conducting survey research and providing advisory services for large health systems and healthcare companies. Jarrett was previously Executive Director of Health Policy at The Health Management Academy, a network of executive leaders from the 100-largest hospital systems across the U.S. In that role, he advised C-Suite hospital system executives on federal policy initiatives and strategy. He also created and led a business unit offering advisory services to health system executives using proprietary survey research data in areas of business development, marketing, budgeting, and health policy. Additionally, he directed a quarterly healthcare survey of 1,500 consumers, sponsored and published by the Royal Bank of Canada (RBC). He regularly speaks to health system and healthcare company boards of directors and leadership teams on the topics of health policy and consumerism in healthcare. Jarrett began his career at Public Opinion Strategies, providing survey research analysis to federal and state campaigns during the 2008 election cycle. He worked for Public Opinion Strategies again during the 2012 election cycle, serving as a strategist and pollster to the Romney for President Campaign from 2011-2012. In that role, Jarrett provided in-depth analysis of internal survey research data to senior campaign officials, including over 300 surveys and 150 focus groups. Jarrett is a RIVA-trained focus group moderator and has moderated or managed over 250 focus groups in his career. He has an MBA from the Fuqua School of Business at Duke University and a BA in Political Science from Clemson University, where he was a member of the men's varsity soccer team.

Kevan Mabbutt
Senior Vice President and Chief Consumer Officer
Intermountain Healthcare

Kevan Mabbutt is the Senior Vice President and Chief Consumer Officer of Intermountain Healthcare. He began serving in this position in August 2017. Mr. Mabbutt brings more than 25 years of consumer-focused experience to this role. As a member of Intermountain's executive leadership team, Mr. Mabbutt is responsible for bringing consumer (patients, members, caregivers, and community) perspectives to the forefront of healthcare design and delivery. He leads Intermountain's efforts to identify what consumers need and expect from healthcare, and to evolve the organization's capability to create and deliver consistent, consumer-centric, digitally-enabled experiences for them. This includes leading the development and rollout of My Health+, Intermountain's digital front door, which empowers patients and members to find, manage, and pay for care in a convenient and seamless way. Mr. Mabbutt also leads Intermountain's marketing, brand, and communications function. Mr. Mabbutt was previously at The Walt Disney Company, based in Los Angeles, where he served as the Global Head of Consumer Insight. He led consumer experience development and transformation for Disney's theme park, cruise line, resort, retail, and digital businesses in the U.S., Europe, and Asia. He was instrumental in defining the guest experience at Disney's first theme park in mainland China (Shanghai Disney Resort) and driving the digital transformation of Walt Disney World in Florida (My Disney Experience portal and Magic Bands). He also helped expand the Disney, Pixar, Marvel, and Star Wars brands globally. Prior to Disney, Mr. Mabbutt held global marketing and strategy leadership roles at Discovery Channel and the BBC and served as a consultant to media companies in the Middle East, Asia, and Europe. He was also a member of Deloitte's consumer practice. In that role, he developed strategies to attract, retain, and satisfy customers in the banking, transportation, and retail sectors. Mr. Mabbutt was born in London, grew up in Africa, and received both his bachelor's and master's degrees from Cambridge University in England.

Sandra Mackey
Chief Marketing Officer
Bon Secours Mercy Health

Sandra Mackey is the chief marketing officer (CMO) of Bon Secours Mercy Health, one of the nation's largest Catholic health systems with 60,000 associates, 50 hospitals and more than 1,200 points of care spanning seven states and two countries. With annual revenues of more than $10 billion, Bon Secours Mercy Health remains true to its mission and contributes more than $2 million a day to benefit the communities it serves. As CMO, she is responsible for marketing, communications, digital, brand and creative strategy to support health care delivery across the ministry. Before joining Mercy Health in 2017 as chief marketing officer, Mackey served as senior vice president of marketing and communications for The Arthritis Foundation, where she was responsible for national strategic marketing initiatives. Previously, Mackey was the executive director of market strategy for Emory Healthcare in Atlanta, where she led a team to support service line and strategic growth initiatives, established a digital marketing platform, and launched a comprehensive brand strategy. Mackey was named 2018 Chief Marketing Officer of the Year by the *Cincinnati Business Courier*. She is a graduate of the Woodruff Leadership Academy and holds a bachelor's degree in nursing from Birmingham University in England. She serves on the board of directors for Conduit Health Partners, Mercy Neighborhood Ministries, and is the Chair of the FC Cincinnati Foundation board.

Paul Matsen
Chief Marketing and Communications Officer
Cleveland Clinic

Paul Matsen joined Cleveland Clinic in 2006. He is responsible for all marketing and communications programs at Cleveland Clinic including global development of the brand, marketing of all U.S. and international locations, and digital marketing. Mr. Matsen also leads Cleveland Clinic's Corporate Communications department. During Mr. Matsen's tenure, the Cleveland Clinic has grown to be one of the most recognized and respected healthcare brands in the world. Under his leadership, Cleveland Clinic has been an innovator in digital and content marketing including the industry-leading ClevelandClinic.org website, social media, mobile apps, and search engine marketing programs. Prior to joining Cleveland Clinic, Mr. Matsen was most recently the Chief Marketing Officer at Delta Airlines. He began his career in New York, working at a number of leading advertising agencies. He is a graduate of Rutgers University, N.J. Paul is an active member of the Cleveland Community and has served as a member of the Board of Directors of the United Way of Greater Cleveland, Destination Cleveland, and Hathaway Brown School. Founded in 1921, Cleveland Clinic is a nonprofit, multidisciplinary care team that cares for patients through 19 patient-centered institutes, caring for 2.45M patients annually with 8.7M outpatient visits in locations around the globe. A 5,996–bed healthcare system with a main campus in Cleveland, it operates 18 hospitals and over 220 outpatient locations, five hospitals in southeast Florida with more than 1,000 beds, a medical center for brain health in Las Vegas, a sports and executive health center in Toronto, and a 394-bed hospital in Abu Dhabi. Cleveland Clinic London will open its 184-bed hospital in 2022. Cleveland Clinic continues to be a national leader among *U.S. News & World Report*'s best hospitals. The Cleveland Clinic heart and heart surgery program has been ranked #1 in the nation since 1995.

Russ Meyer
Brand Strategist
CVS Health

20+ years experience in brand consulting, marketing, and advertising. I specialize in solving complex global brand strategies for companies and organizations in just about every industry. I also have a passion for creating and leading high performing collaborative teams. I like working in industries in transformation, particularly those undergoing consumerization such as healthcare, technology, and energy. I have a passion for helping brands define their purpose and embrace sustainability. A creative strategist at heart who uses both his left and right brain, my specialties include brand strategy, corporate branding, sustainability, social media.

Wendell Potter
Consultant, Author, Former health insurance executive

Wendell Potter is a former health insurance executive, *New York Times* bestselling author, healthcare and campaign finance reform advocate, and authority on corporate and special interest propaganda. He leads two health care reform advocacy nonprofits: the Center for Health and Democracy and Business Leaders for Health Care Transformation, and is the founder of Tarbell.org, a nonprofit journalism organization that investigates corporate and political corruption. An accomplished public speaker and writer, Wendell has spoken at hundreds of public forums and has written for *The New York Times, The Washington Post, USA Today, Los Angeles Times, Chicago Tribune, The Guardian, Newsweek, The Nation, American Journal of Public Health,* the *British Medical Journal,* and many other publications. He also is a frequent guest on CNN, MSNBC, and other national and international news outlets, and has a robust social media following (Twitter: @wendellpotter). In addition, he has testified before several U.S. Senate, House, and state legislative panels on how health insurance companies, in their quest to meet Wall Street profit expectations, contribute not only to the rising number of uninsured and underinsured Americans but also to unsustainable medical costs. Wendell's books include *Deadly Spin: An Insurance Company Insider Speaks Out On How Corporate PR Is Killing Health Care And Deceiving Americans; Obamacare: What's In It For Me — What Everyone Needs To Know About The Affordable Care Act;* and *Nation On The Take, How Big Money Corrupts Our Democracy and What We Can Do About It* (all published by Bloomsbury). His latest book, *For Want of a Dentist: The Rise of the Dental Therapy Movement in Tribal Nations and the U.S.,* will be published by the W.K. Kellogg Foundation in late 2021.

Kyle Rolfing

Kyle is a successful serial entrepreneur and business builder. Kyle's most recent exit, Bright Healthcare, is one of the most spectacular healthcare success stories of the last decade and is Minnesota's all-time largest IPO - resulting in an initial enterprise value of over $10 billion. In addition to Bright, Kyle was a founder and CEO of RedBrick Health, Definity Health, and has served as an investor, board of directors member, and mentor to numerous other successful Minnesota companies including Zipnosis, Wellbeats, Learn to Live, among others. Kyle is currently launching a venture capital fund, TrueNorth Health Ventures, to focus on early-stage companies in Minnesota and the upper Midwest.

Dr. Jaewon Ryu
President and CEO
Geisinger

Jaewon Ryu, MD, JD, is the President and CEO of Geisinger, an integrated delivery system with clinical enterprise, health plan, the Geisinger Commonwealth School of Medicine, and research and innovation functions operating in central and northeastern Pennsylvania. He joined the organization originally as the Executive Vice President and Chief Medical Officer in 2016.

Dr. Ryu came to Geisinger from Humana, where he was the President of Integrated Care Delivery and responsible for the company's owned and joint-ventured care delivery assets. Prior to Humana, he held various leadership roles at the University of Illinois Hospital & Health Sciences System, Kaiser Permanente, and in government at the Centers for Medicare and Medicaid Services, and as a White House Fellow at the Department of Veterans Affairs. He started his career as a practicing corporate healthcare attorney at the international firm McDermott, Will & Emery.

Outside of Geisinger, Dr. Ryu serves on the Medicare Payment Advisory Commission (MedPAC), a body legislatively tasked with advising Congress on payment and other polices governing health plans and providers serving Medicare beneficiaries. He is also a member of the board of Privia (NASDAQ: PRVA), which brings capabilities that help provider practices. He has previously served in other advisory roles, including board positions with My Health Direct, Inc. (acquired by Experian), a provider of digital care coordination solutions, as well as MCCI and JenCare, both organizations managing the financing and delivery of care. He has also served on the Board of Directors of the White House Fellows Foundation and Association.

Dr. Ryu earned his B.A. from Yale University and his M.D. and J.D. from the University of Chicago. He completed his residency training in emergency medicine at Harbor-UCLA Medical Center.

Suzanne Sawyer
Senior Vice President, Chief Marketing and Communications Officer
Johns Hopkins Medicine

Suzanne joined Johns Hopkins Medicine in 2019 as Senior Vice President and Chief Marketing and Communications Officer after more than 25 years of leadership in health care marketing, communications, strategic planning, and business development. In her current role, Suzanne is responsible for leading marketing, digital strategy, brand management, marketing analytics, internal communications, media relations, corporate communications, and reputation management for Johns Hopkins Medicine. Suzanne was previously VP & Chief Marketing Officer of Penn Medicine where she helped to pioneer the practice of precision marketing in US health care. Her prior roles included Vice President of Portfolio Marketing for IBM Watson Health, as well as CMO and leadership positions for University of Rochester Medical Center, Penn State Geisinger

Health System, Penn State's Hershey Medical Center, the American Enterprise Institute, and the National Wildlife Federation. She received her BA from Penn State University in Foreign Service and International Politics. Suzanne is a frequent presenter at marketing and technology conferences. She is the recipient of numerous awards, including 2018 Healthcare Influencer by MM&M and PR Week, one of the Top 100 Women Leaders in Healthcare of 2021 by *Women we Admire*, and she was inducted into the Healthcare Internet Hall of Fame in 2017.

Laura Schoen
President Global Healthcare, and Chair Latin America, Weber Shandwick
Chief Healthcare Officer, DXTRA Health Integrated Solutions

Laura's personal journey has been one of transformation. Morphing from journalism to public relations, living and working in multiple countries, pursuing global opportunities, embracing change, and taking on multiple challenges. In the last 20 years since joining IPG, Laura has led the evolution of the Weber Shandwick healthcare ecosystem, working with the most successful companies in the healthcare industry to transform the understanding and treatment of life-threatening conditions. Laura has also launched successful healthcare agencies like dna communications and Current Health, in addition to acquiring trailblazers like Revive. Now, Laura has embraced a new challenge, as the Chief Healthcare Officer of the recently announced DXTRA Health Integrated Solutions, a collective of 27 best-in-class marketing agencies. Laura's drive goes beyond health. As Weber Shandwick's leader for Latin America, Laura has expanded the agency footprint, adding five wholly owned offices in addition to a strong network of affiliates to the agency's global network. PRovoke Media has recognized the agency's leadership in Latin America with the Agency of the Year Award in Brazil 2015 and Agency of the Year Award in Mexico 2019. Laura was also honored at the PRWeek Global awards as best PR Professional in Latam 2019.

Dr. Erica Taylor
Associate Chief Medical Officer of Diversity, Equity, and Inclusion
Duke Health Private Diagnostic Clinic

As a proud member of the Duke Community, Dr. Taylor is heavily committed to various aspects of leadership, including her service as the Chief of Surgery and Medical Director of Orthopaedic Surgery at Duke Raleigh Hospital. She is the Vice Chair of Diversity and Inclusion for the Department of Orthopaedics, working with colleagues and institutional leaders to develop thoughtful strategy and best practices toward belonging. For over a decade, she has worked closely with pipeline programs and national organizations that strive to promote successful pathways into orthopaedic surgery for populations that are under-represented in this field. Recently, Dr. Taylor was appointed as the Duke Health physician organization's inaugural Associate Chief Medical Officer for Diversity, Equity, and Inclusion. She brings to this role a lifetime of experience, passion, and a proven track record as a leader for change.

Dr. Erica Taylor achieved her Bachelor of Science degree in Biomedical Engineering Science from the University of Virginia in 2002. She obtained her medical degree from the Duke School of Medicine and then returned to the University of Virginia to complete orthopaedic surgical residency training, including a year of productive tissue engineering research. She then went on to complete a fellowship in Hand and Upper Extremity Surgery at The Cleveland Clinic in Ohio. She joined the Duke School of Medicine faculty as a hand surgeon in 2013 and received her Master of Business Administration degree from the Duke Fuqua School of Business in 2020. Inspired by the aforementioned education and experiences, she founded the Orthopaedic Diversity Leadership Consortium, LLC, a pioneering organization whose mission is to elevate the necessary components of inclusive leadership in orthopaedic surgery through network and strategy development.

Scott Weber
Chief Marketing and Design Officer
M Health Fairview

Scott leads marketing and design for M Health Fairview. He is driven by his passion for serving the patient and improving their health care experience. Scott was a managing partner at Accenture, focusing on innovative digital solutions for health care organizations. He has a wide breadth of experience in creative agencies where he helped build national brands like Walmart, Ikea, Samsung, and Capital One. Scott received a bachelor's degree from The Ohio State University and a Master of Business Administration from Georgetown University's The McDonough School of Business.

Kristen Hall Wevers
Senior Vice President, Chief Marketing and Communications Officer
UC Health

Kristen Hall Wevers, MBA, is senior vice president and chief marketing and communications officer at UC Health, the Cincinnati, Ohio region's adult academic health system. Her proven strategic senior leadership roles include brand-building, marketing, media & public relations, corporate & crisis communications, sales, and business development.

Before joining UC Health in 2016, Wevers served for six years at Mercy Health as the chief brand, marketing, and communications officer where she unified 25+ Mercy hospitals and ancillary services across Ohio and Kentucky under a singular corporation and brand name, vision, and promise. Prior to joining Mercy Health, Wevers spent six years as officer and vice president for Messer Construction Co., responsible for all marketing, communications, and sales support for the Midwest commercial construction company. Wevers began her career at The Procter & Gamble Company, spending almost 17 years in sales, marketing, and external relations leadership roles across the United States. She also served as company spokesperson for The Procter & Gamble Company's North America marketing and sales functions.

Wevers earned her bachelor's degree from Denison University, master's in business administration from Xavier University, and is pursuing an EdD in leadership studies at Xavier University. Wevers is active in the community, serving on the board of directors for The Ronald McDonald House Charities of Greater Cincinnati, The United Way of Greater Cincinnati, is a Leaders Circle executive for The Leadership Council for Non-Profits, and serves as a GreenLight Fund-Cincinnati advisory cabinet member. She is a former board member of Impact 100, Cincinnati Arts and Technology Studios, and Xavier University's Women of Excellence.

Wevers was named "2021 Chief Marketing Officer of the Year" by the *Cincinnati Business Courier*, awarded marketer of the year by the American Marketing Association Cincinnati Chapter, and recognized with numerous marketing, communications, and public relations awards. She was named to the list of "Most Powerful & Influential Women" by the Ohio Diversity Council. Wevers has presented at healthcare and industry conferences including Vizient, SHSMD, HMPS, and the National Healthcare Summit for CXOs.

Team 2030 Biographies

Christian Barnett
Senior Vice President, Strategy
Revive

Christian has been wielding the power of insight for the last three decades. As senior vice president of strategy, Christian drives strategic thinking and advocates for innovation across every client engagement. Whether he is debating the latest consumer research or discussing cultural truths, you can always find him in pursuit of the next idea. With deep experience in developing brands across a wide variety of categories, Christian brings a diverse background to any engagement he takes on. He has worked with everyone from LEGO to Dell to Chevron to Colgate. His expertise in unpacking audiences, inspiring creative, and pushing boundaries has helped countless brands reach success. While working at Revive, he has channeled his experience into brands such as Henry Ford Health System, Cincinnati Children's, and Community Health Innovations. There isn't a challenge that Christian doesn't go all-in on, not even when it came to his fight to get milk in the office fridge. He didn't stop asking for it, but instead led the development of a fully integrated campaign and launch throughout the office advocating for real milk.

Sasha Boghosian
Executive Vice President, Head of Insights
Revive

Sasha heads the insights group at Revive, which is responsible for identifying our clients' core challenges and developing breakthrough strategies that chart the right path for solving them. The work requires a diverse group of strategists, planners, and data experts who conduct extensive research and data analysis to deconstruct obstacles and gain deep insights into our clients' customers, markets, and offerings. Sasha leads the team in distilling these core truths into effective strategies to fuel powerful creative ideas and integrated marketing campaigns that produce measurable impact. In addition to his (slightly obsessive) focus on constantly up-leveling the impact of insights at Revive, Sasha has overseen the development of brand strategy and creative campaigns for countless healthcare organizations, helping them achieve their brand and financial goals. Sasha studied international relations at the University of Southern California and aspired to become a diplomat but came to his senses after working in Washington and Sacramento. He found his calling during one of his first public relations assignments when he convinced an iconic news magazine show to devote an hour to telling his client's story to a national television audience.

Desirée Duncan
Client Experience Director
Revive

As a client experience director at Revive, Desirée brings more than a decade of experience in leading integrated marketing communications programs and teams with particular expertise in developing and driving digital strategies geared toward measured success. Her background and skillset in digital media, content development, and marketing lend valuable perspective and support for the Revive team. She also serves as a member of the DEI committee. Desirée has worn many different hats over her career, including leading digital agency teams in recruitment marketing, leading creative and engagement teams at television stations across the U.S., and revamping digital media and communication strategies with B2B companies. Desirée's passion for storytelling had led her to platform for marginalized voices by producing documentaries, hosting television shows for PBS affiliate stations across the country, and hosting a podcast.

Brandon Edwards
Executive Chairman and Founder
Revive

As current Executive Chairman and Founder of Revive, and CEO for 12 years prior, Brandon brings 27 years of experience in healthcare and integrated marketing. Before starting Revive in 2009 along with current Revive CEO Joanne Thornton, Brandon served for eight years as president and COO of a national agency. During his career, he also oversaw operational communications for Tenet Healthcare and served as part of Tenet's Corporate Strategy and Venture Group, which managed the corporate venture fund and analyzed large strategy opportunities. He began his career in politics, managing local, state, and federal campaigns. Brandon earned his MBA from UCLA's Anderson School and is a featured speaker for healthcare industry and marketing communication trade groups.

Bjorn Gunnerud
Formerly SVP, Insights
Revive
(now Chief Experience and Marketing Officer at North Memorial Health)

Bjorn Gunnerud is an accomplished marketing and communications leader recognized for building brands through imaginative ideas and relatable storytelling that create authentic emotional connections with the right people. At Revive, he drives the development of brand strategy for health system clients and facilitates collaboration between Revive's many disciplines to develop integrated marketing programs to solve both financial and marketing goals. Bjorn previously served as vice president of marketing and communications for Children's Minnesota, where he was responsible for all marketing and communications programs, including developing the brand, championing a remarkable end-to-end customer experience, leading clinical marketing and outreach, driving digital engagement, and overseeing corporate communications efforts. Prior to his role at Children's, he was vice president of marketing at MinuteClinic, the largest retail health provider in the country and a subsidiary of CVS Health. There he led early efforts to drive trial and adoption by parents and demonstrate the value of retail health programs for employers. Bjorn started his career in the advertising industry and quickly rose to leadership positions in several top advertising agencies, managing marquee brands, including BMW, Georgia-Pacific, and Citibank. His work has received some of the marketing and communications industry's most recognizable awards, including the first-ever Cannes Titanium Lion. Bjorn is a graduate of Saint Olaf College.

Shannon Hooper
Formerly Executive Vice President; Chief Growth Officer & Interim Chief Financial Officer
Revive
(now Chief Strategy & Product Officer at BehaVR)

Shannon is a healthcare innovation enthusiast and student of healthcare's ever-shifting business models. As Chief Growth Officer and Interim Chief Financial Officer at Revive, Shannon is responsible for the agency's corporate strategy, growth, and finance functions. Her decade-plus of expertise in health technology also positions her as a key subject matter expert and strategist for clients' complex communications and brand challenges. She proudly serves on Revive's DEI Committee to help instill diversity, equity, and inclusion in all facets of the business. A graduate of the Nashville Health Care Council Fellows program and recognized health tech influencer, Shannon is an expert storyteller and passionate voice for healthcare transformation. She is a regular speaker on key healthcare topics, including new payment models and interoperability. She has a strong perspective on why and how healthcare companies must abandon jargon and refocus around operative — not merely disruptive — innovation. Shannon has spent her career in both agency and corporate roles. Before Revive, she served as director of corporate communications for Intel-GE Care Innovations. Her expertise in brand positioning, stakeholder engagement, strategic communications, and reputation management has helped *Fortune* 500 companies enter new markets and reach new audiences around the world. Shannon received her MBA from Duke University's Fuqua School of Business, where she was recognized as a Fuqua Scholar for performing in the top 10% of the graduating class.

Kayla Johnson
Project Management Project Coordinator
Revive

As project coordinator at Revive, Kayla Johnson is responsible for developing and managing multiple, comprehensive project plans to meet targeted deadlines, organizing, and setting clear expectations for all project tasks and deliverables, and working across all aspects of client engagements. Throughout her professional career, Kayla has immersed herself in public affairs, issue navigation, strategic positioning, and payor/provider relations. After working two jobs while receiving her bachelor's degree in strategic communications, she moved to Nashville to pursue a career in healthcare marketing. She strengthened her resourcefulness by working for a crisis communications agency and healthcare consulting firm before joining Revive.

She excels in the fast-paced atmosphere and likes the industry's unpredictable flux. She's passionate about improving healthcare on a national level and staying in the know regarding news and legislation that drives the industry. She continues to blend her communications background with her passion for helping hospitals and health systems function better.

Josh Schoonover
EVP, Client Delivery Group Lead
Revive

As the leader of Revive's client delivery group, Josh oversees the agency's client services functions and capabilities, including creative, content, media, and integrated communications. More importantly, he is responsible for integrating these capabilities to address the most pressing marketing and communications challenges facing healthcare brands. With more than 17 years of experience working in and around healthcare as a journalist, researcher, consultant, and marketer, he uses his understanding of the healthcare industry to derive the insights, messages, stories, and experiences organizations need to leverage to effectively engage with their target audiences. A perpetual learner, Josh's educational pursuits include a master's degree in journalism and doctoral studies in healthcare design at Arizona State University.

Jeff Speer
EVP, Insights
Revive

Serving as a senior strategist for clients, Jeff works with Revive teams and clients to design integrated marketing communication programs, develop

251

strategy and messaging to strengthen brands, improve reputations, and grow market share.

Over the past 20 years, he has worked with provider, service, technology, and device companies across the healthcare spectrum on campaigns targeting consumers, businesses, and physicians. Jeff's tactical areas of expertise include brand strategy and positioning, message development, internal communications, research design and analysis, and concepting.

Jeff graduated from the University of California, Los Angeles with a bachelor's degree in English and a concentration in business administration.

Jared Usrey
Vice President, Strategy
Revive

Obsessed with seeing the world through others' eyes, Jared has been helping organizations make marketing and technology decisions since he started his own business in high school. This drive has spilled over into his professional life, and he is still solving organizational problems. Now, he spends his time digging into the mindsets of prospects and customers to drive impactful insights, fueling the brand, marketing, and campaign strategies he develops for a range of healthcare clients. Before joining Revive, Jared built websites, plans, and marketing materials for more than fifteen years. Most recently, he worked at SMS Holdings, a conglomerate with seven operating companies. There, he led the implementation of multiple marketing strategy and operations initiatives, including vertical and ABM campaigns, website relaunches, marketing automation, a revamped CRM, and updated reporting across operating companies and corporate functions.

Stephanie Wierwille
Senior Vice President, Content Lead
Revive

As senior vice president and content lead, Stephanie helps brands determine what stories to tell and where to tell them across digital, traditional, and emerging channels. Through robust expertise in digital- and social-first full-funnel marketing, she leads healthcare brands to marketing maturity. With ten years of marketing experience across both healthcare and consumer brands, Stephanie's client experience includes Cincinnati Children's, Johns Hopkins Medicine, UNC Health, MD Anderson Cancer Center, American Cancer Society, Delta Air Lines, Amazon, Walmart, Wells Fargo, Coca-Cola, and Chick-fil-A. Her career began when social media was in its infancy, and she pioneered social marketing for TGI Fridays. In her time at The Richards Group, she partnered with MD Anderson Cancer Center to roll out the End Cancer brand campaign to social media. As the digital and social space matured, Stephanie then worked at the change management level, helping Delta Air Lines reshape its organizational structure across the company to prioritize social media for operations, customer service, marketing, and corporate communications. She also worked with QVC and HSN to redefine their business models to prioritize e-commerce and social shopping.

Kris Wickline
Vice President, Strategy
Revive

As vice president of strategy at Revive, Kris is the point person for consulting with her clients on their business challenges and goals and developing marketing strategies and programs to drive results. Kris is a seasoned healthcare marketer skilled in using business and consumer analytics and insights to produce data-driven strategies and quantifiable outcomes. Before her role at Revive, Kris served as vice president of integrated marketing strategy at Healthgrades, where she advised some of the nation's top health systems on integrated, multi-channel consumer acquisition, engagement, and retention programs. Her experience in healthcare began at a *Fortune* 500 health insurer where she led the direct-to-consumer marketing, e-commerce, and lead generation functions for a $65M individual health insurance business. She also applied her consumer marketing expertise in leading a customer retention team, driving improvements in business and customer analytics and insights, customer experience, engagement, and cross-sales to improve the company's bottom line.

Lucy Whitfield
Strategy Coordinator
Revive

As a junior strategist at Revive, Lucy is responsible for uncovering insights that drive effective strategies to deliver against clients' business objectives. She is adept at conducting and analyzing qualitative and quantitative research and works closely with senior strategists on strategy and positioning development, messaging development, and communications and creative brief writing, among other initiatives. Before joining the strategy team, Lucy specialized in health system new business opportunities at Revive — leading the development of integrated responses to Request for Proposals and pitches and managing internal teams and project plans. A Chattanooga, TN native, Lucy graduated from Vanderbilt University with a degree in human & organizational development and a minor in corporate strategy. An avid runner and reader, she is always on the hunt for a new trail to explore or book to curl up with.

ENDNOTES

1   Bevolo, C. (2011). *Joe Public Doesn't Care About Your Hospital.* Rockbench Publishing, p. 12.

2   Bhargava, R. (2020). *Non Obvious Mega Trends.* Ideapress Publishing, p. 29.

3   Diaz, K. (2011). *Pawlenty changes his approach on health care.* [online] The Star Tribune. Available at: https://www.startribune.com/ pawlenty-s-health-care-switcheroo/127073788/

4   Cuthbertson, A. (2020). *Elon Musk claims AI will overtake humans in 'less than five years.'* [online] The Independent. Available at: https://www.independent. co.uk/life-style/gadgets-and-tech/news/elon-musk-artificial-intelligence-ai-singularity-a9640196.html

5   Chebrolu, K., Ressler, D., and Varia, H. (2020). *Smart use of artificial intelligence in health care.* [online] Deloitte Insights. Available at: https://www2.deloitte. com/us/en/insights/industry/health-care/artificial-intelligence-in-health-care.html

6   See 5.

7   Bradley, R. *Blockchain explained... in under 100 words.* [online] Deloitte Perspectives. Available at: https://www2.deloitte.com/ch/en/pages/strategy-operations/articles/blockchain-explained.html

8   Dixon, C. *Introducing a16z crypto.* [online] andreessen horowitz. Available at: https://a16z.com/2018/06/25/introducing-a16z-crypto/

9   NIHCM Foundation. (2020). "Hospital Consolidation: Trends, Impacts & Outlook." Available at: https://nihcm.org/publications/ hospital-consolidation-trends-impacts-outlook

10 Abelson, R. (2021). *Buoyed by Federal Covid Aid, Big Hospital Chains Buy Up Competitors. [online] The New York Times.* Available at: https:// www.nytimes.com/2021/05/21/health/covid-bailout-hospital-merger. html?referringSource=articleShare

11 Furukawa, M. F., Kimmey, L., Jones, D. J., Machta, R. M., Guo, J., and Rich, E. C. (2020). Consolidation of Providers Into Health Systems Increased Substantially, 2016-2018. *Health Affairs, 39*(8). https://www.healthaffairs.org/ doi/10.1377/hlthaff.2020.00017

12 Cohen, J. (2021). *Digital health M&A has already set a record this year.* *[online]* Modern Healthcare. Available at: https://www.modernhealthcare.com/mergers-acquisitions/digital-health-ma-has-already-set-record-this-year?utm_source=modern-healthcare- am&utm_medium=email&utm_campaign=20210801&utm_content=article3-headline (can't access behind paywall!)

13 See 10.

14 Daly, R. (2019). *Only a tiny share of hospital revenue is risk-based: Moody's.* [online] HFMA. Available at: https://www.hfma.org/topics/news/2019/09/only-a-tiny-share-of-hospital-revenue-is-risk-based--moody-s.html

15 O'Brien, J. (2020). *Less than 20% of Medicare Spending Is Value-Based.* [online] HealthLeaders. Available at: https://www.healthleadersmedia.com/finance/less-20-medicare-spending-value-based

16 Kaufman, N. (2021, March). *It is Utter Nonsense to Say that FFS is not Value-based Care and Risk-based Arrangements Are. (In response to MHC).* [Post]. LinkedIn. Available at: https://www.linkedin.com/posts/nathan-kaufman-07b8a03_it-is-utter-nonsense-to-say-that-ffs-is-not-activity-6785327018927104000-iVb9

17 Ajayi, T. (2020). *Industry Voices—The pandemic shows why value-based models are the future of U.S. healthcare.* [online] Fierce Healthcare. Available at: https://www.fiercehealthcare.com/hospitals/industry-voices-pandemic-shows-why-value-based-models-are-future-u-s-healthcare

18 Bestsennyy, O., Gilbert, G., Harris, A., and Rost, J. (2021). *Telehealth: A quarter-trillion-dollar post-COVID-19 reality?* [online] McKinsey & Company. Available at: https://www.mckinsey.com/industries/healthcare-systems-and-services/our-insights/telehealth-a-quarter-trillion-dollar-post-covid-19-reality

19 Boodman, S. (2018). *For millennials, a regular visit to the doctor's office is not a primary concern.* [online] The Washington Post. Available at: https://www.washingtonpost.com/national/health-science/for-millennials-a-regular-visit-to-the-doctors-office-is-not-a-primary-concern/2018/10/05/6b17c71a-aef3-11e8-9a6a-565d92a3585d_story.html

20 Christensen, C. (2011). *A Disruptive Solution for Health Care.* [online] Harvard Business Review. Available at: https://hbr.org/2011/03/a-disruptive-solution-for-heal.html

21 Fabius, V., Kohli, S., Timelin, B., and Veranen, S. M. (2020). *How COVID-19 is changing consumer behavior — now and forever.* [online] McKinsey & Company. Available at: https://www.mckinsey.com/industries/retail/our-insights/how-covid-19-is-changing-consumer-behavior-now-and-forever

22   Galloway, S. (2020). *The Great Dispersion*. [Blog post] No Mercy/No Malice. Available at: https://www.profgalloway.com/the-great-dispersion/

23   Magnan, S. (2017). *Social Determinants of Health 101 for Health Care: Five Plus Five*. [online] National Academy of Medicine. Available at: https://nam.edu/social-determinants-of-health-101-for-health-care-five-plus-five/

24   World Health Organization. (2020). "An ad hoc WHO technical consultation managing the COVID-19 infodemic: call for action." Available at: https://www.who.int/publications/i/item/9789240010314

25   Lohr, S. (2021). *What Ever Happened to IBM's Watson?*. [online] *The New York Times*. Available at: https://www.nytimes.com/2021/07/16/technology/what-happened-ibm-watson.html

26   O'Flaherty, K. (2021). *Apple Issues New Blow to Facebook With Stunning iPhone Privacy Move*. [online] *Forbes*. Available at: https://www.forbes.com/sites/kateoflahertyuk/2021/05/21/apple-issues-new-blow-to-facebook-with-stunning-iphone-privacy-move/?sh=3e5724fb4f4b

27   Davis, J. (2021). *Scripps Health EHR, Patient Portal Still Down After Ransomware Attack*. [online] HealthITSecurity.com. Available at: https://healthitsecurity.com/news/scripps-health-ehr-patient-portal-still-down-after-ransomware-attack

28   CMS.gov. (2020). "National Health Expenditure Data: Historical." Available at: https://www.cms.gov/Research-Statistics-Data-and-Systems/Statistics-Trends-and-Reports/NationalHealthExpendData/NationalHealthAccountsHistorical

29   Kamal, R., Ramirez, G., and Cox, C. (2020). *How does health spending in the U.S. compare to other countries?*. [online] Peterson-Kaiser Family Foundation Health System Tracker. Available at: https://www.healthsystemtracker.org/chart-collection/health-spending-u-s-compare-countries/#item-spendingcomparison_health-consumption-expenditures-per-capita-2019

30   Tikkanen, R. and Abrams, M. K. (2020) *U.S. Health Care from a Global Perspective, 2019: Higher Spending, Worse Outcomes*. [online] The Commonwealth Fund. Available at: https://www.commonwealthfund.org/publications/issue-briefs/2020/jan/us-health-care-global-perspective-2019

31   West Health Institute. (2021). *1 in 5 Americans did not seek needed medical treatment during the pandemic due to cost*. [online] MedicalXpress.com Available at: https://medicalxpress.com/news/2021-03-americans-medical-treatment-pandemic-due.html

32   Panchal, N., Kamal, R., Cox, C., and Garfield, R. (2021). *The Implications of COVID-19 for Mental Health and Substance Use*. [online] Kaiser Family

Foundation. Available at: https://www.kff.org/coronavirus-covid-19/issue-brief/the-implications-of-covid-19-for-mental-health-and-substance-use/

33   Howley, E. K. (2021). *Children's Mental Health Crisis Could Be a Next 'Wave' in the Pandemic.* [online] U.S. News & World Report.com. Available at: https://www.usnews.com/news/health-news/articles/2021-03-04/childrens-mental-health-crisis-could-be-a-next-wave-in-the-pandemic

34   National Alliance on Mental Illness. (2021). "Mental Health By the Numbers." Available at: https://www.nami.org/mhstats

35   Bogusz, G. B. (2020). *Health Insurers Still Don't Adequately Cover Mental Health Treatment.* [Blog post] National Alliance on Mental Illness. https://www.nami.org/Blogs/NAMI-Blog/March-2020/Health-Insurers-Still-Don-t-Adequately-Cover-Mental-Health-Treatment

36   León, J. N. *Big Data in Healthcare 2021.* [online] High-Tech Trends. Available at: https://htechtrends.com/big-data-in-healthcare/

37   See 25.

38   See 25.

39   Mcfarlane, G. (2019). *How UnitedHealth Group Makes Money.* [online] Investopedia.com. Available at: https://www.investopedia.com/articles/markets/043015/how-unitedhealth-group-makes-its-money-unh.asp

40   WebMD. (2020). "What Is Precision Medicine?" Available at: https://www.webmd.com/cancer/precision-medicine

41   Bailey, C. (2020). *Gene therapies offer breakthrough results but extraordinary costs.* [online] Massachusetts Municipal Association. Available at: https://www.mma.org/gene-therapies-offer-breakthrough-results-but-extraordinary-costs/

42   See 41.

43   Guram, J. (2021). *Without Reform, Medicare Policies Will Hamstring New Gene Therapies.* [online] The Evidence Base (USC Schaeffer & USC Dornsife). Available at: https://healthpolicy.usc.edu/evidence-base/without-reform-medicare-policies-will-hamstring-new-gene-therapies/

44   Gelbaugh, C. (2021). *Cheat Sheet: Generational Shifts in Health Care.* [online] The Advisory Board, p. 5.

45   Kesavadev, J., Saboo, B., Krishna, M. B., and Krishnan, G. (2020). Evolution of Insulin Delivery Devices: From Syringes, Pens, and Pumps to DIY Artificial Pancreas. *Diabetes Therapy, 11*(6), 1259-1269. https://doi.org/10.1007/s13300-020-00831-z

46   Bisignani, A., De Bonis, S., Mancuso, L., Ceravolo, G., and Bisignani, G. (2019). Implantable loop recorder in clinical practice. *Journal of Arrhythmia, 35(1)*, 25-32. https://doi.org/10.1002/joa3.12142

47   Mayo Clinic. (2021). "Holter Monitor." Available at: https://www.mayoclinic. org/tests-procedures/holter-monitor/about/pac-20385039

48   Smith, J. (2021). *65 Exciting Things You Can Do With the Apple Watch.* [online] Gottabemobile.com. Available at: https://www.gottabemobile.com/ things-apple-watch-can-do/

49   Etherington, D. (2021). *With iOS 15, Apple reveals just how far Health has come — and how much further it can go.* [online] TechCrunch.com. Available at: https://techcrunch.com/2021/06/16/apple-health/

50   Centers for Disease Control and Prevention. (2020). "National Diabetes Statistics Report, 2020." Available at: https://www.cdc.gov/diabetes/data/ statistics-report/index.html?CDC_AA_refVal=https%3A%2F%2Fwww.cdc. gov%2Fdiabetes%2Fdata%2Fstatistics%2Fstatistics-report.html

51   Future Today Institute. (2021). *2021 Tech Trends Report,* p. 105.

52   Theophanides, A. *Forces of Change: The Future of health.* [online] Deloitte. Available at: https://www2.deloitte.com/za/en/pages/life-sciences-and-healthcare/articles/the-future-of-health.html

53   Vance, A. (2021). *Know Thyself Down To The Neuron. Bloomberg Businessweek,* p. 57.

54   Sezgin, E., Huang, Y., Ramtekkar, U., and Lin, S. (2020). Readiness for voice assistants to support healthcare delivery during a health crisis and pandemic. *npj Digital Medicine, 3(122)*. https://doi.org/10.1038/s41746-020-00332-0

55   Eve. (2020). *Woebot — the bleeding intelligent self-help therapist and companion.* [online] Digital Initiative: Harvard Business School. Available at: https://digital.hbs.edu/platform-digit/submission/woebot-the-bleeding-intelligent-self-help-therapist-and-companion/

56   See 32.

57   Brown, K. (2021). *Something Bothering You? Tell It to Woebot.* [online] *The New York Times.* Available at: https://www.nytimes.com/2021/06/01/health/ artificial-intelligence-therapy-woebot.html

58   The Medical Futurist. (2018). "The Top 12 Social Companion Robots." Available at: https://medicalfuturist.com/the-top-12-social-companion-robots/

59   See 58.

60   See 57.

61 Omada. "Altogether, American Eagle Outfitters Employees Shed 1,251 Pounds." Available at: https://f.hubspotusercontent30.net/hubfs/1775981/2020%20 Assets/Omada_American%20Eagle%20Case%20Study.pdf

62 IQVIA Institute for Human Data Science. (2021). *Digital Health Trends 2021*, p. 15.

63 Christensen, C., Grossman, J., and Hwang, J. (2008). *The Innovator's Prescription*, p. 44.

64 Christensen, C., Grossman, J., and Hwang, J. (2008). *The Innovator's Prescription*, p. 56.

65 Joszt, L. and Caffrey, M. (2020). *Personalized Medicine: The Role of Technology and Diagnostics in Driving Change.* [online] AJMC. Available at: https:// www.ajmc.com/view/personalized-medicine-the-role-of-technology-and-diagnostics-in-driving-change

66 Collins, F. S., Doudna, J. A., Lander, E. S., and Rotimi, C. N. (2021). Human Molecular Genetics and Genomics – Important Advances and Exciting Possibilities. *New England Journal of Medicine, 384*, 1-4. https://doi. org/10.1056/NEJMp2030694

67 Armstrong, M. M. (2020). *Cheat sheet: What is Digital Twin?.* [Blog post] IBM Business Operations Blog. Available at: https://www.ibm.com/blogs/ internet-of-things/iot-cheat-sheet-digital-twin/

68 Garcia, D. A. and Roseman, J. (2021) *How Digital Twin Technology is Disrupting Healthcare.* [online] Plug and Play. Available at: https:// www.plugandplaytechcenter.com/resources/how-digital-twins-t echnology-disrupting-healthcare/

69 Q Bio. (2021). *Q Bio Announces First Clinical "Digital Twin" Platform and Novel Whole-Body Scanner, and Major Investment from Kaiser Foundation Hospitals.* [Press release]. Available at: https://www.businesswire.com/news/ home/20210429005437/en/Q-Bio-Announces-First-Clinical-"Digital-Twin"-Platform-and-Novel-Whole-Body-Scanner-and-Major-Investment-From-Kaiser-Foundation-Hospitals

70 ReviveHealth. (2020). "The End of the Runway: Consumerism Report," p. 31.

71 Koonin, L. M., Hoots, B., Tsang, C. A., Leroy, Z., Farris, K., Jolly, B. T., Antall, P., McCabe, B., Zelis, C. B. R., Tong, I., and Harris, A. M. (2020). Trends in the Use of Telehealth During the Emergence of the COVID-19 Pandemic — United States, January-March 2020. *MMWR Morb Mortal Wkly Rep I, 69*(43), 1595-1599. https://dx.doi.org/10.15585/mmwr.mm6943a3

72 Schroeder, B. (2021). *The Future of Healthcare is Coming Home: Three Major Trends.* [online] *Forbes.* Available at: https://www.forbes.com/sites/

bernhardschroeder/2021/04/05/the-future-of-healthcare-is-coming-home-three-major-trends-to-leverage-for-startups/?sh=d3146a830488

73 See 72.

74 See 72.

75 Intermountain Healthcare. (2021). *Intermountain Healthcare Opens New Hospital ---Without a Building or Walls*. [Press release] Available at: https://intermountainhealthcare.org/news/2018/02/intermountain-healthcare-opens-new-hospital-without-a-building-or-walls/

76 Roth, M. (2021). *Atrium Health's Virtual Hospital Opens Door to New Care Models*. [online] HealthLeaders. Available at: https://www.healthleadersmedia.com/telehealth/atrium-healths-virtual-hospital-opens-door-new-care-models

77 Waddill, K. (2021). *Three Common Characteristics Among Virtual-First Health Plans*. [online] HealthPayerIntelligence.com. https://healthpayerintelligence.com/news/three-common-characteristics-among-virtual-first-health-plans

78 Scott-Dawkins, K. and Syal, M. (2020). "Advertising in 2030," p. 23. [online] Essence. Available at: https://assets.ctfassets.net/puoqjhq4x55s/4oJkK KLs0Zo43btx0t2HaO/7e72188e4eb9ae14c0b92f0290ba5a81/Advertising_in_ 2030_FINAL_4.28.20.pdf

79 Guilford-Blake, R. (2020). *Wait. Will AI Replace Radiologists After All?* [online] *Radiology Business*. Available at: https://www.radiologybusiness.com/topics/artificial-intelligence/wait-will-ai-replace-radiologists-after-all

80 Renken, E. (2020). *As Out-Of-Pocket Health Costs Rise, Insured Adults Are Seeking Less Primary Care*. [online] NPR. Available at: https://www.npr.org/sections/health-shots/2020/02/03/801351890/as-out-of-pocket-health-costs-rise-insured-adults-are-seeking-less-primary-care

81 Meskó, B. and Dhunnoo, P. (2021). *7 Futuristic Professions In Healthcare You Can Still Prepare For*. [online] The Medical Futurist. Available at: https://medicalfuturist.com/future-jobs-in-healthcare/

82 Auken, I. (2016). *Welcome to 2030: I Own Nothing, Have No Privacy And Life Has Never Been Better*. [online] Forbes. Available at: https://www.forbes.com/sites/worldeconomicforum/2016/11/10/shopping-i-cant-really-remember-what-that-is-or-how-differently-well-live-in-2030/?sh=59446db6354f

83 Schiller, B. (2020). *Industry Voices—Healthcare consumerism will be the driving force post-COVID-19*. [online] Fierce Healthcare. Available at: https://www.fiercehealthcare.com/tech/industry-voices-healthcare-consumerism-will-be-driving-force-post-covid

84 Bevolo, C. (2019). "The Case for Building a Post Health System Brand," p. 2.

85   Damberg, C. (2005). *Consumer-Directed Health Plans: Research on Implications for Health Care Quality and Cost.* [online] The Rand Corporation. Available at: https://www.rand.org/content/dam/rand/pubs/testimonies/2005/RAND_CT249.pdf

86   The Rand Corporation. (2011). *Largest Study of High-Deductible Health Plans Finds Substantial Cost Savings, but Less Preventive Care.* [Press release]. Available at: https://www.rand.org/news/press/2011/03/25.html

87   Bevolo, C. (2011). *Joe Public Doesn't Care About Your Hospital.* Rockbench Publishing, p. 8.

88   Wicklund, E. (2021). *Will Telehealth Payment Parity Be Permanent or a Passing Fancy?.* [online] mHealthIntelligence.com. Available at: https://mhealthintelligence.com/news/will-telehealth-payment-parity-be-permanent-or-a-passing-fancy

89   Freed, M., Neuman, T., and Cubanski, J. (2021). *10 FAQs on Prescription Drug Importation.* [online] Kaiser Family Foundation. Available at: https://www.kff.org/medicare/issue-brief/10-faqs-on-prescription-drug-importation/

90   Allied Market Research. (2021). *Medical Tourism Market to Reach $273.72 Bn, Globally, by 2027 at 12.8% CAGR: Says Allied Market Research.* [Press release]. Available at: https://www.prnewswire.com/news-releases/medical-tourism-market-to-reach-273-72-bn-globally-by-2027-at-12-8-cagr-says-allied-market-research-301208332.html

91   Mathews, A. W. (2020). *Physicians, Hospitals Meet Their New Competitor: Insurer-Owned Clinics.* [online] *The Wall Street Journal.* Available at: https://www.wsj.com/articles/physicians-hospitals-meet-their-new-competitor-insurer-owned-clinics-11582473600

92   Aetna. (2021). "Aetna Facts." Available at: https://www.aetna.com/about-us/aetna-facts-and-subsidiaries/aetna-facts.html

93   Tozzi, J. (2021). *UnitedHealth Chases 10,000 More Doctors for Biggest U.S. Network.* [online] Bloomberg.com. Available at: https://www.bloomberg.com/news/articles/2021-03-05/unitedhealth-s-deal-machine-scoops-up-covid-hit-doctor-groups?sref=XTvh2gSR

94   Hughes, L. and Vohra, S. (2021). *Rural health is in crisis – 5 creative ways the Biden administration can help it thrive.* [online] The Conversation. Available at: https://theconversation.com/rural-health-is-in-crisis-5-creative-ways-the-biden-administration-can-help-it-thrive-151205

95   Rau, J. and Huetteman, E. (2020). *Urban hospitals of last resort cling to life in time of COVID.* [online] ModernHealthcare.com. https://www.modernhealthcare.com/hospitals/urban-hospitals-last-resort-cling-life-time-covid

96   Golden, J. N. (2021). *Mercy Hospital Sale Finalized, Saving Historic Bronzeville Hospital From Closing.* [online] Block Club Chicago. Available at: https://blockclubchicago.org/2021/04/05/mercy-hospital-sale-finalized-saving-the-bronzeville-hospital-from-closing/

97   Rosenfeld, J. (2021). *Jaw-Dropping Stats About the State of Retirement in America.* [online] GoBankingRates.com. Available at: https://www.gobankingrates.com/retirement/planning/jaw-dropping-stats-state-retirement-america/

98   The Advisory Board. (2018). "Understanding Consumer Preferences for Healthcare."

99   Mehrota, A., Dean, K. M., Sinaiko, A. D., and Sood, N. (2017). Americans Support Price Shopping for Health Care, But Few Actually Seek Out Price Information. *Health Affairs,* 36(8).https://doi.org/10.1377/hlthaff.2016.1471

100 The Advisory Board Daily Briefing. (2018). "Patients aren't savvy health care shoppers — but here's how providers, insurers can help." Available at: https://www.advisory.com/en/daily-briefing/2018/08/02/health-care-shopping

101 Renfrow, J. (2017). *80% of shoppers compare prices online before shopping in stores.* [online] Fierce Retail. Available at: https://www.fierceretail.com/digital/80-shoppers-do-online-price-comparison-before-store-shopping

102 Bevolo, C. (2017). *Joe Public III: The End of Hospital Marketing.* Rockbench Publishing, p. 135.

103 Gebreyes, K., Davis, A., Davis, S. Shukla, M.. and Rush, B. *Breaking the cost curve.* [online] Deloitte Insights. Available at: https://www2.deloitte.com/xe/en/insights/industry/health-care/future-health-care-spending.html

104 Muoio, D. (2021). *HIMSS21: Hospitals, payers and startups clamoring to be 'digital front door,' and it's overwhelming patients.* [online] Fierce Healthcare. Available at: https://www.fiercehealthcare.com/digital-health/hospitals-payers-startups-numerous-digital-front-doors-overlap-and-overwhelm

105 Dyrda, L. (2021). *Walmart physician-led clinics gain steam: 10 things to know.* [online] BeckersASCReview.com. Available at: https://www.beckersasc.com/leadership/walmart-physician-led-clinics-gain-steam-10-things-to-know.html

106 Ahmed, E. (2021). *Walmart dives into virtual care, decelerates clinic expansion.* [online] eMarketer. Available at: https://www.emarketer.com/content/walmart-dives-virtual-care-decelerates-clinic-expansion

107 Stewart, D. (2021). *Walmart to Open 4,000 Healthcare 'Supercenters' by 2029 That Include 'Comprehensive' Clinical Laboratory Services.* [online] DarkDaily.com https://www.darkdaily.com/2021/05/03/walmart-to-open-

4000-healthcare-supercenters-by-2029-that-include-comprehensive-clinical-laboratory-services/

108 Landi, H. (2018). *Jack Stoddard Tapped to be COO of Amazon-Berkshire-JP Morgan Health Venture.* [online] Healthcare Innovation. Available at: https://www.hcinnovationgroup.com/policy-value-based-care/news/13030674/jack-stoddard-tapped-to-be-coo-of-amazonberkshirejp-morgan-health-venture

109 "Episode 81." (2021). Podcast. *The Prof G Podcast.*

110 Gurdus, L. (2019). *Tim Cook: Apple's greatest contribution will be 'about health.'* [online] CNBC. https://www.cnbc.com/2019/01/08/tim-cook-teases-new-apple-services-tied-to-health-care.html

111 See 49.

112 Pifer, R. (2021). *UnitedHealth returns to normal care levels in Q4, posts $15B in profit for 2020.* [online] Healthcare Dive. Available at: https://www.healthcaredive.com/news/unitedhealth-returns-to-normal-care-levels-q4-posts-15b-in-profit-2020/593605/

113 Definitive Healthcare. "Top 10 Largest Health Systems in the U.S." Available at: https://blog.definitivehc.com/top-10-largest-health-systems

114 Drees, J. (2021). *Optum launches virtual care offering nationwide: 5 things to know.* [online] BeckersHospitalReview.com. https://www.beckershospitalreview.com/telehealth/optum-launches-virtual-care-offering-nationwide-5-things-to-know.html?utm_campaign=bhr&utm_source=website&utm_content=most-read

115 Repko, M. (2021). *Dollar General hires chief medical officer as it looks to become a health-care destination in rural areas.* [online] CNBC. https://www.cnbc.com/2021/07/07/dollar-general-hires-chief-medical-officer-boosts-health-care-items.html

116 Landi, H. (2020). *Primary care is ripe for disruption. Here are the players trying to shake up the market.* [online] Fierce Healthcare. https://www.fiercehealthcare.com/practices/primary-care-ripe-for-disruption-here-are-players-trying-to-shake-up-market

117 Bannow, T. (2021). *Private equity continues to propel urgent-care growth, but some markets reaching capacity. [online]* Modern Healthcare. Available at: https://www.modernhealthcare.com/providers/private-equity-continues-propel-urgent-care-growth-some-markets-reaching-capacity

118 Grand View Research. (2017). "U.S. Retail Clinics Market Worth $7.3 Billion By 2025 | CAGR: 20.3%" Available at: https://www.grandviewresearch.com/press-release/us-retail-clinics-market-analysis

119 Barbella, M. (2021). *U.S. Virtual Care Market to Grow More Than Seven-Fold by 2025*. [online] *Medical Product Outsourcing Magazine*. Available at: https://www.mpo-mag.com/contents/view_breaking-news/2021-03-23/us-virtual-care-market-to-grow-more-than-seven-fold-by-2025/

120 Kennedy, P. and Snowbeck, C. (2021). *Bright Health raises $924M, making it the largest IPO ever in Minnesota*. [online] *The Star Tribune*. Available at: https://www.startribune.com/bright-health-raises-924m-making-it-the-largest-ipo-ever-in-minnesota/600071504/

121 Jercich, K. (2020). *Kaiser Permanente launches 'virtual-first' health plan in Washington*. [online] *Healthcare IT News*. Available at: https://www.healthcareitnews.com/news/kaiser-permanente-launches-virtual-first-health-plan-washington

122 Raths, D. (2020). *Kaiser Permanente Accelerates Social Health Network Efforts*. [online] Healthcare Innovation. https://www.hcinnovationgroup.com/population-health-management/social-determinants-of-health/article/21160594/kaiser-permanente-accelerates-social-health-network-efforts

123 Fox56 Newsroom. (2021). "GIANT company donates $200k to Geisinger 'Fresh Food Farmacy' program." Available at: https://fox56.com/news/local/giant-company-donates-200k-to-geisinger-fresh-food-farmacy-program

124 Vanderbilt Health Affiliated Network. (2021). "Network." Available at: https://www.vhan.com/about/network/

125 Allina Health. (2012). *Allina's new name focuses on health, not hospitals*. [Press release]. Available at: https://www.allinahealth.org/allina-news/2012/02/allinas-new-name-focuses-on-health-not-hospitals

126 Bevolo, C. (2017). *Joe Public III: The End of Hospital Marketing*. Rockbench Publishing, p. 122.

127 Michelson, D. (2019). *The No. 1 takeaway from the 2019 JP Morgan Healthcare Conference: It's the platform, stupid*. [online] Beckershospitalreview.com. https://www.beckershospitalreview.com/hospital-management-administration/the-no-1-takeaway-from-the-2019-jp-morgan-healthcare-conference-it-s-the-platform-stupid.html

128 Winkler, R. (2021). *Apple Struggles in Push to Make Healthcare Its Greatest Legacy*. [online] *The Wall Street Journal*. Available at: https://www.wsj.com/articles/apple-struggles-in-push-to-make-healthcare-greatest-legacy-11623832200

129 Dodge, B. and Livingston, S. (2021). *Walmart is slowing its ambitious push into healthcare, employees and leaked documents reveal*. [online] Business Insider.

130 ReviveHealth. (2020). "The End of the Runway: Consumerism Report," p. 31.

[131] Christensen, C., Grossman, J., and Hwang, J. (2008). *The Innovator's Prescription*, p. 103.

[132] *Winona Daily News.* (2007). "Mayo moving into retail clinic business in Minnesota." Available at: https://www.winonadailynews.com/newsupdate/mayo-moving-into-retail-clinic-business-in-minnesota/article_87e90c21-0a25-5219-80da-52e67a27987a.html

[133] Morse, S. (2017). *Majority of provider-sponsored plans losing money, report says.* [online] *Healthcare Finance.* Available at: https://www.healthcarefinancenews.com/news/majority-provider-sponsored-plans-losing-money-report-says

[134] Dapcevich, M. (2020). *Who are 'America's Frontline Doctors' and Dr. Stella Immanuel?.* [online] Snopes. Available at: https://www.snopes.com/news/2020/07/30/americas-frontline-doctors/

[135] See 134.

[136] Frenkel, S. and Alba, D. (2020). *Misleading Virus Video, Pushed by the Trumps, Spreads Online.* [online] *The New York Times.* Available at: https://www.nytimes.com/2020/07/28/technology/virus-video-trump.html

[137] Sommer, W. (2020). *Trump's New Favorite COVID Doctor Believes in Alien DNA, Demon Sperm, and Hydroxychloroquine.* [online] The Daily Beast. https://www.thedailybeast.com/stella-immanuel-trumps-new-covid-doctor-believes-in-alien-dna-demon-sperm-and-hydroxychloroquine

[138] See 136.

[139] See 137.

[140] Pitofsky, M. (2020). *Doctor retweeted by Trump has warned of alien DNA, sex with demons.* [online] The Hill. Available at: https://thehill.com/blogs/blog-briefing-room/news/509421-doctor-retweeted-by-trump-has-warned-of-alien-dna-sex-with?rl=1

[141] See 137.

[142] Wikipedia. (2021). "1968 Olympics Black Power salute." Available at: https://en.wikipedia.org/wiki/1968_Olympics_Black_Power_salute

[143] Haislop, T. (2020). *Colin Kaepernick kneeling timeline: How protests during the national anthem started a movement in the NFL.* [online] SportingNews.com Available: https://www.sportingnews.com/us/nfl/news/colin-kaepernick-kneeling-protest-timeline/xktu6ka4diva1s5jxaylrcsse

[144] Graham, B. A. (2017). *Donald Trump blasts NFL anthem protestors: 'Get that son of a bitch off the field.'* [online] *The Guardian.* Available at: https://www.theguardian.com/sport/2017/sep/22/donald-trump-nfl-national-anthem-protests

145 Baragona, S. (2021). *Unvaccinated Americans Whiter, More Republican Than Vaccinated.* [online] Voice of America. Available at: https://www.voanews.com/covid-19-pandemic/unvaccinated-americans-whiter-more-republican-vaccinated

146 Bump, P. (2021). *A third of White conservatives refuse to get vaccinated — a refusal shown in polling and the real world.* [online] The Washington Post. Available at: https://www.washingtonpost.com/politics/2021/07/06/third-white-conservatives-refuse-get-vaccine-refusal-shown-both-polling-real-world/

147 McPhillips, D., Almasy, S., and Holcombe, M. (2021). *States with low vaccination numbers had COVID-19 case rates last week 3 times higher than others where people are fully vaccinated.* [online] CNN. Available at: https://www.cnn.com/2021/07/12/health/us-coronavirus-monday/index.html

148 Collinson, S. (2021). *Politics is causing needless deaths in the fight against Covid-19.* [online] CNN. Available at: https://www.cnn.com/2021/07/14/politics/politics-needless-covid-deaths/index.html

149 http Merriam-Webster. "Sect." Available at: https://www.merriam-webster.com/dictionary/sect

150 Fisher, M. (2021). *'Belonging Is Stronger Than Facts:' The Age of Misinformation.* [online] The New York Times. Available at: https://www.nytimes.com/2021/05/07/world/asia/misinformation-disinformation-fake-news.html

151 Packer, G. (2021). *How America Fractured Into Four Parts.* [online] The Atlantic. Available at: https://www.theatlantic.com/magazine/archive/2021/07/george-packer-four-americas/619012/

152 Wong, J. C. (2020). *Down the rabbit hole: how QAnon conspiracies thrive on Facebook.* [online] The Guardian. Available at: https://www.theguardian.com/technology/2020/jun/25/qanon-facebook-conspiracy-theories-algorithm

153 Malinowski, T. and Eshoo, A. (2021). *Opinion: Congress must decide: Will it protect social media profits, or democracy?* [online] The Washington Post. Available at: https://www.washingtonpost.com/opinions/2021/04/26/malinowski-eshoo-congress-social-media-section-230/?utm_campaign=wp_main&utm_medium=social&utm_source=twitter

154 Frier, S. and Kopit, S. (2021). *Facebook Built the Perfect Platform for Covid Vaccine Conspiracies.* [online] Bloomberg Businessweek. Available at: https://www.bloomberg.com/news/features/2021-04-01/covid-vaccine-and-fertility-facebook-s-platform-is-letting-fake-news-go-viral

155 Bond, S. (2021). *Just 12 People Are Behind Most Vaccine Hoaxes on Social Media, Research Shows.* [online] NPR. Available at: https://www.npr.org/2021/05/13/996570855/disinformation-dozen-test-facebooks-twitters-ability-to-curb-vaccine-hoaxes

156 Green, A. (2018). *Facebook's 52,000 data points on each person reveal something shocking about its future.* [online] Komando.com. Available at: https://www.komando.com/social-media/facebooks-52000-data-points-on-each-person-reveal-something-shocking-about-its-future/489188/

157 Curran, D. (2018). *Are you ready? Here is all the data Facebook and Google have on you.* [online] *The Guardian.* Available at: https://www.theguardian.com/commentisfree/2018/mar/28/all-the-data-facebook-google-has-on-you-privacy

158 Hutchinson, A. (2019). *What Does Facebook Know About You Really?* [online] Social Media Today. Available at: https://www.socialmediatoday.com/news/what-does-facebook-know-about-you-really/546502/

159 Faggella, D. (2017). *The ROI of recommendation engines for marketing.* [online] MarTech.org. Available at: https://martech.org/roi-recommendation-engines-marketing/

160 Lewis, M. (2021). *The Premonition: A Pandemic Story.* W.W. Norton & Company, p. 279 (Kindle version).

161 Erdman, S. L. (2020). *A 'building distrust' in public health agencies is 'the elephant in the room,' Fauci says.* [online] CNN. Available at: https://www.cnn.com/2020/10/22/health/fauci-distrust-building-coronavirus/index.html

162 Larsen, A. (2021). *Andy Larsen: Where the CDC went wrong on COVID-19 spread, masks and vaccination benefits.* [online] *The Salt Lake City Tribune.* Available at: https://www.sltrib.com/news/2021/05/13/andy-larsen-biggest/

163 Talev, M. (2020). *Axios-Ipsos poll: Americans won't take Trump's word on vaccine.* [online] Axios. Available at: https://www.axios.com/axios-ipsos-poll-trump-coronavirus-vaccine-06428246-c633-41ba-9081-1f789a90e976.html

164 Jamison, P. (2020). *A top scientist questioned virus lockdowns on Fox News. The backlash was fierce.* [online] *The Washington Post.* Available at: https://www.washingtonpost.com/dc-md-va/2020/12/16/john-ioannidis-coronavirus-lockdowns-fox-news/

165 Lewis, M. (2021). *The Premonition: A Pandemic Story.* W.W. Norton & Company, p. 295 (Kindle version).

166 Picheta, R. (2019). *The flat-Earth conspiracy is spreading around the globe. Does it hide a darker core?.* [online] CNN. Available at: https://www.cnn.com/2019/11/16/us/flat-earth-conference-conspiracy-theories-scli-intl/index.html

167 Hotez, P. (2021). *The Antiscience Movement Is Escalating, Going Global and Killing Thousands.* [online] *Scientific American.* Available at: https://www.scientificamerican.com/article/the-antiscience-movement-is-escalating-going-global-and-killing-thousands/

168 Taylor, L. (2021). *'We are being ignored': Brazil's researchers blame anti-science government for devastating COVID surge.* [online] *Nature.* Available at: https://www.nature.com/articles/d41586-021-01031-w

169 Yahr, E. (2020). *The long and winding evolution of Dr. Drew, back in the spotlight after a coronavirus controversy.* [online] *The Washington Post.* Available at: https://www.washingtonpost.com/arts-entertainment/2020/04/13/dr-drew-pinsky-coronavirus-loveline/

170 Lee, B. Y. (2020). *What Dr. Phil Said About COVID-19 Coronavirus, Here is How Twitter Reacted.* [online] *Forbes.* https://www.forbes.com/sites/brucelee/2020/04/19/what-dr-phil-said-about-covid-19-coronavirus-here-is-how-twitter-reacted/?sh=6a59ebf07d90

171 Walker-Ford, M. (2021). *The World's Top 50 Social Media Influencers by Number of Followers [Infographic].* [online] Social Media Today. Available at: https://www.socialmediatoday.com/news/the-worlds-top-50-social-media-influencers-by-number-of-followers-infogra/601711/

172 Lee, B. Y. (2021). *Joe Rogan's Not Sure Why Younger, Healthy People Should Get Covid-19 Vaccines, Here's Why.* [online] *Forbes.* Available at: https://www.forbes.com/sites/brucelee/2021/05/02/joe-rogan-asks-why-younger-healthy-people-should-get-covid-19-vaccines-heres-why/?sh=1b6e804b68d8

173 Newman, C. (2020). *Big Data Analytics Shows How American's Individualism Complicates Coronavirus Response.* [online] UVAToday. Available at: https://news.virginia.edu/content/big-data-analytics-shows-how-americas-individualism-complicates-coronavirus-response

174 Krugman, P. (2020). *The Cult of Selfishness Is Killing America.* [online] *The New York Times.* Available at: https://www.nytimes.com/2020/07/27/opinion/us-republicans-coronavirus.html

175 Urban Dictionary. (2009). "Dr. Google." Available at: https://www.urbandictionary.com/define.php?term=Dr%20Google

176 American Board of Medical Specialties. (2019). "Patient-driven Data Can Improve Care." Available at: https://www.abms.org/news-events/patient-driven-data-can-improve-care/

177 Howatt, G. (2021). *Minnesota pediatrician disciplined for discouraging childhood vaccines.* [online] *The Star Tribune.* Available at: https://www.

startribune.com/minnesota-pediatrician-disciplined-for-discouraging-childhood-vaccines/600087021/

178 Knowles, H. (2021) A doctor called coronavirus vaccines 'fake.' Now he sits on an Idaho regional health board. [online] *The Washington Post.* Available at: https://www.washingtonpost.com/health/2021/09/16/idaho-covid-gop-ryan-cole/

179 Sayers, D. and Riess, R. (2021) *Arkansas doctor under investigation for prescribing anti-parasitic drug thousands of times for Covid-19 despite FDA warning. [online]* CNN. Available at: https://www.cnn.com/2021/08/26/us/covid-ivermectin-arkansas-doctor/index.html

180 (2021) *Arkansas inmates not told they were given anti-parasitic drug. [online]* Modern Healthcare. Available at: https://www.modernhealthcare.com/safety-quality/arkansas-inmates-not-told-they-were-given-anti-parasite-drug?utm_source=modern-healthcare-covid-19-coverage&utm_medium=email&utm_campaign=20210902&utm_content=article7-headline

181 Aratani, L. (2021). *Judge orders hospital to treat Ohio Covid patient with ivermectin. [online] The Guardian.* Available at: https://www.theguardian.com/us-news/2021/aug/31/ivermectin-covid-ohio-judge-orders-hospital

182 Smith-Schoenwalder, C. (2021). *American Medical Association, Other Groups Warn Against Ivermectin Use for Covid-19. [online]* U.S. News & World Report. Available at: https://www.usnews.com/news/health-news/articles/2021-09-02/american-medical-association-other-groups-warn-against-ivermectin-use-for-coronavirus

183 Stone, P. (2021). *Trump loyalists team up with anti-vax doctors for 'health and freedom' tour. [online] The Guardian.* Available at: https://www.theguardian.com/us-news/2021/sep/03/trump-loyalists-doctors-ministers-reawaken-america-tour

184 Mohsin, M. (2020). *10 Branding Statistics You Need To Know In 2021 [Infographic].* [Blog post] Oberlo.com Available at: https://www.oberlo.com/blog/branding-statistics

185 See 134.

186 Perry, C. (2020). *What Comes After The Coherence Crash?* [online] Media Genius. Available at: https://cperry248.medium.com/what-comes-after-the-coherence-crash-ecbe0f8005b5

187 Peterson-Withorn, C. (2021). *How Much Money American's Billionaires Have Made During The Covid-19 Pandemic.* [online] *Forbes.* Available at: https://www.forbes.com/sites/chasewithorn/2021/04/30/american-billionaires-have-gotten-12-trillion-richer-during-the-pandemic/?sh=5577886f557e

188   Collins, C. (2021). *Updates: Billionaire Wealth, U.S. Job Losses and Pandemic Profiteers.* [online] Inequality.org. Available at: https://inequality.org/great-divide/updates-billionaire-pandemic/

189   Agency for Healthcare Research and Quality. (2019). 2019 National Healthcare Quality & Disparities Report. *AHRQ Pub. No. 20*(21)-0045-EF, p. ES1. Available at: https://www.ahrq.gov/sites/default/files/wysiwyg/research/findings/nhqrdr/2019qdr-cx061021.pdf

190   Agency for Healthcare Research and Quality. (2019). 2019 National Healthcare Quality & Disparities Report. *AHRQ Pub. No. 20*(21)-0045-EF, p. ES2. Available at: https://www.ahrq.gov/sites/default/files/wysiwyg/research/findings/nhqrdr/2019qdr-cx061021.pdf

191   Agency for Healthcare Research and Quality. (2019). 2019 National Healthcare Quality & Disparities Report. *AHRQ Pub. No. 20*(21)-0045-EF, p. O10. Available at: https://www.ahrq.gov/sites/default/files/wysiwyg/research/findings/nhqrdr/2019qdr-cx061021.pdf

192   Agency for Healthcare Research and Quality. (2019). 2019 National Healthcare Quality & Disparities Report. *AHRQ Pub. No. 20*(21)-0045-EF, p. A8. Available at: https://www.ahrq.gov/sites/default/files/wysiwyg/research/findings/nhqrdr/2019qdr-cx061021.pdf

193   Agency for Healthcare Research and Quality. (2019). 2019 National Healthcare Quality & Disparities Report. *AHRQ Pub. No. 20*(21)-0045-EF, p. A24. Available at: https://www.ahrq.gov/sites/default/files/wysiwyg/research/findings/nhqrdr/2019qdr-cx061021.pdf

194   Agency for Healthcare Research and Quality. (2019). 2019 National Healthcare Quality & Disparities Report. *AHRQ Pub. No. 20*(21)-0045-EF, p. A10. Available at: https://www.ahrq.gov/sites/default/files/wysiwyg/research/findings/nhqrdr/2019qdr-cx061021.pdf

195   Agency for Healthcare Research and Quality. (2019). 2019 National Healthcare Quality & Disparities Report. *AHRQ Pub. No. 20*(21)-0045-EF, p. A12. Available at: https://www.ahrq.gov/sites/default/files/wysiwyg/research/findings/nhqrdr/2019qdr-cx061021.pdf

196   Agency for Healthcare Research and Quality. (2019). 2019 National Healthcare Quality & Disparities Report. *AHRQ Pub. No. 20*(21)-0045-EF, p. A22. Available at: https://www.ahrq.gov/sites/default/files/wysiwyg/research/findings/nhqrdr/2019qdr-cx061021.pdf

197   Agency for Healthcare Research and Quality. (2019). 2019 National Healthcare Quality & Disparities Report. *AHRQ Pub. No. 20*(21)-0045-EF, p.

D8. Available at: https://www.ahrq.gov/sites/default/files/wysiwyg/research/findings/nhqrdr/2019qdr-cx061021.pdf

[198] Agency for Healthcare Research and Quality. (2019). 2019 National Healthcare Quality & Disparities Report. *AHRQ Pub. No. 20*(21)-0045-EF, p. D9. Available at: https://www.ahrq.gov/sites/default/files/wysiwyg/research/findings/nhqrdr/2019qdr-cx061021.pdf

[199] Agency for Healthcare Research and Quality. (2019). 2019 National Healthcare Quality & Disparities Report. *AHRQ Pub. No. 20*(21)-0045-EF, p. D13. Available at: https://www.ahrq.gov/sites/default/files/wysiwyg/research/findings/nhqrdr/2019qdr-cx061021.pdf

[200] Agency for Healthcare Research and Quality. (2019). 2019 National Healthcare Quality & Disparities Report. *AHRQ Pub. No. 20*(21)-0045-EF, p. D44. Available at: https://www.ahrq.gov/sites/default/files/wysiwyg/research/findings/nhqrdr/2019qdr-cx061021.pdf

[201] Agency for Healthcare Research and Quality. (2019). 2019 National Healthcare Quality & Disparities Report. *AHRQ Pub. No. 20*(21)-0045-EF, p. D26. Available at: https://www.ahrq.gov/sites/default/files/wysiwyg/research/findings/nhqrdr/2019qdr-cx061021.pdf

[202] Agency for Healthcare Research and Quality. (2019). 2019 National Healthcare Quality & Disparities Report. *AHRQ Pub. No. 20*(21)-0045-EF, p. D50. Available at: https://www.ahrq.gov/sites/default/files/wysiwyg/research/findings/nhqrdr/2019qdr-cx061021.pdf

[203] Agency for Healthcare Research and Quality. (2019). 2019 National Healthcare Quality & Disparities Report. *AHRQ Pub. No. 20*(21)-0045-EF, p. D51. Available at: https://www.ahrq.gov/sites/default/files/wysiwyg/research/findings/nhqrdr/2019qdr-cx061021.pdf

[204] Agency for Healthcare Research and Quality. (2019). 2019 National Healthcare Quality & Disparities Report. *AHRQ Pub. No. 20*(21)-0045-EF, p. D55. Available at: https://www.ahrq.gov/sites/default/files/wysiwyg/research/findings/nhqrdr/2019qdr-cx061021.pdf

[205] Agency for Healthcare Research and Quality. (2019). 2019 National Healthcare Quality & Disparities Report. *AHRQ Pub. No. 20*(21)-0045-EF, p. D64. Available at: https://www.ahrq.gov/sites/default/files/wysiwyg/research/findings/nhqrdr/2019qdr-cx061021.pdf

[206] Ndugga, N. and Artiga, S. (2021). *Disparities in Health and Health Care: 5 Key Questions and Answers.* [online] Kaiser Family Foundation. Available at: https://www.kff.org/racial-equity-and-health-policy/issue-brief/disparities-in-health-and-health-care-5-key-question-and-answers/

207 The Economist. (2020). "Covid-19 has shone a light on racial disparities in health." Available at: https://www.economist.com/international/2020/11/21/covid-19-has-shone-a-light-on-racial-disparities-in-health

208 LaViest, T. A. Gaskin, D., and Richard, P. (2011). Estimating the Economic Burden of Racial Health Inequalities in the United States. *International Journal of Health Services, 41*(2), p. 234.

209 Hamel, L., Lopes, L. Muñana, C., Artiga, S., and Brodie, M. (2020). *KFF/The Undefeated Survey on Race and Health.* [online] Kaiser Family Foundation. Available at: C. https://www.kff.org/report-section/kff-the-undefeated-survey-on-race-and-health-main-findings/#HealthCareSystem

210 Wilson, V. (2020). *Racial disparities in income and poverty remain largely unchanged amid strong income growth in 2019.* [Blog post] Economic Policy Institute, Working Economics Blog. Available at: https://www.epi.org/blog/racial-disparities-in-income-and-poverty-remain-largely-unchanged-amid-strong-income-growth-in-2019/

211 Leighton, H. (2019). *Housing costs have lowered for the rich but risen for the poor, analysis shows.* [online] Rice|Kinder Institute for Urban Research. Available at: https://kinder.rice.edu/urbanedge/2019/05/03/housing-inequality-high-income-see-costs-drop-low-income-higher-rent

212 UCLA School of Law: Williams Institute. (2019). "LGBT Poverty in the United States," p. 2.

213 https://khn.org/news/article/the-pandemic-will-undermine-american-health-for-years/?utm_campaign=KHN%3A%20Daily%20Health%20Policy%20Report&utm_medium=email&_hsmi=135976667&_hsenc=p2ANqtz-8O9-WR5pnjQOYB4x9vIUinTOA1zXC9aZMF_e0cO6MReMr0s4Whe_jEdRua_xDOwN_9QoZHxys0C9E59LYyilQiJHuHLg&utm_content=135976667&utm_source=hs_email

214 Stobbe, M. (2021). *US life expectancy in 2020 saw biggest drop since WWII.* [online] AP News. Available at: https://apnews.com/article/science-health-coronavirus-pandemic-fac0863b8c252d21d6f6a22a2e3eab86

215 Women's National Law Center. (2021). "A Year of Strength & Loss." Available at: https://nwlc.org/wp-content/uploads/2021/03/Final_NWLC_Press_CovidStats.pdf

216 Vogels, E. A., Rainie, L. and Anderson, J. (2020). *Experts Predict More Digital Innovation By 2030 Aimed At Enhancing Democracy.* [online] Pew Research Center. https://www.pewresearch.org/internet/2020/06/30/innovations-these-experts-predict-by-2030/

217 Tepper, N. (2021). *UnitedHealthcare, Cigna, Aetna all unveil new policies restricting biologics use. [online].* Modern Healthcare. Available at: https://www.modernhealthcare.com/insurance/unitedhealthcare-cigna-aetna-all-unveil-new-policies-restricting-biologics-use

218 The Editorial Board. (2021). *Opinion: The U.S. is growing more unequal. That's harmful — and fixable.* [online] The Washington Post. Available at: https://www.washingtonpost.com/opinions/2021/07/16/us-is-growing-more-unequal-thats-harmful-fixable/

219 Ochieng, N.. Schwartz, K. and Neuman, T. (2020). *How Many Physicians Have Opted-Out of the Medicare Program?* [online] Kaiser Family Foundation. Available at: https://www.kff.org/medicare/issue-brief/how-many-physicians-have-opted-out-of-the-medicare-program/

220 Hegedus, H. (2021). *An inside look at the growing field of concierge medicine.* [online] Boston 25 News. Available at: https://www.boston25news.com/news/an-inside-look-growing-field-concierge-medicine/BANPRYX3JNDOBLNPGSEIMXQ5QQ/

221 Weber, D. O. (2019). *How Many Patients Can a Primary Care Physician Treat?* [online] American Association for Physician Leadership. Available at: https://www.physicianleaders.org/news/how-many-patients-can-primary-care-physician-treat

222 Karlis, N. (2020). *Among poorest 20 percent of Americans, one-third of income goes to health care: study.* [online] salon.com. Available at: https://www.salon.com/2020/01/27/among-poorest-20-percent-of-americans-one-third-of-income-goes-to-health-care-study/

223 Kliff, S. and Sanger-Katz, M. (2021). *Americans' Medical Debts Are Bigger Than Was Known, Totalling $140 Billion. [online] The New York Times.* Available at: https://www.nytimes.com/2021/07/20/upshot/medical-debt-americans-medicaid.html

224 Potter, W. (2021). *The $140 billion in the New York Times says Americans owe in medical debt is just the tip of the iceberg.* [Blog post] Wendell Potter NOW. Available at: https://wendellpotter.substack.com/p/nyt-medical-debt?utm_source=substack&utm_medium=email&utm_content=share&token=eyJ1c2VyX2lkIjozNjUwNTA1MywicG9zdF9pZCI6MzkwMzY0NjksIl8iOiJBRG9sSSIsImlhdCI6MTYyNjg4OTkzMywiZXhwIjoxNjI2ODkzNTMzLCJpc3MiOiJwdWItMjU1MTUyIiwic3ViIjoicG9zdC1yZWFjdGlvbiJ9.C0ppXcdYTfutXqs4G8KCMtUjZFsP4vkf2bzYA3dWTE8

225 Konish, L. (2019). *This is the real reason most Americans file for bankruptcy.* [online] CNBC. Available at: https://www.cnbc.com/2019/02/11/this-is-the-real-reason-most-americans-file-for-bankruptcy.html

226 See 44.

227 Muhlestein, D. (2020). *The Coming Crisis For The Medicare Trust Fund.* [Blog post] Health Affairs Blog. Available at:

228 Romig, K. (2020). *What the 2020 Trustees' Report Shows About Social Security.* [online] Center on Budget and Policy Priorities. Available at: https://www.cbpp.org/research/social-security/what-the-2020-trustees-report-shows-about-social-security

229 Scommegna, P. and Mather, M. (2021). *Unequal Health Care Access and Quality Contribute to U.S. Racial Health Disparities Among Older Adults.* [online] Population Reference Bureau. Available at: https://www.prb.org/resources/unequal-health-care-access-and-quality-contribute-to-u-s-racial-health-disparities-among-older-adults/

230 Selassie, G. (2020). *Health Disparities Facing Older Adults of Color amid COVID-19: Guest Blog by Justice in Aging.* [online] National Health Law Program. Available at: https://healthlaw.org/health-disparities-facing-older-adults-of-color-amid-covid-19-guest-blog-by-justice-in-aging/

231 See 299.

232 Vogels, E. (2021). *Digital divide persists even as Americans with lower incomes make gains in tech adoption.* [online] Pew Research Center. Available at: https://www.pewresearch.org/fact-tank/2021/06/22/digital-divide-persists-even-as-americans-with-lower-incomes-make-gains-in-tech-adoption/

233 Logically. (2019). "5 Examples of Biased Artificial Intelligence." Available at: https://www.logically.ai/articles/5-examples-of-biased-ai

234 See 233.

235 Ledford, H. (2019). *Millions of black people affected by racial bias in health-care algorithms.* [online] *Nature.* Available at: https://www.nature.com/articles/d41586-019-03228-6

236 Riganti, C. and Rippey, B. (2021). *U.S. Drought Monitor: West.* [online] National Drought Mitigation Center. Available at: https://droughtmonitor.unl.edu/CurrentMap/StateDroughtMonitor.aspx?West

237 Allhands, J. (2021). *We are just 5 feet away from the possibility of deeper water cuts to save Lake Mead.* [online] azcentral. Available at: https://www.azcentral.com/story/opinion/op-ed/joannaallhands/2021/07/19/lake-mead-5-feet-away-provision-make-deeper-water-cuts/7999245002/

238 Salas, R. N., Friend, T. H., Bernstein, A. and Jha, A. K. (2020). Adding a Climate Lens To Health Policy In The United States. *Health Affairs, 39*(12). https://doi.org/10.1377/hlthaff.2020.01352

239   See 233.

240   Limaye, V. (2021). *Opinion: We must consider the profound toll of climate change on public health.* [online] *The Washington Post.* Available at: https://www.washingtonpost.com/opinions/2021/08/09/true-cost-climate-change-needs-include-health-toll/

241   Kaplan, S. (2020). *Climate change is also a racial justice problem.* [online] *The Washington Post.* Available at: https://www.washingtonpost.com/climate-solutions/2020/06/29/climate-change-racism/

242   Kaplan, S. (2021). *Heat waves are dangerous. Isolation and inequity make them deadly.* [online] *The Washington Post.* Available at: https://www.washingtonpost.com/climate-environment/2021/07/21/heat-wave-death-portland/

243   Armour, S. (2021). *Climate Change to Be Treated as Public-Health Issue.* [online] *The Wall Street Journal.* Available at: https://www.wsj.com/articles/climate-change-to-be-treated-as-public-health-issue-11630315800

244   See 207.

CPSIA information can be obtained
at www.ICGtesting.com
Printed in the USA
LVHW111145120522
718154LV00001B/1/J